THE CHALLENGE OF PROGRESS

CURRENT PERSPECTIVES IN SOCIAL THEORY

Series Editor: Harry F. Dahms

Recent Volumes:

Douglas Kellner
University of California — Los Angeles (Philosophy)

Daniel Krier
Iowa State University (Sociology)

Lauren Langman
Loyola University (Sociology)

Eric R. Lybeck
University of Exeter (Sociology)

John O'Neill
York University (Sociology)

Paul Paolucci
Eastern Kentucky University (Sociology)

Lawrence Scaff
Wayne State University (Political Science)

Steven Seidman
State University of New York at Albany (Sociology)

Helmut Staubmann
Leopold Franzens University, Innsbruck (Sociology)

Alexander Stoner
Salisbury University (Sociology)

Stephen Turner
The University of South Florida (Philosophy)

CURRENT PERSPECTIVES IN SOCIAL THEORY
VOLUME 36

THE CHALLENGE OF PROGRESS: THEORY BETWEEN CRITIQUE AND IDEOLOGY

EDITED BY

HARRY F. DAHMS
University of Tennessee, USA

United Kingdom – North America – Japan
India – Malaysia – China

Emerald Publishing Limited
Howard House, Wagon Lane, Bingley BD16 1WA, UK

First edition 2020

British Library Cataloguing in Publication Data
A catalogue record for this book is available from the British Library

ISBN: 978-1-78714-572-6 (Print)
ISBN: 978-1-78714-571-9 (Online)
ISBN: 978-1-78714-980-9 (EPub)

ISSN: 0278-1204 (Series)

Printed and bound by CPI Group (UK) Ltd, Croydon, CR0 4YY

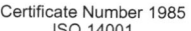

ISOQAR certified
Management System,
awarded to Emerald
for adherence to
Environmental
standard
ISO 14001:2004.

ISOQAR
REGISTERED

Certificate Number 1985
ISO 14001

INVESTOR IN PEOPLE

This volume is dedicated to the memory of Moishe Postone (1942–2018), member of the Editorial Board from 2002 to 2018 and contributor to volumes 19 and 33.

CONTENTS

LIST OF CONTRIBUTORS

Amy Allen	Department of Philosophy, Penn State University, USA
Robert J. Antonio	Department of Sociology, University of Kansas, USA
Patricia Arend	Department of Behavioral Sciences, Fitchburg State University, USA
Katherine Comeau	Department of Sociology, University of Notre Dame, USA
Daniel M. Harrison	Department of Government, Criminology, and Sociology, Lander University, USA
Lawrence Hazelrigg	Department of Sociology, Florida State University, USA
Reha Kadakal	Sociology Program, California State University Channel Islands, USA
Timothy W. Luke	Department of Political Science, Virginia Polytechnic Institute and State University, USA
Karen Ng	Department of Philosophy, Vanderbilt University, USA
Kevin Olson	Department of Political Science, University of California, USA
George Steinmetz	Department of Sociology, University of Michigan, USA
Shawn Van Valkenburgh	Department of Sociology, University of California, USA

INTRODUCTION

Harry F. Dahms

In 2016, two books appeared that shared two aspects: both addressed issues pertaining to the future, and the covers of both books showed a white man in a dark suit in a precarious situation.

One book is about "imagined futures," and the cover shows a white man standing at the edge of a concrete overpass whose construction must have ended abruptly, since there is no evidence in the photo of a continuing construction effort; the overpass ends with a clean cut, in midair, and the man is looking straight ahead, into the distance; we (the observer/reader/photographer) are standing at ground level, looking up. The person at the precipice where the overpass should continue is carrying a briefcase and wearing a business suit, with a white shirt and a reddish tie. The sky above is blue and clear, without a hint of clouds.

The other book promises to address "the end of progress," and its cover shows a man in motion, striding from left to right across a flat concrete surface that has cracked; the photo was taken as the person is moving across a crack that is a few inches wide, which extends beyond the upper edge of the book cover and splits into two cracks in the bottom part of the image, extending beyond the lower edge of the cover. This man also is dressed in a dark suit (black, as far as one can tell) and a white shirt; it is not clear, however, he does not appear to be wearing a formal business suit, and he certainly is not wearing a tie. Like the person on the other cover, he is looking straight ahead, in this case in the direction in which he heading, to a point beyond the (right) edge of the cover. We (the observer/reader/photographer) are hovering slightly above the scene; all the angle of vision allows for is the concrete floor with cracks extending beyond sight, and the man in suit.

On the one hand, it is highly likely that the choice of images for the two books covers (by different publishing houses, to be sure) is purely accidental. On the other hand, as the saying goes, there are no accidents. In this instance, the coincidence is not merely that both books were published during the same year

The Challenge of Progress: Theory Between Critique and Ideology
Current Perspectives in Social Theory, Volume 36, 1–11
Copyright © 2020 Emerald Publishing Limited
ISSN: 0278-1204/doi:10.1108/S0278-120420190000036003

on related topics — in essence: the future, especially the future of the modern world — but more so that the themes of future and progress visually are tied to a sense of precariousness, of no way forward or of the ground under one's feet coming apart, especially the real or imagined precariousness of the position of white men in blacks suits in today's world, as the privileges they have enjoyed up until now appear to be threatened. The most intriguing coincidence between the two book covers, however, is the fact that corresponding books appeared in 2016. Numerous political and cultural trends had been underway up until then which highlighted the weakening commitment to, and waning appeal and deepening crisis of, democracy as well as modernity, among substantial segments of the population in a growing number of countries, such as Brazil, Hungary, the Philippines, and Poland. Yet, the Brexit referendum and the US Presidential election in 2016, on June 23 and November 8, respectively, sent shock waves around the world, among individuals and groups that share, implicitly or explicitly, a constructive and forward-looking perspective on progress and the future. Much has been made of the fact that both the Brexit referendum (e.g., Outhwaite, 2017) and the most recent US Presidential election (e.g., Kivisto, 2017) at least in part were expressions of the intensifying anger on the part of white men in the face of eroding privileges; one might add that modern societies as they emerged historically, with regard to social and economic structures of inequality and as systems of power, resulted from or were strongly influenced by the privileged actions and choices of white men, or rather, by the actions and choices of privileged white men. After all, the privileges of the latter do not just compare to those who are not white or minorities or women, but also to other white men whose identities, however, are wrapped up with their whiteness and the concurrent categorical possibility of their having the potential of becoming privileged as well, or of it having to be someone else's fault that they are not privileged. To be sure, this is neither to suggest that white men determined and controlled the direction of the evolution of economic and social structures, nor that white men were responsible for *creating* capitalism and the kind of progress that came with it, nor that white men do not also constitute their own social and economic structure. Yet, it is undeniable that overall, white men — especially white men *in suits* — benefitted more greatly from the social, political, and economic configurations of modern capitalist societies than any other group.

The books I have been referring to are Amy Allen's *The End of Progress: Decolonizing the Normative Foundations of Critical Theory* (2016) and Jens Beckert's *Imagined Futures: Fictional Expectations and Capitalist Dynamics* (2016). The man hurrying across the cracked cement floor adorns Allen's book, and the man standing on the edge of the incomplete overpass in on the cover of Beckert's book. Both books, in very different ways, acknowledge the fact that we live in a world in which capitalism has become "normal," the singular reality to reckon with, regardless of whether we are envisioning or dreaming of capitalism's impending demise, whether modern capitalist societies constitute an increasingly *destructive* rather than productive totality (if we employ as the relevant reference the planet, humankind, or the biosphere as a whole, rather than modern capitalist societies only), or whether we defend capitalism with fervor. After all, from the outset, "capitalism" was not a static socioeconomic and political system but, more precisely, a system in which static and dynamic dimensions and forces translate into and sustain a reality which — in terms of social theory — constitutes both a moving target of sorts, and a social context that continually must reinvent itself — or rather, its material foundation. As Marx and Engels formulated one of modern societies' defining paradoxes, the bourgeoisie maintains its predominant position in modern society by continuously revolutionizing the means of production. As a consequence, modern societies perpetually are involved in multiple processes of more or less far-reaching adjustments which, in many regards and at the same time, resemble a vast evolutionary process that constitutes a "cosmos" (Weber) that, on the one hand, is resistant to illumination and rational representation and, on the other, is against consistent observation in any meaningful sense. Neither Allen, nor Beckert expects or dreams of capitalism's impending demise, nor do they defend it with fervor, and both are highly cognizant of the fact there is no simple stance to adopt that would provide certainty with regard to "progress," to the fate of modern societies and democracy, or to the future in the broader sense.

Beckert's book is at the intersection of social theory and economic sociology. In the introduction, he writes that:

> The capacity to imagine counterfactual futures is [...] a human characteristic that exists independent of capitalism. Imagined futures are crucial to understanding the development of modernity in general; and they exist, though in different forms, in traditional societies as well. Religious eschatology, for instance, projects futures unrelated to the economy. By the same token, the capitalist economy's orientation toward an open economic future does not exist solely at the level of action orientations: the capitalist economy institutionalizes specific systemic pressures that enforce a temporal orientation toward future economic opportunities and risks. Only by closely examining these institutionalized pressures may we comprehensibly shed light on the role of actors' temporal orientations with regard to economic processes. (Beckert, 2016, pp. 3—4)

The innovative aspect of Beckert's book pertains to the fact that actors in modern economies and societies are not motivated exclusively by the rational pursuit especially of their set economic interests, but that they must make, as it were, leaps of faith regarding the future, in order be able to act and decide and choose at all. Indeed, the book is a sustained argument, based on a related thorough analysis:

> that imaginaries of the future are a crucial element of capitalist development, and that capitalist dynamics are vitally propelled by the shaping of expectations. Institutional trajectories from the past are not irrelevant to outcomes [...] but [...] sociologists [and, we might add, social theorists; H.F.D.] would do well to shift more of their attention to the future, particularly to the images of the future that actors nourish. Furthermore, temporal orientations and perceptions of the future are relevant far beyond the economic realm investigated here [...] "history matters," but the future matters just as much. (Beckert, 2016, p. 6)

The book concludes as follows:

> Modern capitalism entails much more than instrumentally rational actors and calculative devices — it includes the creativity expressed in imagined futures. The infinite new paths they propose are an indispensable part of the eternal process of capitalist renewal, which is fully contingent in its content, and is sporadically interrupted by crisis. This mixture of creativity and destructiveness was described many decades ago by the German-American theologist Paul Tillich in a single word: demonic. (Beckert, 2016, p. 285)

Inevitably, Beckert includes in his considerations and analysis the issue of progress without which modern society would not have emerged and could not function. It is a concept loaded with a broad range of connotations and implications that point in a variety of directions and raise an array of issues.

While Beckert's argument and the object of his investigation are infused with diverse notions of and perspectives on progress, the starting point of Allen's book is Adorno's observation that "progress occurs where it ends," and it is located squarely at the point of tension between the critical theory of the early Frankfurt School and subsequent incarnations of this tradition, especially those of Jürgen Habermas, Axel Honneth, and Rainer Forst.[1] Yet, *The End of Progress* (Allen, 2016) is not about progress approaching its end – empirically, theoretically, or in terms of the imaginaries that guide individuals', social groups' and societies' actions, aspirations, and public policies. Rather, the argument is both more subtle and more disconcerting, as it pertains to the fact that the notion of progress as it informed, legitimated, and accompanied the rise of modern societies has been entangled with colonialism not just in many traditional approaches to telling and analyzing the story of the historical trajectory of modern societies, but in critical approaches also, including in critical theory:

> My main *critical* aim is to show that and how and why Frankfurt School critical theory remains wedded to problematically Eurocentric and/or foundationalist strategies for grounding normativity. My primary *positive* aim is to decolonize Frankfurt School critical theory by rethinking its strategy for grounding normativity, in such a way as to open this project up to the aims and concerns of post- and decolonial critical theory. [...] such an opening up is crucial if Frankfurt School critical theory is to be truly critical, in the sense of being able to engage in the ongoing self-clarification of the struggles and wishes of our postcolonial—by which I mean formally decolonized but still neocolonial—age. (Allen, 2016, p. xii)

The critical theory of the early Frankfurt School started out with the aspiration to spell out standards for, and to attain the most advanced critical consciousness of, its own time (the 1930s and 1940s in the industrially most advanced societies), and to do so for modern society more generally, in a manner that required critical reflexivity with regard to their own positionality. Yet, for its current proponents to continue to be captives of an understanding of and perspective on progress in the twenty-first century that warrants rigorous scrutiny, this does not bode well for the state of social theory, more generally including the social sciences and philosophy, and even less for modern societies. It is in this regard that the events of 2016, Brexit and the US Presidential election, and many elections that have followed, such as in the Philippines, Austria, Italy, and most recently Brazil, are cause for concern, as they highlight in a variety of ways the continuing crises of modernity and democracy. Allen's book is a sustained and rigorous critique of how the writings of *recent* critical theorists that followed in, but also in important ways departed from, the footsteps of Theodor W. Adorno (arguably the most sophisticated and committed representative and promoter of "first-generation" critical theory), continue to adhere to an inherently western European understanding of progress, focusing on Jürgen Habermas as the main representative of the "second generation," Axel Honneth for the "third generation," and Rainer Forst for the "fourth generation." In addition, Allen's perspective is both inspired and informed by the writings of Michael Foucault.

In this volume of *Current Perspectives of Social Theory*, a set of contributions addresses the current state of affairs, in different ways. What we are facing is not just a crisis with regard to the internal functioning and widespread support of democratic values and institutions as it is tied to the dynamics of capitalism, and as far as the commitment to maintaining social, political, economic, cultural, organizational, and technological achievements of the modern age is concerned, but an array of challenges to many dimensions of progress. Part I of this volume assembles four review essays regarding Amy Allen's *The End of Progress*, by sociologists George Steinmetz and Reha Kadakal, philosopher Karen Ng, and political theorist Kevin Olson, followed by a response by Amy Allen.[2] Part II brings together historically situated analyses of challenges to progress, including an examination of the role of the philosophy of Nietzsche in the resurgence of right-wing thought and activism, an analysis of Ridley Scott's 1982 movie, *Blade Runner*, and a re-evaluation of Fukuyama's "end of history" thesis from the vantage point of the early twenty-first century. Part III, finally, presents analyses of the dynamics of progress, focusing on desertification processes in and around Las Vegas, Nevada, of the changing dynamics of traditional marriage proposals in the United States, and of the influence of Francis Bacon on Emile Durkheim.

Among the theorists whose work is included in his volume are several authors who have been actively involved in *Current Perspectives in Social Theory* for some time, whose writings have appeared here before, or whose work is published here for the first time. Robert Antonio, Lawrence Hazelrigg, and Timothy Luke have been associate editors and members of the editorial board for many years, and have each contributed several essays over the years. Especially noteworthy is a well-known essay by Robert Antonio on climate change, which appeared in volume 26 and which sparked two responses and Antonio's reply (in the same volume). Hazelrigg has functioned as coeditor for volumes 27 and 30. Amy Allen's previous book, *The Politics of Our Selves* (2008), was discussed in a special section in volume 29. Previous volumes have included a chapter each from Kevin Olson, Reha Kadakal, and Daniel Harrison, as author or co-author. Karen Ng has been a member of the editorial board since 2015.

Reha Kadakal's chapter is the first review essay in the section on Amy Allen's *The End of Progress*. It constitutes an effort to clarify further the normative foundations of critical social theory by means of a close reading of Allen's critique of current Frankfurt School theory and the alternative methodology it presents. The combination of "problematizing genealogy" and "metanormative contextualism" presents the opportunity to examine whether such a methodology constitutes a viable alternative for the normative grounding of critical theory, focusing on whether Allen's rendering of philosophy of history accurately characterizes related problems in recent Frankfurt School critical theory; whether problematizing genealogy and the notion of "unreason" qualify as true alternatives; and whether the distinction between metanormative and normative levels is tenable for critical theory. Drawing on Allen's reiteration of the mediated nature of categories, Kadakal suggests that the strong distinction between forms of thought underlying first and second-generation Frankfurt School critical theory should be framed against the backdrop of the specific context of the European historical present that informs its normative universe, rather than in terms of philosophy of history.

George Steinmetz's review examines claims made by Allen about the affinity between postcolonial theory and the approaches of Adorno and Foucault for purposes of criticizing the notion of historical progress, as well as her alternative approach to decolonization. He also addresses the status of Habermas' aim to put critical theory on a secure normative footing, Honneth's claim regarding the history of an ethical sphere that constitutes an unplanned learning process kept in motion by a struggle for recognition, and Forst's attempt to reconstruct Critical Theory's normative account via Kant rather than Hegel. Is Allen's claim that her approach is fully in the spirit of Critical Theory and may be seen as a continuation of Critical Theory's first generation, as in Adorno, justified? How does it a "genealogical" approach that draws on Adorno's negative dialectics and critique of identity thinking, along with Nietzsche's conception of genealogy, as developed by Foucault? Steinmetz then focuses on Allen's partial compromise with the idea of progress, critical theory's ability to benefit from engagement with other critical theories and theories of ethics, aside from postcolonial theory, and nonwestern theories that shed a different light on Allen's critique, thus drawing attention to the gesture of decolonizing, the distinctions between colonialism and empire, and the sociology of knowledge production that undergirds a "decolonizing" critique.

Karen Ng recognizes Allen's work as an important intervention in the narrow sense of critical theory *after* the early Frankfurt School, as it set out to reconcile and redeem the philosophies of history found in Kant and Hegel, and regards the book as a sophisticated and compelling challenge to critical theories that are normatively grounded in Eurocentric conceptions of progress. The twofold aims of Allen's book are to extricate the critical theories of Habermas and Honneth from a conception of historical progress that takes European modernity as both exemplary and authoritative, and to rethink the relation between the historical and the normative for purposes of identifying an alternative approach to normative grounding. Ng contends that Allen's positive thesis that critical theory's normative foundations can be reconceived along the lines of metanormative contextualism inspired by Adorno and Foucault is problematic, and that more modest and narrowly focused conceptions of progress would be more productive. Furthermore, Honneth's social ontology as it is central to his early recognition theory can be separated from his stronger statements concerning the teleological progression of history and is more central for his project of normative grounding.

Kevin Olson's essay is motivated by similar intuitions as Allen, despite paths that diverge at times. Allen's critique of the Frankfurt School's tendency toward Eurocentrism, progress-thinking, and historical teleology should be situated in a broader project directed at addressing the struggles and wishes of our age. Olson welcomes Allen's ability to put in stark contrast some significant problems of

Frankfurt School critical theory, and he commends her effort to renew the tradition. Allen's reliance on postcolonial theory to demonstrate how the recent work of the Frankfurt School is entwined with notions of progress. He then asks what can be salvaged from Frankfurt School social theory, beyond its teleology and normative foundationalism, whether it is possible to imagine a theory of the public sphere inspired by Habermas but released from the normative bounds placed on public discourse by the idea of "regulative presuppositions of speech," and what might happen if Honneth's conception of freedom were to be freed from universalistic historicism centered in European modernity, if supporting Forst's notion of public discourse would not come at the prize his approach to justification.

In her response, Allen restates the motivation for and rationale of the book to defend her interpretive claims regarding Adorno, Foucault, Habermas, Honneth, and Forst. Her application of standards drawn from Adorno and Foucault, as they jive with postcolonial critical theory, to the perspectives, claims, and theoretical contributions of Habermas, Honneth, and Forst show how they presume a historical present that has shaped successive generations of Frankfurt School critical theorists. This historical present is be characterized by relative social and political stability as it has come to be typical of the United States and Europe (and, one might add, initially West Germany, and then unified Germany), but not many other societies where anti-colonial struggles, proxy wars, and even genocides occurred in response to persistent legacies of European colonialism, during the twentieth century. According to Allen, critical theory must move beyond its implied second-, third- and fourth-generation sociohistorical reference frame and admit, in productive fashion, how its own critical perspective is situated within the postcolonial present.

As the first contribution to Part II, Robert Antonio's chapter on "Nietzsche after Charlottesville" starts out from the observation that Nietzsche's texts entail diverse and at times contradictory themes that are resistant to straightforward summation and open to conflicting interpretations, not least because Nietzsche was prone to deploying puzzling and disorienting statements intended to provoke readers. Thus, there is not likely to be "one true Nietzsche." Antonio points out that Nietzsche's sociocultural and social psychological arguments regarding German antisemitism and nationalism contradict current *alt-right* views, and theorizes conditions that give rise to this distinctive type of demagoguery. Contentious appropriations of Nietzsche have been part and parcel of conflicts over capitalist crises and reactionary populist revivals for more than one hundred years. Moreover, rampant growth and the expansion of the global economy, especially when compared to the biosphere, have increased material throughput and production of waste, in the process generating a host of increasingly urgent global environmental problems, not least climate change. It is telling that under such circumstances, members of the *alt-right* contend that cosmopolitan people are deracinated, devoid of their cultural particularity, and spiritually lost. By contrast, progressives insist that a stronger commitment to cosmopolitanism will increase diversity, enhance the ability to put oneself in the shoes (and positions) of others, and increase communicative capacities and powers of cooperation. Nietzsche encouraged individuals as human beings to respect nature, and it is important to protect his thought from *alt-right* efforts to utilize his thought and writings, especially for the sake of new political-economic alternatives and forms of collective action that are more conducive to the reconciliation of the natural and social world, including the worlds of politics, culture, and economy.

Lawrence Hazelrigg's essay situates Ridley Scott's 1982 film, *Blade Runner*, which was an adaptation of Philip K. Dick's novel *Do Androids Dream of Electric Sheep?* ([1968]1975) (and which, if I might add, arguably was one of the few adaptations in the history of film that improved upon the literary original) within a general context of critical theory, with two goals in mind: to draw attention to the affinity between themes raised in the film and a set of specific issues that have been important to critical theory, and to examine, criticize, and expand on some of the later issues, specifically the dialectic of identity/difference. The essay is intended as a contribution to studies of specific films in terms of social, cultural, political theory, e.g., considering scenarios and sequences of a plotline and assessing degrees and types of realism at work in cinematic format. Hazelrigg concludes that *Blade Runner* highlighted the evolving meaning of prosthetics and related practical and conceptual-semantic boundaries of what it means to be "human" – a common trope in science-fiction films.

The third contribution to Part II is by Daniel Harrison, who examines the peculiar situation of sociologists at the current historical juncture. As human civilization appears to be threatened by collapse in the medium or long term, the social and natural worlds are in a process of rapid reconfiguration. Individuals are forced to rely on themselves to an increasing extent, the function of government is being redefined, state power is becoming more distant and terrifying at the same time – how are sociologists and social theorists to respond? Harrison's immanent critique of sociology as a profession, vocation, and critical practice points out how sociology is a perilous choice as a vocation, for independent researchers as well as for the contracting professoriate, even though some sociologists are becoming more critical in and of this context. As well they should: as plans in Brazil to shut down sociology and philosophy departments demonstrate, sociology there and elsewhere is especially necessary in the early twenty-first century as both a mode of intervention and a method of inquiry.

Timothy Luke's essay is the first chapter in Part III and an exercise in applied social theory. Las Vegas, Nevada, serves as an indicator for transformations in the age of the Anthropocene. Focusing on the process and threat of desertification, Las Vegas illustrates the logic of such processes in many other places that provide examples for biopolitical spaces and geophysical places that replicate the so-called resonance dilemma of people in search for sustainable lifestyles in global spaces under strain. With human factors that are situated in historical contexts resembling "forces of Nature" in geological history, Luke scrutinizes systems of organized growth that are linked to challenging processes like commercial degradation, urban demography, military development, and nuclear devastation responsible for desertification. Treating Las Vegas as exemplifying the "globalizing neoliberal omnipolitanization" of the surface of the Earth, the consequences of neoliberalism also are visible in metrometabolic exchanges of particular urban environments.

Patricia Arend and Katherine Comeau's study of patterns of social reproduction of traditional heterosexual engagement rituals, specifically the aspect of men proposing marriage to women, with many women surpassing men in educational attainment and access to power, draws on a set of semi-structured interviews with middle-class, heterosexual women. Arend and Comeau identify three types of socioeconomic incentives encouraging women to continue to participate in traditional proposals, and demonstrate that by taking into consideration *social* factors that mediate relationships among women, economic and status incentives contribute to the perpetuation of the traditional engagement ritual. Particularly, heterosexual women who are located socio-economically in middle-class positions turn out, in the context of their female-centered reference groups, to exchange socioeconomic status for involvement in gender-normative relations with their male partners. By implication, progress at the level of socially mediated individual relationships is both more difficult to attain and maintain than many social theorists assumed just a few years ago.

Finally, Shawn van Valkenburgh's examination of Francis Bacon's influence on Émile Durkheim reveals how the theory of mental "idols" presented by the former plays an important role in the work of the latter. During their respective time periods, Bacon, as well as Durkheim, endeavored to demarcate and advocate new methods of inquiry against competitors. They were similarly reluctant to engage both in philosophical abstractions and amateurish obsessions with quick practical results. Van Valkenburgh points out affinities between Durkheim's concern with dangers to sociological knowledge and Baconian idols, and both offer consonant remedies on the basis of deliberate self-restraint. Evidently, Bacon's influence on Durkheim was greater than typically recognized, and warrants close attention.

What, then, of progress? To return to the beginning of this introduction — white men in precarious situations — I would like to quote from Wendy Brown's most recent book, *In the Ruins of Neoliberalism: The Rise of Anti-democratic Politics in the West* (2019), specifically from the fifth and final chapter, "No Future for White Men: Nihilism, Fatalism, and Ressentiment" (pp. 161–188):

> The white male supremacism in contemporary traditional values politics becomes explicit, then, not only because nihilism pulls the moral drapery off those values and makes them contractual and instrumentalizable, but also because this supremacism has been wounded without being destroyed. Its subject abhors the democracy it holds responsible for its wounds and seeks to pull democracy down as it goes. (p. 180)

Wounded creatures typically act purely on instinct, although this is not necessarily so. As many people know from personal experience, when animals — which typically take flight as soon as humans appear in the vicinity — are caught in precarious circumstances, e.g., trapped in situations they cannot escape from on their own, they frequently "play dead" when a person approaches them, become motionless, hold still, to allow the person to free them from their accidental prison, and take off the instant the possibility arises.[3] By contrast, there are humans who, when wounded, even or especially if only symbolically, are determined to strike out, rather than seeking help from others, or indicating a willingness to cooperate with others. Brown continues:

> Perhaps we are witnessing how nihilism goes when futurity itself is in doubt. Perhaps there is a form of nihilism shaped by the waning of a type of social dominance or the waning social dominance of a historical type. As this type finds itself in a world emptied not only of meaning, but of its own place, far from going gently into the night, it turns toward apocalypse. If white men cannot own democracy, there will be no democracy. If white men cannot rule the planet, there will be no planet. Nietzsche was immensely curious about what would come after the two centuries of the intensifying nihilism he expected. But what if there is no "after"? What if supremacy is the rosary held tight as white civilization itself appears finished and takes with it all futurity? What if this is how it ends? (p. 180)

While Wendy Brown's formulations might sound like a rant or hyperbole, unfortunately, indications and evidence appear to suggest that they are far from that. Negative sentiments and resentments clearly are on the rise, and their positive opposites at best are in a neutral and stagnant position. If progress is to be reignited, where will it start? Or will it at all? As Brown closes her book:

> Families become shells, ownership and savings vanish, marriages teeter and break, depression, anxiety, and other forms of mental illness are ubiquitous, religion is commercialized and weaponized, and patriotism is reduced to xenophobic support for troops in aimless, endless wars and useless, but spectacular border barricades. Nation, family, property, and the traditions reproducing racial and gender privilege, mortally wounded by deindustrialization, neoliberal reason, globalization, digital technologies, and nihilism, are reduced to affective remains. To date, these remains have been activated mostly by the Right. What kinds of LEFT political critique and vision might reach and transform them? (pp. 187–188)

In this spirit, this volume is dedicated to the memory of Moishe Postone, who was a member of the editorial board of *Current Perspectives in Social Theory* for many years, who contributed his own writing, and whose overall work and intellectual energy were dedicated to the reinterpretation and continuous application of Marx's critical theory, in the interest of keeping alive the possibility of constructive progress in the form of qualitative social transformation: his *presence* and commitment to advancing our theoretical understanding of the modern world will be missed.

NOTES

1. A related issue is whether the designation, "critical theory," is appropriate for these later representatives of the tradition, or whether qualifications are required. As I have suggested elsewhere (Dahms, 2018), the shift from the early Frankfurt School to Honneth and Forst may better be understood as a project of "critical liberalism."

2. For discussions of Beckert's book, see Rona-Tas (2017), Murray (2017), Harrington (2016), and Kerem Coban (2016).

3. Science writer Sarah Zielinski (2015) referred to modern humans as "superpredators":

> The human species really is unlike any other predator on the planet, especially when it comes to our choice of prey. Across the animal world, predators focus their efforts on juveniles. Humans, by contrast, are far more likely to be killing big strapping adults, particularly among carnivores on land and fish in the ocean.

REFERENCES

Allen, A. (2016). *The end of progress: Decolonizing the normative foundations of critical theory.* New York, NY: Columbia University Press.

Beckert, J. (2016). *Imagined futures: Fictional expectations and capitalist dynamics.* Cambridge, MA: Harvard University Press.

Brown, W. (2019). *In the ruins of neoliberalism: The rise of anti-democratic politics in the west.* New York, NY: Columbia University Press.

Dahms, H. F. (2018). Critical theory derailed: Paradigm fetishism and critical liberalism in Honneth (and Habermas). In V. Schmitz (Ed.), *Axel Honneth and the future of critical theory* (2018, pp. 207−242). New York, NY: Palgrave.

Dick, Ph. K. ([1968]1975). *Do androids dream of electric sheep?* New York, NY: Ballantine Books.

Harrington, B. (2016). The capitalist's imagination. *The Atlantic*, July 13. Retrieved from https://www.theatlantic.com/business/archive/2016/07/the-capitalists-imagination/491009/. Accessed on July 22, 2019.

Kerem Coban, M. (2016). *Book review − Imagined futures: Fictional expectations and capitalist dynamics by Jens Beckert.* LSE Review of Books. September 7. Retrieved from https://blogs.lse.ac.uk/lsereviewofbooks/2016/09/07/book-review-imagined-futures-fictional-expectations-and-capitalist-dynamics-by-jens-beckert/. Accessed on July 22, 2019.

Kivisto, P. (2017). *The Trump phenomenon: How the politics of populism won in 2016.* Bingley: Emerald Publishing.

Murray, M. (2017). On imagined and science fictional futures. *Mediations*, *30*((2) Summer), 99−111. Special issue on "Post-Humanisms Reconsidered." Retrieved from https://www.mediations-journal.org/articles/Fictional_Futures. Accessed on June 22, 2019.

Outhwaite, W. (Ed.). (2017). *Brexit: Sociological responses.* London: Anthem Press.

Rona-Tas, A. (2017). The importance of thinking forward. *Socio-economic Review*, *15*(1), 241−253.

Zielinski, S. (2015). Modern humans have become superpredators. Smithsonian.com, August 20. Retrieved from https://www.smithsonianmag.com/science-nature/modern-humans-have-become-superpredators-180956348/. Accessed on June 22, 2019.

PART I
IDENTIFYING THE CHALLENGE:
A CRITICAL DISCUSSION OF *THE END OF PROGRESS: DECOLONIZING THE NORMATIVE FOUNDATIONS OF CRITICAL THEORY* (2016), BY AMY ALLEN

HISTORY, CRITIQUE, AND PROGRESS: AMY ALLEN'S "*END OF PROGRESS*" AND THE NORMATIVE GROUNDING OF CRITICAL THEORY

Reha Kadakal

ABSTRACT

Allen's critique of current Frankfurt School theory presents the joint methods of "problematizing genealogy" and "metanormative contextualism" as alternative for the normative grounding of critical theory. Through a close reading of Allen's critique, I investigate whether Allen's identification of philosophy of history is an accurate diagnosis of the problems of the normative grounding of current Frankfurt School theory, whether Allen's distinction between metanormative and normative levels is tenable for critical theory, and whether Allen's methodology constitutes a viable alternative for the normative grounding of critical theory. As an alternative, I suggest scrutinizing the grounding strategies of current Frankfurt School theory to expand beyond their genealogy in Enlightenment thought, and address the question of what made the affirmative form of thought underlying current Frankfurt School theory a historical possibility. Expanding on Allen's reiteration of the mediated nature of categories, I suggest that the stark contrast between forms of thought underlying first- and second-generation Frankfurt School critical theory needs to be understood not in relation to philosophy of history but against the

The Challenge of Progress: Theory Between Critique and Ideology
Current Perspectives in Social Theory, Volume 36, 15–36
ISSN: 0278-1204/doi:10.1108/S0278-120420190000036006

backdrop of the specific context of the European historical present that informs its normative universe.

Keywords: Philosophy of history; critical theory; normative social theory; Frankfurt School; genealogy; Hegel

What is the relationship between history and critique? Is critical social theory possible without a conception of historical progress? Where do we seek the normative grounding of critical social theory in an epoch defined as "postmetaphysical"?

In Amy Allen's recent work *The End of Progress* (2016), these and similar questions on the relation of theory, critique, and normativity reassert their significance for a critique of the normative horizon and internal structure of the current generation of Frankfurt School critical theory, as represented in the works of Habermas, Honneth, and Forst. More specifically, Allen points to a fundamental problem of the normative-theoretical framework of current Frankfurt School thought: it remains inadequate, indeed silent on the forms of domination made possible through colonialism, the challenges that followed in its aftermath through the postcolonial period, and the forms of neocolonial domination that characterize the contemporary political landscape. We are compelled to ask how is it that, despite its essential critical and emancipatory intent, Frankfurt School theory has not taken up the questions of colonial domination that have been central to postcolonial critique? The question involves more than simply the problem of the relative shortcomings of a research agenda of the Frankfurt School tradition. Rather, Allen's critique reveals that such a lack of engagement with the fundamental questions of colonization and its legacies emerges from a central problem in the normative foundations of current Frankfurt School thought, namely its strategy of grounding normativity through the notion of historical progress. Allen interrogates such a notion of historical progress, as well as the form of theorizing within which it is envisaged, in the context of the historical relationship between Europe and its colonized "others." For Allen, the commitment to the "idea of historical progress" as a means to "ground normativity" defines the current Frankfurt School's distinctive approach. This is also the "biggest obstacle" to decolonize the Frankfurt School theory (Allen, 2016, p. 3).

In this chapter, I will respond to Amy Allen's critique of the normative foundations of current Frankfurt School social theory. More specifically, I will engage her critique of the notion of progress that Allen takes as a grounding category for its normative claims, and the alternative methodology she offers to counter its problems. In order to better assess Allen's critique, in what follows, I will first delineate the main points of Allen's critique of normativity in current Frankfurt School theory. I will then outline the methodology Allen offers as a means to an alternative normative grounding of critical social theory. This methodology draws on Foucault and Adorno and rests on two key tools, namely *problematizing genealogy* and *metanormative contextualism*. Only after such an account of her overall argument, I will be able to draw out possible implications of these methodological tools for critical social theory. From the outset, it must be pointed out that Allen's work is not a claim for the impossibility of normative ends of social theory, or a rejection of the aims of critical theory in general and Frankfurt School critical social theory in particular. Nor is it an attempt at relativism. In pointing to the problematic grounding of the normative claims of current Frankfurt School theory, and by developing an alternative methodology for normative truth claims, her work seeks to rebuild critical social theory and its normative intent on sound theoretical as well as practical foundations. Allen's critique necessitates reflecting not only on the limitations of current Frankfurt School theory, and the questions of its relevancy for the contemporary moment, but also on the task of critical social theory beyond the Frankfurt School tradition, its foundational questions as well as its normative ends. Nevertheless, it is the premise of this essay that the success of every critical-theoretical paradigm ultimately hinges upon the question of how its methodology measures up against the task it sets for itself from the outset. In the final part of the essay, I will lay out my reservations regarding Allen's methodology and examine in what ways such an alternative methodology may not be viable for the normative ends of critical theory. I will end my discussion of Allen's work by expanding on her emphasis on the question of mediation and will elaborate on its further implications on the current Frankfurt School thought.

HISTORY AND NORMATIVITY

Within the overall work of the current generation of Frankfurt School theory, Allen identifies two main strategies for grounding normativity. The first path represents what Allen refers to as a "neo-Hegelian reconstructivist strategy", embodied in the works of Jürgen Habermas and Axel Honneth, where "historical progress and sociocultural learning and development" serve as the central ideas. The second path represents a "neo-Kantian constructivist strategy", where normativity is grounded in a foundationalist conception of "practical reason", as exemplified in the work of Rainer Forst (Allen, 2016, p. xv). While each of these strategies consists in a conception of history that informs a particular paradigm of normativity, and hence constitutes the subject—matter of Allen's critique, in this chapter I will limit my discussion to the fundamental questions arising from Allen's critique of Habermas and Honneth – that is, those theorists she identifies with a neo-Hegelian tradition. The issues arising from Allen's critique of Forst's work, on the other hand, involve an exposition of the fundamental problems of Kant's philosophy, the kind of social theory it informs, and its limitations in providing a philosophical horizon for critical social theory, and as such, requires a separate treatment that I will not tackle at the moment.

As Allen conceives it, the main tenets of Habermas' and Honneth's overall theoretical-normative framework build on the argument that "our current communicative or recognitional practices represent the outcome of a cumulative and progressive learning process and therefore are deserving of our support and allegiance" (2016, p. 3).

For Allen, the cornerstones of Habermas' and Honneth's strategy, namely communicative consensus and recognition, consist in a "progressive, developmental understanding of history as a way of grounding normativity" (2016, p. 3). Evidently, the notion of history-as-progress is not new to the history of ideas. In fact, as Allen points out, such a concept of progress occupied prominent roles in the forms of philosophy of history running through Kant, Hegel, and Marx (Allen, 2016, p. 8). Central to this philosophy of history was a notion of an end of history or *telos*, a "metaphysically loaded conception" that designates a goal of history and the direction of its progress variously conceived as "the kingdom of ends" (Kant), the "Absolute" (Hegel), or "communist utopia" (Marx) (Allen, 2016, p. 8). Allen points out that, while current Frankfurt School thinkers do not adhere to a philosophy of history and its idea of historical progress in the traditional sense of the concept, she nevertheless observes that there are remnants of such a philosophy of history in their grounding strategy (2016, pp. 8–9). Accordingly, unlike the traditional form of philosophy of history, the notion of progress as it figures into current Frankfurt School theory is "contingent rather than necessary, disaggregated rather than total, and postmetaphysical rather than metaphysical" (Allen, 2016, p. 9). For Allen, these postmetaphysically conceived notions of progress in history are expressed in the form of "sociocultural development, historical learning, and moral-political progress that inform Habermas' and Honneth's conceptions of modernity" (2016, p. 9). I will return to the question of Allen's depiction of philosophy of history and its larger implications for social theory in the second half of this essay. For the moment, however, it is important to specify how a philosophy of history, as Allen conceives it, relates to the problems of normativity in current Frankfurt School theory.

For Allen, the conception of progress raises fundamental questions in relation to the normative-theoretical framework of critical theory. To begin with, Allen points out that such normative aims are grounded in a "developmentalist, progressive reading of history," and such a reading, in turn, is immanently interrelated with the "civilizing mission of the West" and its inherent connection to power (2016, p. 3). In adopting a progressive reading of history as a grounding strategy, however, the current Frankfurt School theory not only brackets this idea of the "civilizing mission of the West" and its relation to power, but also ignores the fact that this "civilizing mission" emerged from, and is, in turn, inseparable from the European Enlightenment. That Enlightenment legacy served not only to justify colonialism and imperialism but also "continues to underwrite informal imperialism or neocolonialism" (Allen, p. 3). Against such an affirmative model of "history-as-progress," Allen reminds us of Horkheimer's fundamental distinction between critical and traditional theory, and asserts that critical theory must "hold open the central tension between power, on the one hand, and normativity and rationality, on the other" (2016, p. xiv). It is such a tension between power and normativity, along with its accompanying forms of rationality, that separates critical theory's understanding of the critical subject, as Allen puts it, as "self-consciously rooted in and shaped by the power relations in the society that she nevertheless aims self-reflexively and rationally to critique" (2016, p. xiii). Only when seen from this standpoint at the intersection of power, rationality and normative claims do the inadequacy of the notion of history-as-progress that underlies the normative grounding of current Frankfurt School theory become clear. For Allen, resolving this tension either through power (the ultimate standpoint of political realism) or through normativity amounts to a form of theory that builds on idealizing presuppositions, and as such, it would be in contradiction with the task of critical theory (Allen, 2016, p. xiv). "History-as-progress," accordingly, manifests a fundamental shortcoming of the normative-theoretical framework of the current Frankfurt School theory. Whereas both Habermas and Honneth attempt to ground normativity through what Allen calls a "backward looking story of historical progress" (2016, p. 13), Allen invokes Adorno to argue that for a critical social theory that is "truly critical," it is in fact necessary to "[call] into question the conception of progress as a historical 'fact'" (2016, p. 198). For Allen, one result of this inadequate approach to grounding normativity is that "a gulf has opened up between the Frankfurt School approach to critical theory and critical theory done under the heading of postcolonial theory" (2016, p. xv).

Nevertheless, the fundamental shortcomings of the current Frankfurt School theory vis-à-vis the critical and political needs of the present are not only discernible from the standpoint and purposes of postcolonial theory. Allen's critique also scrutinizes the grounding strategies of Habermas and Honneth against the measure of the very goals of the Frankfurt School tradition of critical social theory. As Allen states, the object of the Frankfurt School tradition of critique extends from "political economy" and "social-cultural analysis" to "theories of self or individual" simultaneously (2016, p. xiii). Put this way, the failure of the normative foundations of critical theory is not only a matter of abstruse theory construction. What is at stake is also the practical aspect of critical social theory and the interest in human freedom that distinguishes critical theory from other theoretical endeavors. As such, a truly critical normative-theoretical alternative to what is currently available in the Frankfurt School tradition is crucial for the contemporary relevance of critical theory (Allen, 2016, p. xiv). The challenge that Allen identifies for critical theory, then, is how to integrate a fundamental critique of Eurocentric and colonial history and its accompanying discourses of "progress" while also grounding the normative and emancipatory aims of critical theory. In Allen's account, the task of "decolonizing" is already inherent in the very purpose of critical theory.

Given Allen's critique, where do we seek a conception of history, and with it, alternative standards with which to ground the normative horizon of critical theory? Allen pursues such an alternative normative grounding through a synthesis of Adorno and Foucault, specifically in their respective insights into the relationship between history and normative truth claims (2016, p. 186). In reading Adorno and Foucault together, Allen's goal is to rethink the relationship between history and normativity through a new theoretical and conceptual framework (2016, p. 165). Through this synthesis, Allen not only problematizes the very idea of historical progress that ignores, among other things, the immanent relation of the notion of "progress" to the "logic of colonialism," but also offers a methodology for critical theory to decolonize itself (2016, p. 201). In what follows next, I will briefly outline the main features of her alternative methodology that draws on Adorno and Foucault, followed by my critical assessment of the viability of that methodology.

THE ENTANGLEMENT OF REASON AND POWER

For Allen, Foucault's and Adorno's thought converge at a point where they each express a fundamental skepticism about the concept of "progress" as a means to understand the history of modernity and its underlying "a-temporal point of view." They both consider such a view to be a "metaphysical illusion" (Allen, 2016, pp. 163–164). In so doing, both Foucault and Adorno, according to Allen, offer a break with the tradition of philosophy of history and its underlying notion of dialectics that had defined Hegel's conception of history (2016, p. 164). As such, they both represent an attempt to "think through Hegel but also beyond him" (Allen, 2016, p. 164). That attempt, as Allen points out, is guided by a desire for the fuller realization of normative content through a broader framework of "immanent critique" (2016, pp. 164–165). For Allen, this immanent critique involves a normative intent: it demands that the contemporary representatives of Enlightenment thought "live up more fully to its own normative ideals of freedom, inclusion and respect for the other" (2016, p. 165). It is because of such normative content, Allen points out, that it is crucial to recover the immanent critique in Foucault and Adorno as a possible means to decolonize critical theory (2016, p. 165).

Drawing on this notion of immanent critique, Allen builds an alternative methodology by reconstructing the main thesis of *Dialectic of Enlightenment*. Allen points out that in the *Dialectic of Enlightenment* (Horkheimer & Adorno, 1994), where Adorno and Horkheimer identify Enlightenment rationality as the sources of "totalitarian repression," the Enlightenment does not stand for simply a particular epoch of history; rather the object of their critique is the whole process of "regressive rationalization" whose outcome is the increasing domination not only of nature but also of human beings, and whose origin is captured in the notion of "will to mastery" (Allen, 2016, pp. 166–169). Allen stresses that for Adorno and Horkheimer, the "will to mastery" does not originate in the Enlightenment. Rather, the latter represents its full fruition. Arguing against Habermas' interpretation of the main thesis of *Dialectic of Enlightenment* as "a totalizing critique or abstract negation of the normative content of Enlightenment modernity" (2016, p. 164; also see Habermas, 1992, p. 126), Allen asserts that the main thesis of the work is in fact to show history as "both progress and regress at the same time" (2016, p. 164). Furthermore, Allen points out that the main standpoint of *Dialectic of Enlightenment* is not simply the "identity of power and reason," which is a form of critique that Horkheimer and Adorno point to in the example of Nietzsche. Rather, *Dialectic of Enlightenment* is a "critical problematization of our present historical moment" instead of an unreflexive affirmation of it (2016, p. 166). Its goal is to compel Enlightenment thought to reflect on itself, and in so doing, to open up a chance to bring into light the dominating and repressive dimensions at work through its history. In Allen's reinterpretation, then, the main thesis of *Dialectic of Enlightenment* is constituted by the question of "the possibility of breaking through the limits of enlightenment" (2016, p. 168). Enlightenment, accordingly, is constituted by totalitarian and regressive overall tendencies, as well as reflective and emancipatory aims simultaneously. It is the dialectical relationship between the two, as Allen points out, that constitutes one of the main arguments of Horkheimer and Adorno's work (2016, p. 169). The structure of this argument is built around the notion of "aporia" or contradiction, whose significance will come up again in my final discussion later (Allen, 2016, p. 169).

For Allen, a similar concern over the inherent link between rationality and power also guides Foucault's critique of reason. Arguing against an interpretation of Foucault's thought as "a rejection of reason in favor of a romantic embrace of unreason or madness," Allen asserts that the "fundamentally ambivalent stance toward reason" that characterizes Foucault's work is driven by a desire "to open up a space of freedom between ourselves and our historical a priori" (2016, p. 177). In Allen's account, Foucault's critique of modernity is an attempt to transform its underlying philosophy of history and its inherent notion of the "progressive rationalization of reason" in order to "open up spaces of freedom," whose effect, among others, is to show "not only that our present is contingent but also how it has been contingently made up through complex historical events" (2016, pp. 177–178). Put differently, for Allen, Foucault's intent, among other things, is to "*historicize* Hegel's philosophy of history, to offer a genealogy of the Hegelian notion of History" (2016, p. 178), and to reveal history without a "teleology of knowledge" (2016, p. 164). In Allen's reading, Foucault's central claim, accordingly, is not one of the "historicity of reason" or of knowledge (2016, p. 179). Rather, Foucault argues that the notion of History – that is, history with a capital H – is in fact "a structure of thought" that becomes "modern historical a priori [to] modern forms of rationality" (Allen, p. 179). In Allen's account, central to Foucault's attempt is the notion of "unreason." For Foucault, "unreason" remained "outside of history and linear temporality," which allowed it to "open up the possibility of reflection on the limits of its own Hegelian, Historical modernity" and to "resist recuperation within the Hegelian dialectic" (2016, pp. 181–182). Unreason, accordingly, stands in for that which "can be neither fully conceptualized in the language of reason nor reconciled in the dialectical unfolding of History" (Allen, 2016, p. 183). Rather, unreason as the "figure of the outside [...] serves to open up and illuminate lines of gaps and fissures [...] in our own historical a priori" (Allen, 2016, pp. 183–184). In this reconstruction of Foucault's thought, Allen argues that the idea of "unreason" allows a "distance" between ourselves and our system of thought (2016, p. 185). Such distance is the space that is created *within*, the "space of freedom" (Allen, 2016, p. 184). Put differently, Foucault's critique is not a rejection of reason. Rather, for Allen, it reveals the ambivalent nature of reason, and most importantly for a project of decolonial emancipation, his work shows how reason is "ambivalently entangled with power relations" (2016, p. 185).

In Allen's reconstruction, then, both Foucault and Adorno offer a critique of history understood as the "progressive rationalization of reason" (2016, p. 186). Accordingly, such a critique does not amount to a "totalizing critique" of reason as Habermas would have it. Rather, such critique shows that it is not possible for critical social theory to "identify a use or a stratum of reason that is not so entangled" (Allen, 2016, p. 186), as to be found, for instance, in Habermas' attempt with the paradigm of system and lifeworld separation, and still remains truly critical. As Allen writes, "the task of philosophy, as Adorno understands it, is to reflect on its own activity as a rational enterprise and in so doing to attempt to transcend itself" (2016, p. 186).

What exactly would such transcendence mean for critical social theory? How does the self-transcendence of philosophy relate to a normative standpoint? From the outset, Allen points out that such transcendence does not imply a "concept of utopia [as] above identity and above contradiction" (2016, p. 187). For Adorno, what constitutes the normative standpoint of a theory is not an idea of a future society based on a notion of the reconciliation of contradictions conceived as a positive concept. Likewise, for Foucault, there can be no such claim as to "have access to a point of view outside of power relations" (Allen, 2016, p. 188). Rather, for both Foucault and Adorno, the notion of good life and good society – even when thought of as utopia – can only be conceived negatively. As Allen puts it, for both Foucault and Adorno:

> any vision of the good life offered from within a society structured by relations of domination is likely to reproduce those power relations, to be infected by them, so they both eschew utopian speculations about what kind of content the "good life" might have. (2016, p. 188)

In this reconstruction, however, the impossibility of conceiving a future society in the sense of a positive utopia is not an impediment to normativity. Rather, it allows for an "open-ended conception of the future" (Allen, 2016, p. 188). More specifically, for Allen, rejecting a positive concept of utopia opens up the possibility of imagining a kind of future society based on a radically different normative grounding than those that are available in current Frankfurt School theory. Within the latter, the forms of normative grounding ultimately boil down to ideals such as "more transparent liberal democracy" (Habermas), "more inclusive forms of recognition" (Honneth), or "political systems through rational justification" (Forst) (Allen, 2016, p. 188). All of these ideals, however, for Allen express the idea of a "better and fuller realization of our *existing normative ideals*" (2016, p. 188, emphasis added) rather than their radical reimagining, which is in fact what the task of truly critical social theory consists in (2016, pp. 189–203). Accordingly, untangling reason and power presents a particular challenge to the normative grounding of social theory: If reason is so entangled with power, and hence any rational enterprise must first attempt to transcend itself, and if such transcendence must reject the existing normative ideals as a positive reconciliation of the contradictions, how can we conceive of normativity? How can we establish the normative foundations of critical theory *critically*, and more successfully than current Frankfurt School theory?

PROBLEMATIZING GENEALOGY AND METANORMATIVE CONTEXTUALISM

The central premise of Allen's alternative method for normative grounding of social theory consists in the notion of a "historically situated conception of rationality" as applied to the "historico-philosophical enterprise itself" (2016, p. 189). For Allen, this is a method that historicizes History itself. Its premise draws on Foucault and Adorno, as I sketched above. Foucault's problematization of history with a capital H, "as the progressive unfolding of a rationalization process," reveals that not only is the idea of History itself historically contingent, but also that such a notion of history excludes and dominates "those who are deemed unreasonable" (Allen, 2016, p. 188). Likewise, Adorno's engagement of Hegel in *Negative Dialectics* expresses a similar concern, and reveals for Allen that "we have to locate the concept of history in history rather than in existence" (2016, p. 189).

Nevertheless, how can critical theory problematize the "historical present" without becoming relativist on the one hand, or falling back to the philosophy of history on the other hand? What methodological tools do we have in order to avoid submitting to either? As an alternative to both of these hazards, Allen expounds the method of "genealogy as problematization," a methodology that Allen intends as self-reflexive of the entanglement of reason and power (p. 190). Such genealogy seeks to uncover the historically contingent nature of the totality of processes that led to specific values or moral standpoints, and thus it seeks to problematize these very standpoints. For Allen, the goal of this genealogy is the "critical problematization of our historical present" (2016, p. 190), and to show in what ways "our normative commitments are entangled with relations of power and domination" (2016, p. 205). In so doing, Allen asserts, genealogy in fact serves the normative perspective of the Enlightenment (2016, p. 204). This is because genealogy as problematization asserts "the legacy of the Enlightenment" not through an affirmation of the present but, as Allen argues, "in and through its radical transformation" (2016, p. 191). As such, it is an attempt to provide an alternative normative grounding of critique.

In Allen's account, such an alternative methodology stands at the intersection of Adorno and Foucault's thought, or rather, where Adorno's thought meets Foucault's method in their approach to critique and normativity, and differences in their conceptual frameworks notwithstanding. Allen points out that while genealogy is not a part of Adorno's overall conceptual framework, his emphasis on history as simultaneous domination and the possibility of freedom can be understood as a form of "problematizing genealogy" (2016, p. 193). Accordingly, both Foucault and Adorno offer us what Allen refers to as necessary "critical distance" (2016, p. 197) that would enable such a problematization

of the present, as well as a standpoint *within*, a standpoint from which to critically reflect on "history with a capital H" — that is, history that presents itself as
historical a priori, or "Historical historical a priori," as Allen calls it (2016,
p. 179). In Allen's reading of Foucault and Adorno, such a critical distance is
conceptualized through the notions of "unreason" and "nonidentity," respectively. While each of these notions would require a much longer and in-depth
discussion, for the purposes of this essay, I will simply assume their respective
outcome as Allen construes it in regard to normativity. Accordingly, central to
this outcome, among others, is the argument that unreason and nonidentity
bring into light the relationship of history and power that otherwise may not be
possible to recognize nor to problematize. Put this way, both "unreason" and
"nonidentity" offer a means to search for truth through what Allen refers to as
"the fragmentary, non-systematic, and experimental work of critical thought"
(2016, p. 194). As such, both Foucault and Adorno, as Allen notes, share a fundamentally normative standpoint: *"a fuller realization of a central normative
ideal of the Enlightenment: freedom"* (2016, p. 196, emphasis original).

For Allen, the method of "problematizing genealogy" shows not only "the
contingency of our beliefs and normative commitments" but also "the ways that
those commitments have been contingently made up of complex relations of
power, domination, and violence" (p. 209). It is important to note the distinction
Allen draws between problematizing genealogy and what she refers to as "subversive genealogy." For the latter, genealogy is reduced to the task of "showing
how our normative ideals and principles get entangled with power relations
when they are applied in the real world" (2016, p. 206). For Allen, the purpose
of genealogy, in contrast, is not simply to point out "how normative ideals go
wrong in practice" (p. 206), nor the subversion of normative ideals, but their
problematization.

Nevertheless, if there is such a connection between the immanent normativity
of forms of life and the forms of power invested within them, how can critical
theory maintain the distinction between the two? The second feature of Allen's
methodology, metanormative contextualism, intends to address this very question. Accordingly, Allen's approach requires that we differentiate between "first-
order normative principles and the metanormative stance we take with respect
to them" (2016, p. 202). In differentiating the normativity of forms of life and
forms of power, Allen argues that the method of "rational reconstruction" currently put forward (i.e., rational reconstruction of communicative structures, as
in Habermas) is "more hindrance than help" (2016, p. 209). This is because for
Allen the progressive reading of European modernity that underlies such a
method of rational reconstruction already understands a form of life that it takes
as paradigmatic to be developmentally superior to those that we label pre- or
nonmodern (2016, p. 229). In so doing, Allen argues, such a progressive reading
of European modernity collapses the space necessary for reflexivity about our
paradigms of normativity.

For Allen, such a lack of clarity between metanormative and normative levels
is obviously the case, for example, with Habermas, which leads to a problematic
grounding of normativity (2016, p. 210). On the one hand, the progressive

reading of history advocates a universal significance and validity of normative claims through context-transcendence (i.e., the validity of the normative ideals of European modernity beyond their historical context). On the other hand, it ignores the fact that this very claim is only possible on the underlying reasoning that:

> premodern or traditional forms of life are developmentally and cognitively inferior to our own, insofar as they haven't learned something that we now know, which is that their world-view is just that, a view of the world, and not the ultimate truth. (Allen, 2016, p. 210)

For Allen, such an intellectual stance founded on the "progressive readings of European modernity" as it figures into current Frankfurt School theory, "places insuperable cognitive burdens on those who would aspire to engage in genuinely open intercultural dialogue across the colonial divide" (2016, p. 202), even as such a stance aims for a dialogue that might prove things to be otherwise. Put differently, the fundamental space between metanormative and normative commitments seems to be already filled by a notion of "progress in history." Accordingly, Allen argues, rather than separating the two levels of normative commitment, current Frankfurt School critical theory, as it stands, already assumes an affirmative standpoint vis-à-vis its own history.

As a means to differentiate between these two different levels of normative commitments, Allen expounds the method of metanormative contextualism. The central premise of metanormative contextualism consists in the assertion that, as we hold on to normative commitments, such as freedom and equality, we also understand that at the metanormative level, these commitments are to be "justified immanently and contextually, via an appeal to specific historical context rather than via an appeal to their putatively context-transcendent character" (Allen, 2016, p. 211). For Allen, such a "contextualist conception of normativity" allows for the separation of the moments of the "fuller realization of normative commitments" (such as the expansion of gay rights in the West, to cite Allen's example) from the affirmation of the historically constituted social forms within which "such normative commitments are embedded" (2016, p. 229). Allen points to the theoretical and practical hazard in this "tendency to self-congratulation [that] can be so seductive and so dangerous for a critical theory that aims to reflect on its own investment in relations of power" (2016, p. 229). In view of her critique, Allen calls for "ongoing and relentless problematization [of] our local and contextual judgments about progress in history" (2016, p. 229). For Allen, while progress should serve as "moral-political imperative," it also requires "a relentless and ongoing problematization [...] of the normative standards by which such progress could be measured" (2016, p. 228).

Allen's diagnosis of the problems of normativity in current Frankfurt School theory intends to challenge contemporary critical social theory to reflect on its Enlightenment genealogies, and to overcome the obstacles that genealogy creates for shared normative-theoretical projects with an emancipatory and decolonial intent. To succeed over these obstacles, Allen in effect asks critical theory to leave behind the idea of normative foundationalism and, instead, suggests that we seek the foundations of this project in contingent, context immanent

normativity. The methods of problematizing genealogy and metanormative contextualism intend to serve such a purpose. Such a diagnosis of current Frankfurt
School theory and the reconstruction of the main tenets of Foucault's and
Adorno's thought would obviously constitute the subject for a lively debate
among critical social theorists. What I would like to focus on here, however, is
the methodology that Allen puts forward as a means to overcome the problem
of normative grounding for critical social theory, namely the joint methods of
"problematizing genealogy" and "metanormative contextualism." In what follows, I will tackle Allen's diagnosis and her alternative reconstruction of a normative grounding not only as a critique of current Frankfurt School theory but
also a possible answer to a question that Adorno once put forward, namely the
question of where to find effective tools to do theory in the modern world (see
Adorno, 2000). Reading this alternative methodology from the standpoint of
how to do theory will allow me to engage Allen's critique beyond its implications on current Frankfurt School thought and toward a possible reconstruction
of normative foundations as well as of the ends of critique.

HISTORY, CRITIQUE, AND MEDIATION

More specifically, I will expand here on three interrelated points of critique. My
first point concerns whether the question of philosophy of history is an accurate
diagnosis of the problems of normative grounding for current Frankfurt School
theory. Second, I will tackle whether problematizing genealogy and the notion
of unreason could serve as an alternative methodology for critical theory. The
third and related point concerns whether the distinction between metanormative
and normative levels as suggested by Allen is tenable for critical theory. Finally,
I will end my critique by expanding on Allen's reiteration of the mediated nature
of theoretical categories and its implications for current Frankfurt School
theory.

As I briefly introduced earlier, Allen argues that the notion of "history-as-
progress," whose socio-historical and cultural origins can be identified in the
European Enlightenment, manifests itself in the form of philosophy of history,
and its remnants are still to be found in the grounding strategies of the current
generation of Frankfurt School social theory. As an alternative, Allen then seeks
the sources of alternative conception of history in Adorno's and Foucault's
thought. There are several concerns that issue from this depiction of a philosophy of history in its "non-traditional" form that figures, as Allen argues, into
current Frankfurt School theory. Needless to say, philosophy of history, regardless of its form, is not compatible with critical social theory and its normative
grounding. Nevertheless, if such a philosophy of history is "contingent, disaggregated and postmetaphysical," to what extent can it still be meaningfully
referred to as a philosophy of history? Put differently, is it philosophy of history,
albeit of a non-traditional form, that underlies the current Frankfurt School theory's notion of progress? In fact, I would like to argue that the problematic status of progress issues from precisely the lack of philosophy of history in current
Frankfurt school theory, and that what underlies its grounding strategy is the

explicit awareness that an appeal to philosophy of history in a postmetaphysical universe is no longer available. If that is the case, however, where do we seek the conceptual sources of the problem of a normative grounding for current Frankfurt School theory? Obviously, one can claim, in agreement with Allen, that even if there is such awareness, the current Frank School theorists are simply unsuccessful in overcoming any remnants of philosophy of history. Nevertheless, for a more accurate diagnosis of the problems of normative grounding in Frankfurt School social theory, I believe it is necessary to differentiate more accurately the forms of thought that Allen draws together under philosophy of history.

Philosophy of history is an attempt to comprehend the universal history of humanity, its course, its development, as well as its future, within a philosophical-speculative framework that incorporates not only epistemological but also ethical and moral standpoints. With the Enlightenment, such a standpoint turned into a template for understanding the entire history of humanity and its development (see Heller, 1982, p. 224). While Allen points out that a philosophy of history runs through Kant, Hegel, and Marx, we should not disregard the fundamental differences among these — the differences that effect divergent foundations of normative categories in the kind of social theories they inform, and hence are central to the argument at hand regarding the conceptions of progress and freedom. Kant's philosophy of history centers around the idea that there is a rational process that is intelligible to reason. For Kant, discovering this purpose through a priori rules for the study of history, which covers topics such as the idea of civil society and the autonomy of reason, among others, also serves as the guiding principles of history, including the development of history from "barbarism to culture" (Kant, 1991[1784], p. 44). In contrast to this a priori philosophy of history, with which Habermas' reconstructive paradigm has a close affinity, Hegel's philosophy of history is not only historical but also permeated with a manifest logic of History. That such a logic resolves itself in the "Absolute" is obviously one of the most contentious claims of his philosophy of history. But the form of thought that such a philosophy of history involves, that is, the logic of contradictions, clearly distinguishes Hegel's thought from the rest of the philosophical tradition that is somewhat crudely called German Idealism. That logic conceives the individual as both the subject and object of history, and permeates the relation between consciousness and history (Hegel, 1956[1899], pp. 1–79). As is well known, such a relationship between consciousness and history was later turned "right side up" by Marx. When read against this backdrop, I would emphasize, contrary to Allen, that in contradistinction to both Kant and Hegel and the forms of idealism each construes, Marx's mature social theory has no philosophy of history. In fact, what we find in Marx's overall thought is a counterpoint to such a philosophical-speculative framework for understanding history. In his mature theory, Marx offers an account as well as a critique of how capitalist modernity, in its commodity form as a social form, in fact recasts its own history as if it represented universal human history in the natural course of its development. Put differently, the break with philosophy of history is already presented in Marx's social theory.

I would like to stress, however, that my intent is not to play up Marx against every given contemporary theoretical debate. Rather, I would like to point out that such a crucial difference in Marx's social theory would be consonant with the conceptual sources of methodology that Allen seeks in Adorno, especially the notion of nonidentity. I will expand on the implications of this alternative approach to history later. The point I would like to emphasize here arises from Allen's question of the relationship between philosophy of history and critical theory, but I pursue the conceptual sources of the problem – the problem of normative grounding – in a different direction than that of Allen's: the differences between a priori vs historical structure notwithstanding, what is common to all of these otherwise diverse philosophies of history was the idea of universalism. The idea of universal history, along with the conception of the course of its development (progress!), is the cornerstone of philosophy of history both in Kant and in Hegel, as a normatively oriented, speculative-philosophical framework. The conception of universalism, in other words, along with the course of history's development as progress are two facets of the same, historically specific European philosophy of history.

The differences between its individual representatives notwithstanding, the current Frankfurt School theory is defined by alertness to the problems of universalism as an attempt to legitimate normative truth claims. In fact, both Habermas' theory of communicative action (Habermas, 1989) as well as Honneth's notion of recognition (Honneth, 1995b) can be taken, at a methodological level, precisely as attempts to arrive at "universalizable" standards without appealing to any philosophy of history. The fact that they strive to substantiate progress retrospectively (what Allen calls "backward-looking philosophy of history") is not due to their conception of history but due, I would argue, to their conception of the present. I will tackle the question of why such a retrospective account of the present appears to progress in the final section. For the moment, it is necessary to note that my emphasis on the question of universalism also allows for an alternative reading of Habermas' appeal to what Allen refers to as the context-transcendence of normative claims. Such an appeal to context-transcendence is founded on the conviction that in a postmetaphysical universe, normativity can indeed be built on quasi-transcendental foundations, that is, through postmetaphysical categories that are socio-historically specific in origin and yet can be taken to be universal in their validity. Context-transcendence, in other words, aims not to realize but to avoid any appeal to philosophy of history.

Obviously, one must still ask whether universalism, even if not grounded on a philosophy of history, can still be taken as a paradigmatic conception of normativity. That is, even if we put aside the question of their historical origin, and accept the quasi-transcendental grounding of normative categories, there is still the question of how they can possibly coalesce in history, when taken paradigmatically as universalizable. In fact, the history of colonialism reveals, precisely, that universalism does not mean equality; it means rather than difference becomes irrelevant at best, and anathema at worst. Such history – the history of the "civilizing mission of the West" – shows that that which seeks to be universal is inherently intolerant, and "intransigence has always defeated tolerance"

(Todorov, 1992, p. 106). On this point, I agree with Allen, though on different grounds, regarding the inadequacy of current Frankfurt School theory's grounding strategy! For, the notion of progress, even when conceived postmetaphysically and quasi-transcendentally, comes with a critical blind spot for European self-understanding – the one implied by colonialism, which is the point that Allen successfully demonstrates.

My next question concerns Allen's suggestion of problematizing genealogy as an alternative methodology: How exactly can genealogical problematization continue, as Allen argues, the normative implications of Enlightenment ideals by transcending them? Allen does offer a convincing argument as to how such a methodology can show that normative claims are in fact infused with power in their genealogy, and thereby it can problematize the existing normative truth-claims. Nevertheless, that problematization would be possible only if we already have a normative criterion that is fundamentally different than that which is being problematized. For normative, categories themselves cannot be derived from such genealogy, nor from the demonstrative value of the genealogical method itself, except, obviously, negatively. Negative, however, is hardly the same as transcendent. The recognition of domination and power in the world already assumes what freedom and autonomy entail, as well as their difference from unfreedom and domination. The value of genealogical problematization, conceivably, resides in its self-reflective character – i.e., rather than unproblematically accepting the normative categories of progress, it would allow us to reflect on their problematic history laden with power and domination. In order to serve as a method of critique, however, genealogy must already assume a theory, if not a philosophy, of history. Furthermore, if the aim of genealogy is to uncover the historically contingent nature of specific values or moral standpoints, is the problematization of normative commitments the same as the grounding of alternative normative commitments that are less entangled with power and domination? It is not fully clear in Allen's account how genealogy, even if it is not a subversive kind as Allen formulates it, could adequately serve as a method that not only offers a critique of Enlightenment ideals but also their transcendence.

Furthermore, in demonstrating the critical value of such genealogy, Allen builds on Foucault's and Adorno's thought as the sources for a radical break with the philosophy of history, for the problematization of modernity's self-understanding, and as such, for advancing a kind of critical theory that is not moored in any speculative-philosophical framework of history for the legitimacy of its normative truth-claims. To these ends, Allen enlists Foucault's notion of unreason and Adorno's notion of nonidentity. Nevertheless, not only are these two notions fundamentally different in terms of the theoretical frameworks within which they developed, it is questionable that one can enlist the two unproblematically for the same critical ends. Whereas Allen argues, invoking Foucault, that "unreason" remained "outside of history and linear temporality," it is not clear how this notion of "outside" is to serve the normative grounding of critical theory. In Allen's reading of Foucault, unreason can be tasked with putting a distance between ourselves and a system of thought that is a form of domination through rationality. But this is not to say that the latter – domination through reason – is the only form of domination, even if it is its most prevalent form in modernity. While the notion of unreason would allow a space outside of the sphere of domination by reason, it is not clear how such space "outside" necessarily amounts to a space of freedom. Even if Allen's critique is limited to the form of domination by reason specific to modernity, a critique that is "truly critical" must also recognize that unreason can be a realm of domination just as well as reason can. While attempting to counter philosophy of history by remaining "outside of history and linear temporality," the notion of unreason, ironically, seems to be limited by a similar dichotomy of "modernity and its other," and rather than transcending it, it appears to be determined by modernity's prevalent form of domination. As a form of thought, this form of critique seems to be as linear as its object. What is further, it is not clear how unreason, in remaining "outside," would recognize which historical processes that create domination would also bring about the conditions of their overcoming, in theory as well as in practice – a shortcoming that ultimately expresses the fundamental distinction between critical theory and the forms of thought that underlie traditional forms of theory. Can we really task unreason, then, with serving as a standpoint of critique? It seems to be the case that, despite its adoption for aims of critique, unreason as a particular reading of history that "remains outside of its linear temporality" comes with the hazard of an equally linear reading of history, even when the purpose of such a reading is ultimately to show the problematic nature of our normative truth claims. If the goal of such a methodology, among others, is an immanent critique that also allows for a concept of history that cannot be assumed from the outset, as Allen argues, neither to be progress or regress, then, rather than remaining "outside" of it, the notions that we enlist to serve as a critique must immanently engage the relationship of reason and history, comprehending both in their contradiction. Adorno's notion of non-identity, I would argue, can serve as a better conceptual tool to that end, as well as the end of critical theory as a normatively oriented social theory. Unlike unreason, with the notion of non-identity, the metaphor is not spatial but processual; it delineates not a "space" but a "moment." It is not a standpoint. Although when unreconciled it is experienced as "negativity," such negativity passes to "critical self-reflection." As Adorno puts it, "The less identity can be assumed between subject and object, the more contradictory as the demands made upon the cognitive subject, upon its unfettered strength and candid self-reflection" (Adorno, 1995, p. 31).

In showing a discrepancy between the aims of critical theory and the strategy of grounding normativity in Habermas' appeal to context-transcendence, Allen asks us to sincerely engage a question of whether "a genuinely open dialogue across lines of cultural difference" is really possible (2016, p. 211). As Allen points out, such a dialogue would only be possible if we could conceive of the relation of our commitments on metanormative and normative levels differently than it currently stands. Metanormative contextualism, accordingly, offers a solution to a problem that current Frankfurt School theory is not able to resolve. As Allen puts it:

our normative principles can be justified relative to a set of basic normative commitments that stand fast in relation to them, but because there is no context-transcendent point of view from which we can determine which contexts are superior to which others, those basic normative commitments must be understood as contingent foundations. (2016, p. 215)

But how exactly can critical social theory maintain and reflect on such a difference between "metanormative or second-order" and "first-order commitments"?

Let me elucidate this question by first stressing that Allen's critique unequivocally shows the problem with taking the specific realization of normative commitments as an affirmation of particular (i.e., European) history as "developmentally superior to pre- or non modern forms of life" (Allen, 2016, p. 229). Such an inference would undermine the *critical* element of the normative-theoretical framework of critical theory, leaving the latter with moral perspectivism rather than with critique. This implies that the realization of normative commitments, and the question of whether such a realization is an affirmation of a specific, given historical form of life as "progress-in-history" must be held to occupy analytically and substantively different levels within the normative-theoretical framework of critical social theory. Rather than advocating relativism, Allen's metanormative contextualism asserts that "we can envision external modes of critique in which justificatory standards that are held fast in one context are brought to bear in those of another, and vice versa" (2016, p. 218). Invoking Adorno and Hegel, accordingly, Allen argues that metanormative contextualism "is beyond the alternatives of relativism and absolutism" (2016, p. 216). Rather, Allen reiterates, the normative horizon of Enlightenment modernity includes both "openness to other normative horizons" as well as "critique and self-reflexivity."

Nevertheless, how is this openness to be realized? What forms of praxis are we to submit to, in order to accomplish such "openness to other normative horizons"? Are we to revert back to paradigms of the rationality of linguistic communication and mutual recognition? Habermas and the consensus theory of truth? Second, and equally important, can metanormative contextualism really avoid falling back to relativism? In her account of the normative ends of critique, Allen already succinctly shows the open-ended nature of the future as an ideal. With metanormative contextualism, however, it is not only the future but also the past and the present, that is, history itself, that must be conceived of as open-ended, subject to interpretation and reinterpretation. If normative commitments can be justified at the metanormative level, and only contextually, via "appeal to [...] historical context," this leaves our normative commitments in the precarious position of being a function of subjectivity and its fundamentally unresolvable questions, conceptually as well as practically. This theoretical problem is in fact in close affinity with the problems of Weber's method. One can perhaps conceive of metanormative contextualism as another, perhaps a more indeterminate capitulation of the fundamental historicity of our normative categories and commitments. In fact, the historicity of our moral, ethical, and epistemological categories is central to the task of critical social theory. This was one of the central implications of the distinction between traditional and critical theory, and of the notion of theory's reflection on its own conditions of possibility.

Nevertheless, historicity is not the same as relativism, and one must draw a stronger distinction between the argument for relativity and the argument for the historicity of our normative commitments than context-dependency can afford. One must agree with Allen that the fuller realization of normative commitments cannot serve as an affirmation of the existing social reality. Neither, for instance, could the successful pursuit of gay rights (Allen's example) be conceived of as "progress in history" in a totally alienated society. But such theoretical necessity would not demonstrate the context-dependency of such normative commitments and the contingency of their foundations, as Allen seems to be suggesting. Rather, it would be due to the fact that critical theory that envisages reality affirmatively would in fact be oblivious to the inherent contradiction of existing social reality. That is to say, the expansion of LGBTQ rights, for instance, is progress independent of the context within which it takes place (can there be a context where it would not be progress?). But such progress should not be an affirmation of what would in fact be a totally alienated society.

My reservations on the viability of metanormative contextualism and problematizing genealogy notwithstanding, as a final point, I will conclude my discussion by expanding on what I consider to be a crucial contribution of Allen's critique, namely her emphasis on the idea of mediation. In contrast to current Frankfurt School theory's strategy of grounding normativity, Allen highlights a feature of critical theory that is indeed central to its emancipatory ends:

> For Adorno, just as for Hegel, there is no unmediated access to things in themselves; rather our access is always mediated thorough concepts, which themselves contain the sedimentations of history, social practices, and culture. (2016, p. 217)

Further consideration of the mediated nature of categories — including the normative categories that ground critical social theory — might help in assessing historically specific conditions underlying the problematic grounding of normativity in current Frankfurt School theory.

In seeking for alternative sources of normative grounding, Allen reminds us that understanding the history of modernity as progress was a very problematic idea for Adorno and Horkheimer, who, in turn, responded to such history, to its inherent contradictions, and to its relations of domination with a critical theory defined by its aporiatic form of thought. In contrast to such aporiatic thought, in both Habermas and Honneth, one sees a form of thought whose conception of history is affirmative, even while their particular assessments are normative, such as the internal colonization thesis, the idea of communicative structures of a lifeworld free of domination, and the diagnosis of misrecognition. Such affirmative thought stands in stark contrast to the critical stance of their first-generation predecessors. How do we explain this eschewing of aporia — the theoretical form that had defined the previous generation of critical theory — in current Frankfurt School theory? Why does modernity appear to be less problematic, and history appear more easily as progress? What I would like to tackle as my last point is the question of what made such affirmative theory, and its underlying affirmative thought, a historical possibility. More specifically, what I would like to suggest is that Allen's emphasis on the mediated nature of concepts as sedimentations of history and culture necessitates questioning the existing paradigms of normativity in the current generation of Frankfurt School theory, along with their grounding strategies, even beyond their genealogy in Enlightenment thought. Perhaps we can read this stark contrast between Adorno and Horkheimer on the one hand, and the current representatives of the Frankfurt School (Habermas, Honneth, and Forst), on the other hand, against the backdrop of the specific context of the European historical present as it informs the normative foundations of theory.

Following Allen, if we take the emphasis on learning, recognition, and progress — the central categories of current Frankfurt School theory — as "sedimentations" of a historical present, it is clear that such history has been a period of relative social and political stability, underlined by the welfare state as its most prominent political form, hitherto an exceptional period in European history. My intent is not to sociologize philosophy, nor to make a reductionist turn to the sociology of knowledge. Rather, the goal is to understand social theory's immanent relation with its time, and thereby to ask what such a stark contrast between the two generations of critical theory discloses about the mediated nature of theory, and about its fundamental concepts. To sketch in rather rough outlines, the specific history of Europe since the Second World War is defined by the state's obligation to support its citizens, alleviate the risks to society defined by exchange, mitigate the consequences of (dare I say?) class conflict, and effectively subside the contradictions that had defined the previous period of liberal capitalism by absorbing these contradictions into its own structures (see Offe, 1994). While such a model of "political solutions to social contradictions" was once adopted more or less across all post-war European societies (Offe, 1994, p. 147), the very idea of simultaneously reconciling otherwise multi-faceted and structurally contradictory ends also led to an "overburdening" (read determining) of social and institutional structures that could not maintain this absorption by political management without their own transformation. Post-war European societies, accordingly, their individual differences notwithstanding, were defined by conflictual outcomes of the political management of post-war capitalist modernity under a liberal-democratic political form. How does such a society experience its contradictions? Where does it seek its solutions? The fundamental categories of social theory that we refer to as current Frankfurt School theory express these very transformations, experiences, and their perceived solutions in notions such as "undistorted communication" and "mutual recognition." What Habermas captures rather arcanely under the term "steering media" in fact expresses the conversion of structural contradictions that had defined a prior phase of capitalist modernity into conflicts emanating from problems of management through the state and other formally independent structures and their capacities. In a society constituted as such, the fundamental conflicts are experienced variously as intrusions of the processes of management into the "horizon of meaning" (the analytical core of the so-called internal colonization thesis) or as conflicts emanating from constraints on mutual recognition due to disruptions in the reproduction of social life (Honneth, 1995a, 1995b, pp. 92–93). The responses and solutions to such conflicts, in turn, appear to be captured through normatively grounded ideas of communicative action, inherent rationality of language, and recognition.

This theoretical form displays a stark contrast with aporiatic thought. As Allen already puts it in regard to the structure of *Dialectic of Enlightenment*, aporiatic thought is central to critical theory that comprehends capitalist modernity in its contradictions (2016, p. 169). Aporia, in other words, is an adequate theoretical expression of such a structure of reality. The outcome of this theoretical comprehension of the immanent contradiction is such that, "Enlightenment rationality is both freedom and unfreedom or domination at the same time [and ...] this contradictory truth can only be expressed through an aporiatically structured argument" (Allen, 2016, p. 170). The critical essence of the thesis of *Dialectic of Enlightenment* consists of its grasp of this relationship between thought and reality. As Allen points out:

> central to Adorno's dialectical conception of progress is the idea that the belief in progress as a historical "fact" – the idea that humanity has progressed in the past and that our present form of life is the result of such progress – stands in the way of progress as a forward liaising moral-political imperative. (2016, p. 174)

The mediated nature of our fundamental categories, including the normative categories that ground critical social theory, in fact underscores one of the central themes of Lukács' reconstruction of Hegel's philosophy, a theme that constituted one of the core ideas of critical theory as Adorno and Horkheimer conceived it: concepts, in critical theory, are products of history (Horkheimer, 1995; see also Abromeit, 2011, p. 321). If, following Lukács, we were to bracket Hegel's idealist framework, we find a philosophical account of this idea articulated as the relationship between reason and history – not by staying outside it, as in Foucault, but by comprehending both reason and history in their contradiction (see Lukács, 1975). Arguably, it was such a philosophical breakthrough that opened up a space for social theory between philosophy on the one hand and history on the other hand (see Marcuse, 1941). Critical theory of the relations between thought and reality, of philosophy and its historical possibility, shows not just the historicity of thought, but also the possible untruth of all metaphysics including the metaphysics of the philosophy of history.

Within the historical context of post-war European modernity, in contrast, the critical-theoretical questions that could only be tackled through aporiatic thought and its categories are replaced with a form of thought that rather simply submits to concepts of "reflection" in the Hegelian sense. The contradictory nature of social reality, in other words, instead of leading to their resolution in higher categories, is replaced with a notion of conflict, and its resolution is modeled as consensus, either through the rationality of linguistic communication or through recognition. Conflict thus replaced contradiction, and the dialectic is abandoned for a consensus theory of truth. The significant blind spots of this form of affirmative thought involve, among others, Europe's own historical relations with its "other" – that is, the history of colonization and its catastrophic outcomes – that cannot be neatly absorbed within such an affirmation of modernity. As Allen's work suggests, postcolonial critique is not only an invaluable but also a necessary interlocutor to help remedy such a blind spot and to enable critical theory to realize its normative ends toward true "progress" by radically scrutinizing its own normative foundations.

Allen's insistence on "truly critical" thought on the one hand, and the Enlightenment heritage on the other hand, enables her to hold that inheritance accountable to its own standards. According to those standards, what constitutes progress can never be settled before thought. For as Allen shows, to assume what progress entails while arguing for "progress" is not a *critical* social theory. This is not to say that the socio-historical and culturally specific categories – i.e., progress and universalism – are inessential to critical theory. From the normative-theoretical standpoint of critical social theory, however, the affirmative nature of these categories needs to be inverted. That is to say, progress and universalism ultimately gain their analytic importance in demonstrating a fundamental discrepancy between how a given form of social life, with its normative truths, appears to us, and how, and on whose expense such social life is made possible historically. The task of the normative categories is to serve critical thought rather than an affirmative one and to show us this discrepancy – the discrepancy, that is, between how we appear to ourselves, and what we really are.

In scrutinizing its normative foundations, Allen's work compels us to consider, among other things, the extent to which the current generation of Frankfurt School theory can in fact be understood within the same normative framework of critical social theory that originally emerged from the Institute for Social Research. In so doing, Allen challenges current Frankfurt School theory to be accountable to its own aims while also remaining within the intellectual tradition of critical social theory. Her argument pushes us to reconsider not only the normative foundations of critical social theory, but more importantly, the possibility of building emancipatory futures upon those foundations.

BIBLIOGRAPHY

Abromeit, J. (2011). *Max Horkheimer and the foundations of the Frankfurt school*. New York, NY: Cambridge.

Adorno, T. W. (1995). *Negative dialectics*. New York, NY: Continuum.

Adorno, T. W. (2000). *Introduction to sociology*. Stanford, CA: Stanford University Press.

Allen, A. (2016). *The end of progress: Decolonizing the normative foundations of critical theory*. New York, NY: Columbia University Press.

Habermas, J. (1989). *The theory of communicative action* (Vol. 2). Boston, MA: Beacon Press.

Habermas, J. (1992). *The philosophical discourse of modernity*. Cambridge: MIT Press.

Hegel, G. W. F. (1956). *The philosophy of history*. New York, NY: Dover Publications.

Heller, A. (1982). *A theory of history*. London: Routledge & Kegan Paul.

Honneth, A. (1995a). *The fragmented world of the social*. Albany, NY: State University of New York Press.

Honneth, A. (1995b). *The struggle for recognition*. Cambridge, MA: Polity Press.

Horkheimer, M. (1995). *Critical theory*. New York, NY: Continuum.

Horkheimer, M., & Adorno, T. W. (1994). *Dialectic of enlightenment*. New York, NY: Continuum.

Kant, I. (1991). Idea for a universal history with a cosmopolitan purpose. In *Kant: Political writings* (2nd ed., pp. 41–53). New York, NY: Cambridge University Press.

Lukács, G. (1975). *The young Hegel.* Cambridge, MA: MIT Press.

Marcuse, H. (1941). *Reason and revolution: Hegel and the rise of social theory.* London: Routledge & Kegan Paul.

Offe, C. (1994). *Contradictions of the welfare state.* Cambridge, MA: The MIT Press.

Todorov, T. (1992). *The conquest of America: The question of the other.* New York, NY: Harper Perennial.

INHERITING CRITICAL THEORY: A REVIEW OF AMY ALLEN'S *THE END OF PROGRESS: DECOLONIZING THE NORMATIVE FOUNDATIONS OF CRITICAL THEORY*

George Steinmetz

ABSTRACT

This review of Amy Allen's book, The End of Progress *(2016), first addresses the structure of the book and focuses on specific points made in individual chapters, including the affinity between postcolonial theory and the approaches of Adorno and Foucault in subjecting the notion of historical progress to "withering critique," and Allen's alternative approach to decolonization; Habermas' aim to put critical theory on a secure normative footing; Honneth's stance that the history of an ethical sphere is an unplanned learning process kept in motion by a struggle for recognition; Forst's attempt to reconstruct Critical Theory's normative account through a return to Kant rather than Hegel; and Allen's claim that her approach is fully in the spirit of Critical Theory and could be seen as continuation of Critical Theory's first generation, as in Adorno, and how it is a "genealogical" approach that draws on Adorno's negative dialectics and critique of identity thinking, as well as on Nietzsche's conception of genealogy, as developed by Foucault. The second part of my response raises three issues: (1) Allen's partial compromise with the idea of progress; (2) whether critical theory would profit from engagement with other critical theories and theories of ethics, beyond postcolonial theory; and (3) nonwestern theories shed a different light on the question of Allen's critique, a theme that also draws attention to the gesture of*

The Challenge of Progress: Theory Between Critique and Ideology
Current Perspectives in Social Theory, Volume 36, 37–48
Copyright © 2020 Emerald Publishing Limited
ISSN: 0278-1204/doi:10.1108/S0278-120420190000036008

decolonizing, the distinctions between colonialism and empire, and the sociology of knowledge production.

Keywords: Critical theory; progress; decolonization; empire; colonialism; Amy Allen; Theodor W. Adorno; Jürgen Habermas; Axel Honneth; Rainer Forst

Amy Allen's *The End of Progress* is a landmark effort to decolonize Critical Theory.[1] The book's goal, more specifically, is to criticize the work of contemporary critical theorists and to bring the insights of postcolonial and decolonial thought, along with Adorno and Foucault, to bear upon the problem of the normative foundations of Critical Theory. Amy Allen argues that Adorno and Foucault, despite their ostensible Eurocentrism, offer resources that complement postcolonial theory in this project of decolonizing Critical Theory. The book does not argue that postcolonial theory is an extension of European critical theory or that Critical Theory offers resources for postcolonial theorizing. Instead, this is an intervention into the normative program of Critical Theory.

To understand what Allen means by "decolonizing" Critical Theory, we need to understand what she means by Critical Theory. Allen edits the Columbia University Press series "New Directions in Critical Theory" in which the current book appears. As she explains, Critical Theory sees itself as being:

> rooted in and constituted by an existing social reality that is structured by power relations that it therefore also aims to critique by appealing to immanent standards of normativity and rationality. (Allen, 2016, p. xiii)[2]

Allen approvingly quotes Nancy Fraser's definition of Critical Theory — drawing on a phrase from Marx — as "the self-clarification of the struggles and wishes of the age" (Allen, 2016, p. 4).[3] At the heart of Critical Theory's normative project is therefore the idea of immanent critique, a "postmetaphysical stance" that is contrasted with projects based on a constructivist justification of abstract transcendent normative principles (Kant), realist definitions of foundational norms or virtues (Aristotle), or normative relativism (although Adorno suggests that relativism is a pseudoconcept; see later). Allen concludes that if we

> assume that struggles around decolonization and postcolonial politics are among the most significant struggles and wishes of our age, then the demand for a decolonization of critical theory follows quite straightforwardly from the very definition of critical theory. (Allen, 2016, p. 4)

More than half of the book is devoted to arguing that *progress* is a core metanormative assumption of Critical Theory since Adorno. The reasons for critical theorists' belief in "our" past as progress are complex and cannot be reduced to racism or adherence to an imperialist culture. Without this assumption, Allen argues, these theories lose any grounding for their moral philosophy. Yet the problems with these assumptions are many. If normativity is grounded in the social world, how can Critical Theory avoid the charge of endorsing whatever normative standards happen to be accepted at a given time and place? Why should we believe that the normative perspective that emerges from an analysis of social relations "is itself valid and deserving of our support?" (Allen, 2016, p. 81). How can Critical Theory avoid the charge of promoting as universal values that are in fact local and contingent? How can a vision of the good life offered from within a society structured by relations of domination not reproduce its power relations? (Allen, 2016, p. 188). And in an era of postcolonial critique, how can such a theory justify promoting as universal values that have been thoroughly entangled with projects of imperial domination and colonial conquest, from the "repugnancy standards" in British colonial law to the French colonial "civilizing mission," by way of the various "protectorates" and structures of western tutelage of "barbarian" cultures? Critical theorist Allen writes:

> should be given serious pause by the very fact that their conception of historical progress overlaps with the neoconservative political worldview to such a degree that spelling out the differences between the two becomes necessary in the first place. (Allen, 2016, p. 116)

The book's first chapter is given over to a discussion of the idea of progress in Critical Theory and social theory and modern history more generally, and to the postcolonial critique of ideas of progress. Edward Said stated bluntly that "Frankfurt School critical theory [...] is stunningly silent on racist theory, anti-imperialist resistance, and oppositional practice in the empire" (Said, 1993, p. 278). Some critical theorists, Allen notes, have simply expanded "the canon of critical theory to include such thinkers as Frantz Fanon [...]" (Allen, 2016, p. 2), but without systematically exploring the theories' complementarities and incompatibilities. A cornerstone of Allen's argument is the idea that there are two views of progress: a forward-looking version, or "progress as imperative," and a backward-looking variant, "progress as fact" (Allen, 2016, p. 12). Critical Theory since Adorno has been committed to the latter, the idea of progress as fact. This commitment has stemmed from the internal demands of Critical Theory's normative program, specifically its commitment to immanent critique, and not from any triumphalist western ideology or racist commitments. But the results have been the same – an implicit and often explicit assumption of the moral superiority of the cultures of the global North, or even more specifically, of Western Europe. According to Critical Theory, it is possible to derive normative standards with universal validity from "our" current social world insofar as that world is assumed to be "the outcome of a process of progressive social evolution," or cumulative social learning, through which "a socially instantiated reason is progressively purified of power relations" (Allen, 2016, pp. 14, 88). Each generation is therefore able to "enrich and build upon the heritage that it inherits from previous generations" (Allen, 2016, p. 87). This is a "situationally engaged" form of practical reason (Allen, 2016, p. 42). The result, for Critical Theory, is a requirement to assume that modern societies are in some respects superior to non-modern ones. But the idea of progress, as countless colonial historians and critics of empire and modernization theory have argued, for more than half a century, was used to justify colonial conquest and imperial domination (Bhambra, 2007; Friedmann, 1936). Postcolonial theory agrees with

Adorno and Foucault in subjecting the notion of historical progress to "withering critique" (Allen, 2016, p. 201).

Allen's alternative approach is sketched in the first chapter and elaborated over the course of the book, culminating in the final chapter. What is required for decolonization of Critical Theory and for a postcolonial normativity, she argues, is "openness to *unlearning*" (p. 31; emphasis added). This stance does not require a rejection of the reflexivity afforded us by the resources of modernity, but a further elaboration of those resources. According to Allen, we can reject progress as a general basis for norms while admitting there has been progress in history in specific domains, as judged by standards that are historically and contextually grounded. Her approach is not one of debunking or vindication, but of critically *problematizing* our norms. Decolonizing critical theory, she argues, requires a posture of genuine respect for the other (Allen, 2016, p. 32). Modernity's salvageable values also include modesty or humility toward moral certainties. More on this are discussed later.

At the heart of the book are chapters on three leading contemporary critical theorists – Jürgen Habermas, Axel Honneth, and Rainer Forst. Habermas' key aim, discussed in Chapter 2, is to put critical theory on a secure normative footing. Habermas understands modernity as a process of social evolution and moral-political learning – as progress – and this evolution validates the critical standards of his critical theory. Habermas sees himself as working in the tradition of Marx, specifically Marx's opposition to the utopian socialists and his understanding of critique as building on existing possibilities and only setting tasks for which it is historically prepared (Allen, 2016, pp. 41–43). Habermas' critiques of Marx target his reduction of progress to productive forces and his theory's lack of a clear normative foundation (Allen, 2016, p. 45). Habermas broadens the definition of progress to include, alongside productive forces, moral practical development, which encompasses communicative rationality, ego development, and reflexivity.[4] The rationalization of communicative action requires eliminating systematically distorted communication by extirpating relations of force. Progress thus occurs within both realms – the productive forces and moral practical knowledge – and is measured against validity claims in both: Truth and the Rightness of Norms. Universal pragmatics, which concerns the universal and unavoidable validity presuppositions of speech, justifies these general claims of progress.

The aim of Habermas' subsequent *Theory of Communicative Action* (1984–1987) is again a critical theory that validates its own critical standards. Here, Habermas argues that there is a universal core to communicative competence, involving three sorts of validity claims: to truth, normative rightness, and sincerity. Every utterance raises at least one of these validity claims, which are connected to the objective, intersubjective, and subjective worlds (Allen, 2016, p. 50). Understanding any utterance requires "taking a yes-no position on the reasons that might be adduced to support the validity claims." Habermas' method for reconstructing these speech acts "proceeds by way of a systematic reconstruction of the intuitive knowledge of a very specific group of people, namely, 'competent members of modern societies'." Since this knowledge is by no means universal, it is clear that the normative potentials "represent the implicit telos toward which language universally aims" (Allen, 2016, p. 51). McCarthy (1991, p. 145; quoted in Allen, 2016, p. 52) notes that Habermas is implicitly privileging a Western "conception of the end point of the history of reason." Allen briefly summarizes Habermas' more recent work, and concludes that although he now accepts the concept of "multiple modernities," he still assumes that the West is superior but that its culture is also fallibilist, meaning that it is open to engage in dialogue with Others who are less progressive (Allen, 2016, p. 4). Habermas also distinguishes between modern and so-called mythical understandings of the world, describing the latter as the "savage mind" while losing all of Lévi-Strauss' irony, and comparing "savage thought" to the "onto-genetic stages of cognitive development" (Habermas, 1984–1987, vol. 1, p. 46). Habermas argues that mythical worldviews fail to differentiate the objective, social, and subjective worlds and hence cannot distinguish claims to truth, normative validity, and sincerity. Indeed, mythical worldviews are non-reflexive and do not identify themselves as worldviews or cultural traditions at all (Allen, 2016, p. 54). More recently, he has continued to ask how the West can continue to act as a "civilizing force" in the rest of the world (Habermas, 2006, p. 16).

Chapter 3 discusses the work of Axel Honneth. In contrast to Habermas' approach, which reconstructs "the implicit know-how of competent communicative actors," Honneth seeks to identify "values and norms that have been immanently justified through historical learning processes" (Allen, 2016, p. 92). Specifically, Honneth posits three realms of recognition: family, legal rights, and social esteem, each of which plays a role in individual autonomy, through self-confidence, self-respect, and self-esteem. In *Freedom's Right* (2014, pp. 3–10), Honneth posts four fundamental principles: (1) the reproduction of society is based on shared principles and values; (2) the theory of justice draws normativity from those values; (3) the method of the theory of justice is normative reconstruction; and (4) this is not an apology for the status quo because there is always room for critique of the ways ideals that are universally shared are imperfectly realized. This is an immanent critique, not a project based on constructivist justification of abstract transcendent normative principles (Allen, 2016, p. 91). The content of normativity is provided, for Honneth, by Hegel's theory of recognition. Honneth's philosophical anthropology is based on psychoanalytic theory, positing a basic human drive for recognition and arguing that suffering impels people to seek emancipation (Allen, 2016, p. 117). For Honneth, the history of an ethical sphere is an unplanned learning process kept in motion by a struggle for recognition (Allen, 2016, pp. 111–113).

As in Hegel's *Philosophy of Right*, Honneth's *Freedom's Right* reconstructs the social conditions under which our normative conception of freedom can be realized (Allen, 2016, p. 94). Methodologically, Honneth argues that the normativity of the social world is only accessible from the internal, first-person reconstructive point of view of the participant in a normative social order (Allen, 2016, p. 106). This approach is juxtaposed to the objectivizing, third person, and external viewpoint of positivist social science. But by relegating power to the external, third-person point of view, Allen argues, Honneth preserves the "pernicious fiction of a power-free normative lifeworld" (Allen, 2016, p. 106) – a fiction that we have already encountered in Habermas and that is so strangely at odds with the very idea of a critical social theory. Allen concludes Chapter 3 by arguing that Critical Theory can do without "the robust notion of historical progress that Honneth advocates" (Allen, 2016, p. 121). A better approach, one that is less vulnerable to postcolonial critique, involves a "thoroughgoing meta-normative contextualism." What this means is explained in Chapter 5.

Allen first turns to Rainer Forst in Chapter 4. Forst has attempted to recon-struct Critical Theory's normative account through a return to Kant rather than Hegel. Rather than summarizing Allen's discussion of Forst, which is less cen-trally involved in the main argument here, it is sufficient to move to her conclu-sion. While Forst avoids Honneth's historical Hegelian approach, with its tendential legitimation of the status quo and purging of power from the life-world, Allen argues that Forst ends up:

> in much the same place: implicitly relying on a thick, historically specific conception of the good that undergirds his conception of practical reason and that is deeply bound up with tele-ological progress narratives while disavowing those very connections. (Allen, 2016, p. 155)

After this detailed discussion of the central role of progress in the thinking of Habermas, Honneth, and Forst, Allen elaborates her alternative approach. She contends that her method is fully in the spirit of Critical Theory, and could even be seen as a continuation of it – especially of Critical Theory's first generation, represented here by Adorno. If Critical Theory is based on a "conception of the critical subject as self-consciously rooted in and shaped by the power relations in the society that she nevertheless aims self-reflexively and rationally to critique," then the "best way to do justice to this tradition is not to remain faithful to its core doctrines or central figures but rather precisely to inherit it," meaning "to take it up while simultaneously radically transforming it" (Allen, 2016, p. xiii).[5] She suggests further that it is possible to partially "inherit" the normative legacy of the Enlightenment while rejecting its imperialist and authoritarian tendencies, which have been so decisively criticized by Horkheimer and Adorno (1944/2002), Foucault (1984), and postcolonial theorists (Chakrabarty, 2000). This critical inheritance requires a different relationship to history, according to Allen, one that is neither subversive nor vindicatory, but *problematizing*. This problematiz-ing approach would point to a fuller realization of the normative inheritance of modernity, rather than a merely negative rejection (Allen, 2016, p. 165).

Allen's alternative is also a "genealogical" approach that draws on Adorno's negative dialectics and critique of identity thinking, and on Nietzsche's concep-tion of genealogy, as developed by Foucault. Although Foucault's approach to the Enlightenment is often read as an entirely negative, subversive one, Allen argues that Foucault "situates his own problematizing critical method within the philosophical ethos of critique that forms the positive normative inheritance of Enlightenment" (Allen, 2016, p. 191). Especially important for Allen's account is Foucault's figure of "unreason." Allen points out that *unreason*, not *madness*, is idealized as freedom by Foucault in his first book, *Folie et déraison*.[6] The paired concept in Adorno, for Allen, is the "non-identical," that which "points outside itself" and away from the rationalized object (Palamarek, 2007, p. 76; note 121). Unreason and the non-identical suggest ways of opening up and illuminating "lines of gaps and fissures," "lines of fragility," or "kinds of virtual fracture" in our historical but naturalized a priori categories of thought (Allen, 2016, pp. 183–184).

In lieu of an approach that reconstructs "the implicit know-how of competent communicative actors" (Habermas) (Allen, 2016, p. 90), then, or one that seeks "values and norms that have been immanently justified through historical learning processes" (Honneth) (Allen, 2016, p. 92), Allen suggests a different approach rooted in *problematization* and *genealogy*. According to Allen, the genealogical method has three different modes: subversion, vindication, and problematizing. Vindication is associated in her account with Habermas, Honneth, and other critical theorists who build on the Enlightenment. Subversion, the position that some attribute to Foucault, would leave us rudderless, lacking any normative starting point and therefore veering inevitably into normative relativism. Allen is adamant that her position is not a relativist one. She accepts Adorno's critique of relativism as a "pseudoproblem" and a correlate of moral absolutism.[7]

The third alternative, problematizing, is defined as showing how particular historical conditions led us to develop specific values and to see certain historically constituted objects as natural and unchangeable. Problematizing reveals this level of "second nature" as historically contingent and thus changeable. Allen's approach thus involves revealing the historical contingency of our own point of view and showing how that viewpoint is connected to power, while at the same time taking up that viewpoint as our normative starting point. The existing normative viewpoint is thus both assumed and transformed (Allen, 2016, p. 190). In this respect, Allen preserves the immanentism of critical theory's normative theory. She proposes a "reflexive, historically contextualized critical methodology that understands critique as the wholly immanent and fragmentary practice of opening up lines of fragility and fracture within the social world" (Allen, 2016, p. 201). This approach dovetails with postcolonial thought not only in its understanding of theory as fracturing imperialist systems of thought, but also in terms of its modesty or humility, its unwillingness to brandish its own normative viewpoint as superior. Allen summarizes this argument:

> [We] take the position that we are committed at a first-order, substantive level to these normative principles inasmuch as our form of life and sense of ourselves as practical moral agents depend on them, but [...] we simultaneously acknowledge, at a second-order, metanormative level, that those very ideals themselves demand of us an awareness of the violence inherent in them and also a fundamental modesty or humility regarding their status or authority. (Allen, 2016, p. 202)

In an approach that recalls Bourdieu's (1978) notion of "participant objectivation," Allen draws on Foucault to endorse an "internal ethnology" that situates itself within our own normative world and "drawing on its normative content while simultaneously viewing it with the detached and objectivating glance of the outsider" (Allen, 2016, p. 207).[8] This form of self-questioning of one's own reality "involves a combination of 'external' and 'internal' reflection, that is [...] observer and participant perspectives" (Allen, 2016, p. 208).

Are we then left with no guidance other than openness to the uncontrolled fracturing of our normative world by external realities? Allen softens this blow near the end of the book, writing that there are "two important features of the normative horizon of Enlightenment modernity that mitigate against what might seem like the arbitrariness implied" by the picture of an uncontrolled fracturing of norms by external realities (Allen, 2016, p. 218). The first is that "like all horizons, this normative horizon is open and not closed, permeated by and formed in interaction with other normative horizons." Second, and even more importantly, our normative horizon "takes openness to criticism and reflexivity as normative goals, and hence as a form of life it requires me to be open to being changed, including when that means learning to unlearn" (Allen, 2016, p. 218).

QUESTIONS AND CRITIQUES

Amy Allen's *The End of Progress* is a tour de force, the product of an immense, sustained labor and exceedingly careful readings of texts. I want to offer three points for discussion. The first is based on what I see as Amy Allen's partial compromise with the idea of progress. The second asks whether Critical Theory might profit from engagement with other critical theories and theories of ethics, beyond postcolonial theory. My third point asks whether nonwestern theories shed a different light on the question of Allen's critique. My final point concerns the gesture of decolonizing, the distinctions between colonialism and empire, and the sociology of knowledge production undergirding a "decolonizing" critique.

The first section of Allen's book discloses a concession to the theorists criticized in the rest of the book. If our normative horizon "takes openness to criticism and reflexivity as normative goals," aren't these just the sorts of orientations that thinkers like Habermas have understood as defining the distinctiveness of the modern, liberal West? Aren't they the opposite of the positions Habermas defined as "modern fundamentalism," for example (Habermas, 2001, 2006)? When Habermas juxtaposes European religions' "self-reflexive accomplishment of a religion that learned to see itself through the eyes of others" and contrasts it with the "repression of cognitive dissonances" in the "Arab world" and Islam (Habermas, 2006, pp. 10−11), it is difficult not to see a connection to the idea of "openness to criticism and reflexivity." By granting this much to the Enlightenment, Allen may be opening the door to being decolonized herself. On the other hand, I can entirely understand why the author introduces this idea. In a normative world that is constantly being buffeted by fractures, fissures, and external shocks, openness to criticism and reflexivity may be ones only life raft.

This leads to my second question, which is whether the author has built too cunning a trap for herself by sticking too closely to postcolonial theory, Foucault, and Adorno as her main resources for "unlearning" progress. One position that is barely alluded to in Allen's book is moral realism (Railton, 1986). Cultural anthropologists have suggested that it is possible to combine a view of ethics as universal, not learned, but also as variable across cultures (Keane, 2016). If normativity is grounded in innate, universal human capacities, this would seem at least to ward off the challenge from postcolonial theorists. Another approach that is not discussed at all in *The End of Progress* is neo-Aristotelean virtue ethics (Annas, 2011; Hursthouse, 1999; Hursthouse & Pettigrove, 2016; MacIntyre, 1999). Again, this position may be problematic for other reasons, but it cannot be faulted for being biased toward western world-views, since the precise definition of virtues varies according to the theorist.

In my third point, I want to probe the trope of "decolonizing." This idea originally appeared in countries in the throes of actual decolonization, and where postcolonial intellectuals were engaged in struggles to take control of their means of intellectual production, their schools, universities, journals, and scientific institutions, and to rid themselves of ideas that were explicitly linked to western colonial domination (Steinmetz, 2017). In the intervening decades, however, the notion of decolonizing has been applied to any and all theoretical systems deemed to be noxious. Nor is colonialism the same thing as imperialism, or empire (Steinmetz, 2014), although these terms and processes are often equated in the discourse of decolonizing. But decolonizing theory may not involve the same thing as removing imperial, or imperialist, traces from it. Neither is racism always associated with empire, even if racism originated in the context of modern colonialism and colonial slavery (Steinmetz, 2015). Some European powers possessed only a single overseas colony, which hardly qualifies those states as empires.[9] Conversely, some empires, like the American one, are largely informal, with a minimal present-day engagement in territorial colonialism (Mann, 2003; Steinmetz, 2005). German critical theorists like Habermas and Honneth may belong to a broadly post-imperial Europe, but Germany has never really been postcolonial, since the *Reich* lost its overseas colonies before anticolonialism was a dominant global ideology. I am not sure how these distinctions would change Allen's critique of the discourse of progress in Critical Theory, but at the very least but they point to the need for a more nuanced critical vocabulary around "decolonizing."[10] We need to ask which aspects of a given body of thought are specifically colonial or imperial, which aspects are saturated with values linked to domination other than colonial/imperial ones (e.g., class or gender domination), which aspects are culturally specific but not systematically linked to ideologies of domination, and which aspects are culturally neutral or universal.

This brings me to a related issue, which is the sociology of knowledge production undergirding Allen's "decolonizing" criticism. On the one hand, the method of *The End of Progress* consists of careful close readings of central philosophical texts. But for the critique to be plausible, we also need to understand how and why these critical theorists fell so routinely into this trap. I suggested my own interpretation of this tendency earlier: the demands of their theory required adopting the progress narrative. An alternative reading would be more contextual, in the sense of *Wissenssoziologie* or intellectual history. Put differently, there does seem to be a difference between a figure like Habermas, who explicitly and openly defends the idea of progress and of the West as civilizing, and Forst, who sidesteps these issues and for whom recourse to progress is only implicit. And there seems to be a major difference between all of these critical theorists and members of the imperial foreign policy establishment, not to mention nostalgists bemoaning the loss of the British Empire. Intellectual history and the sociology of knowledge cannot operate at this level, which elides differences among producers, texts, and the contexts of production. Yet I recognize that Allen's critique is fundamentally a philosophical one, despite her openness to interdisciplinarity, and I am therefore hesitant to insist on the procedures of these extrinsic disciplines.

CONCLUSION

These criticisms in no way diminish my respect and even awe before the enormous achievement represented by Amy Allen's *The End of Progress*. This is a hugely important work of social theory, social philosophy, and ideological criticism. It should be carefully read by anyone interested in Critical Theory, critical theories, postcolonial studies, and the work of Habermas, Honneth, Forst, Adorno, and Foucault. It may not be an exaggeration to state that *The End of Progress* does for Critical Theory what Edward Said's *Orientalism* (1978) did for Oriental studies, what Said's *Culture and Imperialism* (1993) did for cultural studies, what Dipesh Chakrabarty's *Provincializing Europe* (2000) did for historiography, what Gayatri Spivak's "Can the Subaltern Speak?" (1988) did for feminism, and what Spivak's *In Other Worlds: Essays in Cultural Politics* (1987) did for literary studies.

NOTES

1. For previous efforts to decolonize Critical Theory, see Cornell (2008) and McCarthy (2009).
2. Here Allen is drawing on Zurn (2000).
3. From Fraser (1989, p. 138, note 1).
4. Habermas (1979). Allen argues for an essential continuity in Habermas' thinking from this early work through his most recent work, at least with respect to the basic assumption of progress. In other respects, as she acknowledges, moving from universal pragmatics and communicative ethics to the theory of communicative action, to a neo-Kantian discourse ethics, and most recently to an embrace of Eisenstadt's multiple modernities framework. Common to all of these, Allen argues, is a belief in the developmental superiority of modernity (p. 61).
5. Allen draws here on Derrida's discussion of theoretical "inheritance" in *Specters of Marx* (Derrida, 1994).
6. The full title of Foucault's (1961a, 1961b) book was *Histoire de la folie à l'âge classique: folie et déraison*; in the shortened version from the same year, the title and subtitle were reversed as *Folie et déraison: histoire de la folie a l'âge classique*. Both titles suggest that Foucault intended to signal a distinction between *folie* and *déraison*, which is the key point for Allen. This implies that the book's title has been mistranslated, first as *Madness and Civilization: A history of Insanity in the Age of Reason* (Foucault, 1965), and more recently as *History of Madness* (Foucault, 2008). Both of these renderings eliminate the term that is primary, for Allen – *déraison* or unreason – or else they mistranslate *déraison* as "insanity." *Déraison* is a literary term, according to French dictionaries, while insanity is simply an alternative translation of *folie*, along with "madness." Foucault's discussion of Nietzsche, Nerval, Artaud, and Van Gogh suggests that that the modern world condemns "to madness *[folie]* all those who have tried the test of Unreason *[déraison]*" (Foucault, 2008, p. 352).
7. Adorno (2001, p. 175), quoted by Allen (2016).
8. Up to this point, Allen's approach is indistinguishable from that of Bourdieu, who calls on analysts to break with their "spontaneous sociologies" and engage in "genesis

explanations" in order to disrupt the apparent naturalness of social arrangements by reconstructing the arbitrary conditions of their social genesis. Unlike Bourdieu, Allen's procedure is systematically linked to normative analysis. Allen's procedure is also more realistic than Bourdieu's about the impossibility of stepping outside of the assumptions that Bourdieu calls "spontaneous." Unlike the critical theorists Allen is criticizing, however, Bourdieu did call attention explicitly to the need to decolonize sociology, and he attacked what he called *"imperialist reason."* See Bourdieu (1976), Bourdieu and Wacquant (1998), and Steinmetz (2011). Indeed, there are many complementarities between Bourdieu and Foucault, as Bourdieu remarked (Bourdieu, 2007, p. 79). Bourdieu's program of denaturalizing contemporary forms of domination by analyzing their contingent *genesis* in ways that reveal their arbitrariness recalls Foucault's genealogies. *Pascalian Mediations* (Bourdieu, 2000) includes a chapter entitled "The Historicity of Reason." Both thinkers shared a radical historicism with regard to forms of knowledge and social arrangements that are typically "seen as natural or omnihistorical" (Vazquez Garcia, 2002, pp. 349–350). Both were briefly attracted to structuralism but quickly rejected structuralism's reduction of human subjects to mere supports of larger structures; both developed post-Saussurian, non-structuralist theories of practice that avoided falling back into a phenomenology of the subject or common-sense views of action as resulting from conscious, intentional, rational deliberations (Vazquez Garcia, 2002, pp. 356–357). They both rejected disciplinary boundaries, conceptual dichotomies, and the Sartrian model of the "general intellectual."

9. One would not speak of the Danish colonial empire, for example, despite the existence of Greenland, or of an Italian empire in the 1950s, even though Italy temporarily regained control over Somalia. The idea of a Belgian colonial empire is only slightly less jarring, before 1960, since Belgium had a total of three colonies.

10. I admit that I have also engaged in this sort of conceptual blurring, having edited an issue of Postcolonial Studies entitled "Decolonizing German Theory" (Steinmetz, 2006).

REFERENCES

Adorno, T. W. (2001). *Problems of moral philosophy*. Stanford, CA: Stanford University Press.

Allen, A. (2016). *The end of progress: Decolonizing the normative foundations of critical theory*. New York, NY: Columbia University Press.

Annas, J. (2011). *Intelligent virtue*. Oxford: Oxford University Press.

Bhambra, G. K. (2007). *Rethinking modernity: Postcolonialism and the sociological imagination*. New York, NY: Palgrave.

Bourdieu, P. (1976). Les conditions sociales de la production sociologique: sociologie coloniale et décolonisation de la sociologie. In H. Moniot (Ed.), *Le mal de voir* (pp. 416–427). Paris: Union Gén.

Bourdieu, P. (1978). Sur l'objectivation participante. Réponses à quelques objections. *Actes de la recherche en sciences sociales, 23*, 67–69.

Bourdieu, P. (2000). *Pascalian meditations*. Stanford, CA: Stanford University Press.

Bourdieu, P. (2007). *Sketch for a self-analysis*. Cambridge: Polity Press.

Bourdieu, P., & Wacquant, L. J. D. (1998). Sur les ruses de la raison impérialiste. *Actes de la recherche en sciences sociales, 121/122*, 109–118.

Chakrabarty, D. (2000). *Provincializing Europe: Postcolonial thought and historical difference*. Princeton, NJ: Princeton University Press.

Cornell, D. (2008). *Moral images of freedom: A future for critical theory*. Lanham, MD: Rowman & Littlefield.

Derrida, J. (1994). *Specters of Marx: The state of the debt, the work of mourning, and the new international*. New York, NY: Routledge.

Foucault, M. (1961a). *Folie et déraison; histoire de la folie a l'âge classique*. Paris: Union générale d'éditions.

Foucault, M. (1961b). *Histoire de la folie à l'âge classique; folie et déraison*. Paris: Plon.

Foucault, M. (1965). *Madness and civilization: A history of insanity in the age of reason*. New York, NY: Pantheon Books.

Foucault, M. (1984). What is enlightenment? In P. Rabinow (Ed.), *The Foucault reader* (pp. 32–50). New York, NY: Pantheon Books.

Foucault, M. (2008). *History of madness*. London: Routledge.

Fraser, N. (1989). What's critical about critical theory? The case of Habermas and gender. In N. Fraser (Ed.), *Unruly practices: Power, discourse, and gender in contemporary social theory* (pp. 113–143). Minneapolis, MN: University of Minnesota Press.

Friedmann, G. (1936). *La crise du progrès*. Paris: Gallimard.

Habermas, J. (1979). *Communication and the evolution of society*. Boston, MA: Beacon Press.

Habermas, J. (1984–1987). *The theory of communicative action* (2 Volumes). Boston, MA: Beacon Press.

Habermas, J. (2001). Glaube, Wissen – Öffnung. Zum Friedenspreis des Deutschen Buchhandels: Eine Dankesrede. *Süddeutsche Zeitung* no. 237, October 15, 17.

Habermas, J. (2006). Fundamentalism and terror. In C. Cronin (Ed.), *Jürgen Habermas, the divided west* (pp. 3–25). Cambridge: Polity Press.

Horkheimer, M., & Adorno, T. W. ([1944] 2002). *Dialectic of enlightenment: Philosophical fragments*. Stanford, CA: Stanford University Press.

Hursthouse, R. (1999). *On virtue ethics*. Oxford: Oxford University Press.

Hursthouse, R., & Pettigrove, G. (2016). *Virtue ethics. The Stanford encyclopedia of philosophy* (Winter). Edward N. Zalta (ed.). Retrieved from https://plato.stanford.edu/archives/win2016/entries/ethics-virtue/

Keane, W. (2016). *Ethical life: Its natural and social histories*. Princeton, NJ: Princeton University Press.

MacIntyre, A. C. (1999). *Dependent rational animals: Why human beings need the virtues*. Chicago, IL: Open Court.

Mann, M. (2003). *Incoherent empire*. London: Verso.

McCarthy, T. (1991). *Ideals and illusions: On reconstruction and deconstruction in contemporary critical theory*. Cambridge, MA: MIT Press.

McCarthy, T. (2009). *Race, empire, and the idea of human development*. Cambridge: Cambridge University Press.

Palamarek, M. K. (2007). Adorno's dialectics of language. In D. A. Burke (Ed.), *Adorno and the need in thinking: New critical essays* (pp. 41–77). Toronto: University of Toronto Press.

Railton, P. (1986). Moral realism. *Philosophical Review*, *95*(2), 163–207.

Said, E. (1978). *Orientalism*. New York, NY: Vintage.

Said, E. (1993). *Culture and imperialism*. New York, NY: Knopf.

Spivak, G. (1987). *In other worlds: Essays in cultural politics*. New York, NY: Methuen.

Spivak, G. (1988). Can the subaltern speak? In C. Nelson & L. Grossberg (Eds.), *Marxism and the interpretation of culture* (pp. 271–313). Urbana, IL: University of Illinois Press.

Steinmetz, G. (2005). Return to empire: The new U.S. imperialism in theoretical and historical perspective. *Sociological Theory*, *23*(4), 339–367.

Steinmetz, G. (2006). Decolonizing German theory: An introduction. *Postcolonial Studies*, *9*(1), 3–13.

Steinmetz, G. (2011). Bourdieu, historicity, and historical sociology. *Cultural Sociology*, *5*(1), 45–66.

Steinmetz, G. (2014). The sociology of empires, colonialism, and postcolonialism. *Annual Review of Sociology*, *40*(July), 77–103.

Steinmetz, G. (2015). Colonialism, modern, and race. In A. D. Smith, X. Hou, J. Stone, R. Dennis, & P. Rizova (Eds.), *The Wiley Blackwell encyclopedia of race, ethnicity, and nationalism* (pp. 1–3). Hoboken, NJ: Wiley-Blackwell. Retrieved from https://doi.org/10.1002/9781118663202.wberen641

Steinmetz, G. (2017). Sociology and Colonialism in the British and French empires, 1940s–1960s. *Journal of Modern History*, *89*(3), 601–648.

Vazquez Garcia, F. (2002). La tension infinie entre l'histoire et la raison: Foucault et Bourdieu. *Revue internationale de philosophie*, *56*(220), 343–365.

Zurn, C. (2000). Anthropology and normativity: A critique of Axel Honneth's 'formal conception of ethical life'. *Philosophy & Social Criticism*, *26*(1), 115–124.

BACK TO ADORNO: CRITICAL THEORY'S PROBLEM OF NORMATIVE GROUNDING

Karen Ng

ABSTRACT

This chapter offers a review of Amy Allen's The End of Progress: Decolonizing the Normative Foundations of Critical Theory *(2016) and presents the book as having both a negative and positive aim. Its negative aim is to offer a critique of the Eurocentric narratives of historical progress that serves the function of normative grounding in the critical theories of Jürgen Habermas and Axel Honneth. Its positive aim is to provide a new approach to the normative grounding of critical theory that eschews Eurocentric narratives of progress through the idea of metanormative contextualism. For Allen, metanormative contextualism is developed through an engagement with the works of Adorno and Foucault. This chapter raises some critical questions concerning the position of metanormative contextualism, arguing that there are significant differences between Adorno and Foucault that render the position unstable. Specifically, Adorno's normative conception of truth, alongside his critical naturalism presented through the notion of natural history, makes him ill-suited as a representative of Allen's metanormative contextualism and complicates the contributions of Foucault's genealogical analyses. The chapter concludes that a careful consideration of Adorno's views reveals him to be opposed to the two central tenets of metanormative contextualism as defined by Allen.*

Keywords: Critical theory; progress; decolonization; Amy Allen; Theodor W. Adorno; Michel Foucault; Jürgen Habermas; Axel Honneth; Rainer Forst; metanormative contextualism

The Challenge of Progress: Theory Between Critique and Ideology
Current Perspectives in Social Theory, Volume 36, 49–59
Copyright © 2020 Emerald Publishing Limited
All rights of reproduction in any form reserved
ISSN: 0278-1204/doi:10.1108/S0278-120420190000036009

The intellectual battle in critical theory between the methods and analyses of the first generation and those of its subsequent (second, third, and now fourth) generations has long served as a site of heated debate concerning a wide variety of questions related to social critique. In its roughest outline, the most heated debate between the first and subsequent generations of critical theory has been the following: if we accept that history and historical analyses are central to any adequate form of social critique, what then, are the normative foundations of that critique, the criteria by which we judge the successes and failures, the rights and wrongs, of a historically specific social formation? One prominent answer to this question, found in the works of Jürgen Habermas and Axel Honneth, has been to suggest that the unassailable normative progress of European modernity, which can be ascertained from the development of its moral and legal institutions, can itself serve as a basis for the critical assessment of modern societies. As Allen documents in her new book, *The End of Progress: Decolonizing the Normative Foundations of Critical Theory* (2016), the securing of normative foundations on the basis of a progressive understanding of European history has come at a huge critical cost, one that arguably renders Frankfurt School critical theory complicit in Eurocentric and neocolonial discourses of historical development that have long been criticized by post- and decolonial thinkers — not to mention first-generation critical theorists, such as Benjamin and Adorno.

Allen's book is an important and overdue intervention in what she terms the narrow sense of critical theory, namely, the "German tradition of interdisciplinary social theory, inaugurated in Frankfurt in the 1930s," which, after its first generation, sought to redeem the philosophies of history found in Kant and Hegel, despite abandoning their so-called metaphysics (Allen, 2016, p. xi). By contrast, critical theory in the wider, more capacious sense — which includes feminist and queer theory, critical race theory, and post- and decolonial theory, as well as French poststructuralist and psychoanalytic theory — has largely been founded upon challenging many of the central tenets of enlightenment thinking, including its conceptions of reason, subjectivity, and history, of which Kant and Hegel are often represented as characteristic proponents and culprits. Although this characterization of critical theory in the broad sense surely risks oversimplification, it points to a larger, disciplinary dispute within philosophy and the humanities concerning how canonical thinkers and their ideas ought to be inherited. With respect to critical theory in the narrow sense, Allen charges that Habermas, Honneth, and Rainer Forst, who are the main contemporary representatives of the Frankfurt School in Germany, have been far too sanguine in their inheritance of Kantian and Hegelian ideas, particularly concerning the idea of progress. Her central line of argument distinguishes between two conceptions of progress: a forward-looking conception of progress as a moral-political imperative that has emancipation from domination and injustice as its goal, and a backward-looking conception of progress as a historical "fact" reflected in the moral and rational superiority of European modernity over and against its predecessors and its non-Western contemporaries (Allen, 2016, pp. 11–12). According to Allen, the problem with critical theory since Habermas is that the former has come to be normatively and definitively grounded in the latter. If it turns out that the latter conception of progress can no longer be defended, then critical theory will need a different account of normative grounding, one that retains the importance of historical insight without resorting to large-scale claims concerning European modernity's superiority and progress.

Allen's book thus has both a negative and positive aim. Negatively, Allen aims to show that the critical theories of Habermas and Honneth are normatively grounded in, and cannot be successfully extricated from, a conception of historical progress that takes European modernity as both exemplary and authoritative. Rather than reading Habermas as a neo-Kantian constructivist for whom normativity is self-grounding according to idealized procedures of rational deliberation, Allen contends that Habermas' critical theory, from his universal pragmatics to his discourse ethics, relies upon a Eurocentric theory of modernity as its necessary normative ground. In the case of Honneth's neo-Hegelian project, his flagship conception of social freedom − institutionalized forms of mutual recognition that are the conditions for individual autonomy − is grounded upon a strongly teleological conception of historical progress as an ineliminable, transcendental assumption. Allen's claim is that the critical theories of Habermas and Honneth are not only grounded in large-scale theories of European progress, but further, that without these theories, the normative claims of both thinkers would fail according to their own self-delimited criteria. That is, *with* their progressive theories of modernity, Habermas and Honneth cannot answer the charges of parochial Eurocentrism; however, *without* their progressive theories of modernity, neither can successfully navigate the dilemma between context-transcendence and relativistic conventionalism, which their theories of modernity are meant to address and resolve. Allen's positive aim is to rethink the relation between the historical and the normative in order to find an alternative approach to the normative grounding of critical theory. (Forst's theory, according to Allen, avoids the problematic conception of historical progress but relies on a Kantian conception of practical reason that sacrifices the methodological distinctiveness of critical theory. In addition, Allen contends that Forst is still subject to the charge of Eurocentrism on account of presenting a uniquely Western conception of practical reason as something universal, beyond the reach of power relations. I will leave aside Allen's critique of Forst in what follows.)

Central to Allen's positive aim of rethinking the relation between the historical and the normative is her defense of metanormative contextualism, a position inspired by the works of Adorno and Foucault. In line with Allen's earlier work, Foucault is enlisted as a thinker who is both an ally of and an underappreciated resource for critical theory, and here, Allen names Foucault (rather than Derrida) as Adorno's "other son" (Allen, 2016, p. 164). What Adorno and Foucault share in common for Allen's purposes is their opposition to progressive philosophies of history, which results in a genealogical method that aims at "a critical problematization of our present historical moment" (Allen, 2016, p. 166). Rather than understanding the development of enlightenment reason and its institutions as representative of normative progress, Adorno and Foucault present genealogies that reveal the deeply ambivalent nature of modernity in which pairs such as progress and regress, freedom and domination, reason and unreason are simultaneously present. Specifically, Allen defends Adorno and Foucault against Habermas' reading of their projects as conservative, negative philosophies of history, or *Verfallsgeschichten*, that present the history of modernity's development as "a process of decline and fall" (Allen, 2016, p. 164). With respect to Adorno and Horkheimer, Allen reminds us that the critique of the dialectic of enlightenment was at the same time an attempt to rescue the normative potential of enlightenment's promise of freedom. On her reading, Adorno and Horkheimer aim to demonstrate that the positive and negative elements of the enlightenment are inextricably intertwined. In her words, there is a:

> dialectical relationship between the negative, totalitarian, regressive, barbaric, and amoral aspects of enlightenment and its positive, reflective, and emancipatory aspects, between enlightenment as domination and enlightenment as the capacity for rational self-reflection. (Allen, 2016, pp. 168–169)

Or again: "enlightenment rationality is both freedom and unfreedom or domination at the same time" (Allen, 2016, p. 170). If this is the case, then two things follow. First, the story of European enlightenment as a process of moral-practical learning is, at best, a partial and one-sided view of modernity, and at worst, serves to both obscure and justify its negative aspects. Second, given the necessary entwinement of the negative and the positive in the development of modernity, the best strategy for securing progress as a moral-political imperative is to come to an understanding of this dialectic, rather than viewing this development as a clear instance of progress as a historical "fact."

Similarly, Foucault's *History of Madness* should not be read as "advocating a rejection of reason in favor of a romantic embrace of unreason or madness"; rather, in writing a history of reason that demonstrates its entanglement with the pathologization of madness as mental illness, Foucault's aim "is to open up a space of freedom between ourselves and our historical a priori" (Allen, 2016, p. 177). Again, to present this ambivalent history as a history of progress would be to be present a one-sided view of things that obscured the negative effects of reason's development, along with the yet-to-be-determined potential for freedom contained within this history — the productive side of power. Thus, Allen presents Adorno and Foucault as offering an alternative approach to historicized normative theorizing. Their genealogies are "critical problematizations" that, in demonstrating the limits and blind spots of a particular historical self-conception, have the normative aim of "the fuller realization of the normative inheritance of the Enlightenment, in particular, the norms of freedom and respect for the other" (Allen, 2016, p. 166).

In what follows, I will focus on Allen's positive thesis that the problem of the normative foundations of critical theory can be reconceived along the lines of metanormative contextualism inspired by Adorno and Foucault. I am generally sympathetic with Allen's negative thesis *contra* Habermas and Honneth concerning their large-scale narratives of European moral and institutional progress, and agree that such narratives are both highly problematic and unnecessary as normative grounds for critique. However, it may also be the case that more modest, localized, and contingent conceptions of progress may be sufficient and unavoidable in many instances, which perhaps makes me less skeptical than Allen concerning judgments of progress in general.[1] I would also defend aspects of Honneth's social ontology that form the core of his early recognition theory, which I believe are separable from his stronger statements concerning the teleological progression of history, and are more central for his project of normative grounding than suggested by Allen in her book (see Allen, 2016, pp. 81–82 and 117–119). Nonetheless, I will focus on the question of what it would mean to return to Adorno in order to rethink the relation between history and normativity, and raise two challenges concerning Allen's reading of Adorno and the alliance with Foucault. Specifically, I will suggest that Adorno's commitment to a normative conception of truth and irrationality, alongside his critical naturalism and materialism, makes him potentially ill-suited as a representative of Allen's metanormative contextualism, and complicates the contributions of Foucault's historical analyses. That is, although Adorno's critique of the concept of progress fits in neatly with Allen's negative thesis against Habermas and Honneth, other aspects of Adorno's work pose potential problems for her positive thesis of proposing metanormative contextualism as an approach to normative grounding in critical theory.

In addition to the discussed contributions from Adorno and Foucault, metanormative contextualism for Allen consists of two claims.

> First, moral principles or normative ideals are always justified relative to a set of contextually salient values, conceptions of the good life, or normative horizons—roughly speaking, forms of life or life-worlds. Second, there is no über-context, no context-free or transcendent point of view from which we can adjudicate which contexts are ultimately correct or even in a position of hierarchical superiority over which others. (Allen, 2016, p. 215)

The key to understanding Allen's thesis is a distinction between first-order normative claims and second-order metanormative ones. At the first-order level, we can be committed to values such as "freedom, equality, and solidarity with the suffering of others" (Allen, 2016, p. 211). These first-order normative claims are justified relative to our form of life, and may even form an essential part of our self-conception as moral agents (Allen, 2016, p. 202). However, at the metanormative level, Allen suggests that we must be aware "of the violence inherent" in our first-order normative claims as well as take a position of "fundamental modesty or humility regarding their status and authority" (Allen, 2016, p. 202). That is, our higher-order, meta-level reflections on the status of our first-order claims ought to be made with an awareness of their necessarily contingent foundations. If we accept the thesis that there is no über-context from which we can adjudicate, with absolute certainty, the status of our first-order claims, then a normative and epistemic humility with respect to those claims, such as claims about the superiority of European modernity, seems to follow as a result. Borrowing from work in contextualist epistemology by Michael Williams and Linda Martín Alcoff, Allen argues that, importantly, metanormative contextualism does not entail first-order relativism, and further, that the worry about relativism is itself a pseudoproblem derived from a false dichotomy between relativism and absolutism (Allen, 2016, pp. 212, 216). In other words, accepting metanormative contextualism need not undermine our ability to endorse first-order normative claims, and in fact, only does so on the presumption that there exists an absolute, context-transcendent point of view from which to adjudicate those claims in the first place.

Allen's suggestion that worries about relativism often correlate with the assumption of absolutism sounds right, and in making her case, she draws on Adorno who contends that the opposition to false absolutes is much more pressing from the perspective of moral thinking than the (entirely futile) search for absolute and foundational values. However, Adorno's rejection of an absolute standpoint or über-context is complicated by further philosophical commitments that may not fit entirely with Allen's (and Foucault's) metanormative contextualism. First, although Adorno rejects the presumption of a context-transcendent, absolute point of view, he nonetheless continues to hold onto a normative conception of truth and irrationality. Brian O'Connor puts the point in the following way:

> [For Adorno] there is a *normativity of correctness* [...] of *how we ought to think* [...] in order to get experience right this is what one must think. (O'Connor, 2004, pp. 1–2)

That is to say: there is a right and wrong way to think, and this correlates with our ability to make correct and incorrect judgments about ourselves and about the world. Adorno's incessant critique of idealism, for example, can thus be roughly understood as suggesting that idealism takes the wrong approach to thinking, operates on false assumptions, and generates false judgments about ourselves and the world. His own preferred approach of negative dialectics, or what Jay Bernstein calls "the complex concept" (see Bernstein, 2001, chapter 6) would be the right approach to thinking endorsed by Adorno, one that would generate true judgments about ourselves and the world (for example, "The whole is the false," or "Wrong life cannot be lived rightly," or "Culture has failed," etc.).

Without pretending to do justice to Adorno's complex view here, we can provisionally draw two conclusions from this normative view of truth. The first is simply that this doesn't seem to fit in well with Foucault, and although Allen does not aim at a full-scale reconstruction or reconciliation of their views, I think this particular difference between Adorno and Foucault is one that matters to their respective approaches to historical critique. In Adorno and Horkheimer's negative dialectical presentation of the development of enlightenment modernity, the judgment of this history is that it has produced a barbaric, damaged, and inhuman form of life – a wrong life – and they endorse this judgment as the correct view of things such that other judgments (for example, enlightenment as moral progress) would be false. Foucault's presentation of the history of reason and its relation to madness serves the function of "creat[ing] distance between ourselves and our system of thought, our historical a priori," where this distance constitutes the "space of freedom" (p. 184). This suggests that they draw entirely different conclusions from the insight that there is no context-transcendent, absolute point of view: for Adorno, accepting this is compatible with a normative account of truth and first-order judgments about society's wrongness and irrationality; for Foucault, accepting this means that critique and resistance can only consist in creating distance between ourselves and our historical a priori, but not a judgment about whether a particular power/knowledge order is ultimately right or wrong. Foucault's approach to historical critique requires a certain *suspension of judgment* (and arguably, more optimism about the productive possibilities of power), whereas Adorno's approach to historical critique aims at *true judgments* concerning our past and present.[2] This allows us to see, secondly, that the normative view of truth is in fact in conflict with the second claim of metanormative contextualism, namely, that the lack of a context-transcendent point of view entails that we cannot judge the correctness or incorrectness of particular contexts or make comparative judgments in which one context is judged to be superior or inferior to another. Foucault may accept this claim, but not Adorno. There may even be an Adornian critique of this claim, where the suspension of judgment is itself a symptom of our generally reduced capacities for both empathy and thought.

The normative view of truth brings us to a second complication brought by Adorno to metanormative contextualism. Given that Adorno endorses a normative view of truth, what exactly forms the basis of truth, if there is no context-transcendent point of view? (And even more problematically, what is the basis of truth when we live a *Verblendungszusammenhang*, a context of delusion?) While the full answer to this question is, as expected, highly complex, the short answer is his negativistic critical naturalism or materialism.[3] Very roughly, Adorno contends that the basis of truth can be discerned by attending to the priority of the object, insofar as concepts can never exhaust the content of the objects they conceive. Two particular types of objects are especially relevant: nature that is external to us, and ourselves as natural creatures with acute needs and desires. The wrongness evidenced by the dialectic of enlightenment consists partly in the instinct for self-preservation gone terribly awry, where the taming and domination of nature (initially through myth, and then through the conceptual apparatus and technology brought by enlightenment reason), so important for our survival, have resulted in a context that threatens our very survival − both in that our technology and the destruction of nature threaten to make the earth uninhabitable for humans and other life-forms, and in that the knowledge and technology brought about by modernity (most notably, the capitalist form of exchange) fail to satisfy our basic needs and desires and even come to deform them entirely, despite their promise and potential to do exactly the opposite. This means that the truth content of the judgment that enlightenment has led to a new kind of barbarism is indexed to nature in both cases, although in a highly mediated and qualified sense.

Adorno's dialectical approach to naturalism (sometimes also called his materialism) is best understood through his Marxian concept of natural history.[4] Allen explains the first half of Adorno's thesis as follows:

> Adorno's complicated account of the relationship between nature and history is the idea that historically constituted objects come, over time, to seem natural and therefore unchangeable. Revealing this "second nature" to be historically contingent and therefore changeable is a crucial task of critical theory for Adorno. (p. 195)

Here, the aim of critique is to reveal the historically contingent character of things that appear to us as "natural" − things that appear (via unreflective habits and ideological reinforcement) as non-historical, eternal, unchanging, and necessary. This is a central feature of Adorno's dialectical critique of enlightenment rationality, which aims to reconstruct its historical development and trajectory. But there is a second feature of Adorno's natural history approach that Allen omits in her account, which claims, at the same time, that everything historical also has its basis in the natural, that history itself is a "natural outgrowth," which is concealed by certain historical self-understandings (Adorno, 1973, p. 358). The natural history thesis aims to demonstrate the dialectical interrelation of two opposed claims: on the one hand, everything is historically mediated and critique needs to denaturalize what appears as second nature; on the other hand, all history is an outgrowth of and thoroughly conditioned by nature, a condition that is likewise concealed and damaged by unreflective forms of historicism. Because there is no unmediated, non-historical, access to either external or human nature, and human nature itself is both unrealized and distorted, what critique can do is to help us attend to and become aware of history's repressed natural origins, which are most perspicuous in their negative, damaged form. Bernstein puts the point in the following way:

> In a way from which he never deviated, Adorno regards culture as a *part* of the natural world, albeit an intensely historicized part whose fundamental forms of activity cannot be reduced to their natural origins or counterparts, but whose origins and counterparts provide the conditions of possibility of their cultural elaboration as well as their genealogical intelligibility. (Bernstein, 2001, p. 189)

Nature (mediated, historicized, damaged, dominated, appearing in the negative, but still expressive of natural needs, functions, and desires) provides the conditions not just for culture, but also for its genealogical intelligibility; that is, without reference to nature, there would be no basis for truth, history, culture, or genealogical critique or self-understanding. So although Allen is right in suggesting that Adorno's appeal to inhumanity and the reality of suffering "cannot be indicative of a naïve or straightforward realism or objectivism about moral truths or values," the appeal is likewise idle without a reference to our existence as natural creatures in a natural environment with natural needs and desires, all of which only manifest themselves in a historically mediated, arguably damaged form, but none of which can be entirely erased by the concepts and practices of institutionalized enlightened reason that seek to obliviate it (p. 217).[5] All of this is a result of Adorno's normative theory of truth grounded in the priority of the object thesis. What Allen refers to as the method of historical problematization in Adorno thus makes necessary reference to nature as the basis of historical truth.

What are the implications of Adorno's critical naturalism for the thesis of metanormative contextualism? Again I think we can draw two provisional conclusions. The first (again) concerns the divergence between Adorno and Foucault and their respective approaches to historical critique. Traditionally, Foucault has been viewed as a representative of strong social constructivism in which language and discourse come to eclipse any talk of nature or materiality, but more recently Foucault has been viewed as a potential resource for thinkers associated with the "new materialism." Here is a characteristic passage from Foucault concerning the body:

> We believe, in any event, that the body obeys the exclusive laws of physiology and that it escapes the influence of history, but this too is false. The body is molded by a great many distinct regimes; it is broken down by the rhythms of work, rest, and holidays; it is poisoned by food or values, through eating habits or moral laws; it constructs resistances [...]. Nothing in man—not even his body—is sufficiently stable to serve as the basis for self-recognition or for understanding other men. The traditional devices for constructing a comprehensive view of history and for retracing the past as a patient and continuous development must be systematically dismantled. (Foucault, 1984, pp. 87–88)

Some of what Foucault says here fits in well with Adorno's conception of natural history: our physical bodies are molded by history and social practices, but no power regime can ever fully discipline the body such that it does not construct resistances, such that pleasures and perversions do not arise that create a distance from power, even while not being outside of or beyond it. However, Adorno draws significant moral conclusions from his natural history approach ("arrange thoughts and actions so that Auschwitz will not repeat itself"), whereas Foucault consistently and deliberately abstains from moral prescriptions, and would not ever ground moral claims on the basis of bodies and how they are molded by specific power regimes. Like Allen, my point is not to compare and contrast Adorno and Foucault, but I would contend that whereas natural history is a source of normativity for Adorno and a sufficient normative ground for critique, Foucault would reject this approach to normative grounding entirely. He may even reject the very idea that we need normative grounds for critique, and contend that the very debate over normative grounding in critical theory is largely a psuedoproblem. Where does metanormative contextualism fit in here? Does it side with Adorno, turning to natural history as a normative ground, or does it side with Foucault, who does not appear to have the problem of finding normative grounds at all? For Adorno, the potential success of the appeal to inhumanity and suffering depends upon the natural history thesis. Without it, the appeal lacks the necessary explanatory and normative force to make a genuine moral claim.

The second issue concerns how Adorno's critical naturalism complicates the first claim of metanormative contextualism, which states that:

> moral principles or normative ideals are always justified relative to a set of contextually salient values, conceptions of the good life, or normative horizons—roughly speaking, forms of life or life-worlds. (p. 215)

Given Adorno's rejection of a context-transcendent point of view, this must be right. However, Adorno's account may be less pluralistic than is suggested by this claim: the dialectic of enlightenment has a totalizing reach, its destruction of external nature and unrealized human nature knows no bounds, and capitalism is the form of life shared by humanity across the globe. If this is right (a big if), then contextualism is less contextual than it first appears, insofar as all of humanity is implicated in the wrong life. To put the point in Adorno's negative terms: suffering and inhuman practices are wrong everywhere, even if the grounds upon which we make this claim are shifting, contingent, and historically mediated foundations, as Adorno's own attempts at grounding surely are. Negative dialectics itself is, for Adorno, the right way of thinking about wrong life, but it is only right insofar as the conditions of wrong life continue to obtain. This is indeed a form of contextual justification, but when that context is total, the truth of contextualism loses some of its critical edge.

To conclude, none of what I have said implies that Adorno's account is correct, or that critical theory *must* return to Adorno, however, we come to interpret his controversial approach to historical critique. I have tried to draw out some of the implications that I think follow if we do indeed wish to return to Adorno's method of normative grounding, and raise some questions as to whether Adorno's method is compatible with metanormative contextualism. Allen has put forward a sophisticated, powerful, and undeniable challenge to critical theories that are normatively grounded in Eurocentric conceptions of progress. While the need to reject such parochial narratives is clear, critical theory's way forward continues to be open for debate.

NOTES

1. Allen also holds open the idea of more localized and contingent judgments of progress, calling this "progress in history." See Allen (2016, pp. 228–229). One question we could raise is whether progress in history (as opposed to historical progress) would be sufficient, in principal, to normatively ground the critical theories of Habermas and Honneth.

2. On Foucault's conception of critique and the suspension of judgment, see Butler (2002). Butler also draws a connection between Adorno's and Foucault's conceptions of critique, but I disagree with her that Adorno's conception of critique can also be understood along the lines of the suspension of judgment. Note also that Adorno's judgments are generally negative. For a sophisticated defense of Adorno's epistemic negativism which claims that we can only know the wrong, bad, false, inhuman, and so forth, see Freyenhagen (2013, esp. chapters 2 and 8).

3. I agree with Freyenhagen that we can also characterize this as a negative Aristotelianism. See Freyenhagen (2013, chapter 9).

4. Deborah Cook refers to Adorno's natural history approach as critical materialism. See Cook ([2011] 2014, chapter 1).

5. Although I cannot enter the debate as to whether Adorno is a realist of some sort, Alcoff and Shomali (2010) refer to Adorno as a dialectical realist. They also draw a connection between Adorno's conception of constellations and Foucault's conception of an *episteme*.

REFERENCES

Adorno, T. W. (1973). In E. B. Ashton (Trans.), *Negative dialectics*. New York, NY: Continuum.

Alcoff, L., & Shomali, A. (2010). Adorno's dialectical realism. *Canadian Journal of Continental Philosophy*, *14*(2), 45–65.

Allen, A. (2016). *The end of progress: Decolonizing the normative foundations of critical theory*. New York, NY: Columbia University Press.

Bernstein, J. (2001). *Adorno: Disenchantment and ethics*. Cambridge: Cambridge University Press.

Butler, J. (2002). What is critique? An essay on Foucault's virtue. In D. Ingram (Ed.), *The political: Readings in continental philosophy* (pp. 212–226). London: Blackwell.

Cook, D. ([2011] 2014). *Adorno on nature*. New York, NY: Routledge.

Foucault, M. (1984). Nietzsche, genealogy, history. In P. Rabinow (Ed.), *The Foucault reader* (pp. 76–100). New York, NY: Pantheon Books.

Freyenhagen, F. (2013). *Adorno's practical philosophy, living less wrongly*. Cambridge: Cambridge University Press.

O'Connor, B. (2004). *Adorno's negative dialectic*. Cambridge, MA: MIT Press.

DECOLONIZING CRITICAL THEORY

Kevin Olson

ABSTRACT

This chapter rethinks the future of critical theory by engaging Amy Allen's recent work. Allen does the Frankfurt School a great service by drawing a sharp-edged picture of some significant problems. I aim to think along with her in a spirit of shared sympathies that follow sometimes divergent paths. I agree with Allen's critique of Frankfurt tendencies toward Eurocentrism, progress thinking, and historical teleology. However, I also argue that critical theory must be more thoroughly reconfigured to adequately address the struggles and wishes of our age. Specifically, recent work of the Frankfurt School displaces critique in two important ways. The first is a tendency to work at a paradigmatic, meta-level of analysis rather than focusing on concrete problems. The second is a tendency to rely on democratic procedure for normativity without taking account of the tensions and contradictions in actual political cultures. In place of these uncritical tendencies, we need more interpretive and freely experimental critical strategies. One example is an interpretive approach that problematizes political cultures, revealing the tensions ignored by proceduralism. Another example lies in the rich archives of postcolonial thought that have had such a large impact on contemporary political and social life. Postcolonial critique is a non-dogmatic and flexible form of interpretation that has great potential to address problems of racism, international inequality, and the false universalism of many of our ideals.

Keywords: Critical theory; decolonization; postcolonial theory; progress; Amy Allen; Michel Foucault; Jürgen Habermas; Axel Honneth; Rainer Forst; Frankfurt School

Critical theorists like to quote Karl Marx's remark that critical theory should aim at "the self-clarification of the struggles and wishes of the age."[1] In this

The Challenge of Progress: Theory Between Critique and Ideology
Current Perspectives in Social Theory, Volume 36, 61–72
ISSN: 0278-1204/doi:10.1108/S0278-120420190000036011

light, it is somewhat singular that critical theory – or more precisely, that of the Frankfurt School – has occupied itself so much with philosophy recently at the expense of struggles and wishes. The seductions of theory-production have given us highly nuanced accounts of democracy, rights, recognition, and justice, with a corresponding lack of focus on concrete social problems or issues that might characterize this particular age.

A quick glance at the news reveals a very different picture. Refugee flows, economic crises, populist anger, and racial and ethnic tensions all loom large in the domestic news of the United States. Great Britain has just voted to leave the European Union, amidst a wave of anti-immigrant xenophobia that is washing across many other European countries as well. The Middle East is convulsed by Islamic insurgencies and political violence, causing mass dislocations that include many of the refugees currently troubling Europe. China is destabilizing the Western Pacific in a bid for territorial expansion, and Russia seems bent on reclaiming the imperial status vacated by the Soviet Union. The globe is warming, while global capitalism busily provides us with new ways to use resources and expand consumption. At the same time, the global economy pursues an ever-greater polarization between wealth and poverty.

For those who see potential in the critical approaches of the Frankfurt School, the question is how they can be better brought to bear on an unruly, problematic social reality that is desperately in need of criticism. The genres of philosophy produced by Frankfurt thinkers often seem too distant and abstract to comment effectively on these urgent and specific challenges. It is not surprising, then, that this approach is frequently met with indifference or invective in many areas of the humanities and social sciences. Such a reaction might be traced to what is often seen as the Frankfurt School's focus on metatheory, proceduralism, and lack of substantive engagement with urgent issues. Stronger reactions add the charge that this work is implicitly or explicitly foundationalist: that it overstates its claims, narrows the bases of critique, and fails to acknowledge its own investments in power. From this perspective, the Frankfurt School is dismissively characterized as "rationalist" with a wave of the hand indicating that nothing further needs be said.

Amy Allen's *The End of Progress* arrives on this scene as a welcome corrective. Allen theorizes the problems of the Frankfurt School as "colonial" in a particular way. They are problems of epistemology and power that narrow critique and bias it toward a particularly Eurocentric orientation. She charges the Frankfurt School with recapitulating in epistemic terms what European colonialism did in political ones. That is, privileging European norms, ideals, and practices over those of others, and universalizing and valorizing them in the process. In Allen's estimation, this happens particularly through ideals of progress. For Frankfurt thinkers, these ideas are part of an emancipatory teleology; for Allen, they are imposed with a quiet and unnoticed power that arrives with the best intent but also with damaging and distorting consequences. A critical theory built on false universalism and power fails to be adequately critical. The Frankfurt School, from this perspective, must be "decolonized." That is to say, it must stop privileging European, Enlightenment norms, ideals, and practices, and stop valorizing European forms of modernity as developmental goals, in favor of a less dogmatic, more open-ended form of critique.

Allen's criticism of the Frankfurt School is simultaneously incisive and generous. She exercises great interpretive care in delineating problems and blind spots. She understands and appreciates the emancipatory intent of these authors and seeks to hold them to their best intentions. That Allen is able to zero in on a tension between such intentions and their theoretical expression is potentially rectifying rather than dismissive. In this sense, her criticism is a generous one. She does the Frankfurt School the great service of drawing a sharp-edged picture of some significant problems, making it possible to take stock of the damage and salvage what is left. Rather than dismissing this work, she aims at renewal in a way that is quite rare among critical theory's critics.

In what follows, I will enter into dialogue with Allen about several points of her argument. I am highly sympathetic to the line of thinking pursued in *The End of Progress*, both its overall arc and detail. Thus, my comments will not follow the rituals of academic swordplay — thrust and parry, attack and riposte. Rather, I aim to think along with Allen about some of the issues she has raised. This is a matter of shared sympathies that follow sometimes divergent paths. Allen specifically targets the Frankfurt School's tendency toward Eurocentrism, progress-thinking, and historical teleology. While agreeing with this criticism, I see a broader project implied there as well, one that could be quite useful in addressing the struggles and wishes of our age. I put it forward as a helpful expansion of Allen's ideas, though I also reserve her the privilege of disavowing some of the directions in which I take her ideas, rejecting unwarranted additions, and dampening some of my wayward enthusiasm.

PROGRESS-THINKING AS SYMPTOMATIC

Allen draws on postcolonial theory to show how thoroughly notions of progress are threaded through the recent work of the Frankfurt School. This allows her to pose issues of comparative historicism with great precision. The question becomes one of the inner structure of various historicisms: whether they are animated by a negative dialectics (Adorno), genealogy aimed at problematization (Foucault), notions of progress that are themselves normative (Habermas, Honneth), or are generated out of other normative commitments (Forst). This has the benefit of arraying the various approaches Allen examines on the same tableau of comparison. It provides clear grounds to see how Foucault and Adorno can provide a more flexible, open-ended set of critical commitments than can Habermas, Honneth, and Forst.

This is a well-drawn, rich, and insightful discussion. Tracing out its criticisms and consequences, I believe that Allen's line of thinking, particularly its focus on normativity, power, and postcoloniality, opens the Frankfurt School to a broader line of critique. I tend to see progress-thinking as symptomatic of deeper problems in their recent work. Here, I would like to pick up the threads of an earlier discussion with Allen (2016, pp. 226–227, 257n35). I would say that the Frankfurt School's fixation on progress is symptomatic not only of teleology or an overly rigid historicism, but a whole set of assumptions about critical method and normativity. In this regard, I think that decolonizing the normative foundations of critical theory requires a somewhat wider angle of view.

Methodologically, individual Frankfurt thinkers have tended toward building a holistic critical apparatus around one particular concept or paradigm: the pragmatic presuppositions of discourse, for instance, or recognition, or justification. One can quickly see the problems with such an approach by thinking about the contemporary social and political scene that I characterized earlier. Climate change, economic crisis, and global political instability are complex problems that cannot be theorized from a single common perspective. When Frankfurt thinkers try to do so, they are forced into a standpoint that is narrowly procedural. Rather than exploring concrete social issues in an open-ended way and searching for new concepts that might open them up to scrutiny, they retreat to thinking about the discursive processes that one might use to criticize these problems. This kind of thin proceduralism declines the challenge of substantive social criticism while also aiming at an implicitly reductive basis for critique.

Normativity is a similar issue. Allen ably shows that Frankfurt thinkers take a subtle and self-conscious approach to issues of critical normativity, yet still arrive at positions that are foundational, quasi-foundational, exclusionist, and/ or invested with power relations. Allen does us the great service of tracing the power dynamics that underlie this approach: its implicit imperialism, its overstated universalism, and its bias toward European ideals and practices. I see this normative heavy-handedness as symptomatic of more general set of normative attitudes and commitments. This is the sense in which various Frankfurt approaches suffer from what Ronald Dworkin calls the "one right answer thesis": the idea that a cultural interpreter, looking into a complex mixture of social norms and practices, can produce a "right answer" that binds or corrects those practices (Dworkin, 1977, pp. 104, 279–290). Dworkin is talking about legal interpretation, but much the same attitude seems to hold in strands of critical theory. Insofar as it aims at finding a normative "right answer," critical theory attempts to arrive at a correct critical standpoint *ex-ante*, from a purely rational perspective. The power dynamics implicit in such an approach, well-characterized by Allen, add up to a kind of normative heavy-handedness. They bias critique by trying to stipulate a correct critical perspective from the start. Even when this commitment is fallible and procedural, it still constitutes an assertion of epistemic authority and a narrowing of critical modalities.

My comments about methodology and normativity in no way impugn Allen's careful diagnosis of the problems of progress-thinking. Rather, I am inclined to see in that diagnosis more general problems of method and normativity. I believe that these more general problems constitute additional impediments to clarifying the struggles and wishes of the age. My orientation, then, is to build on Allen's critique. In this sense, I think we are headed in the same direction. To the extent that Allen and I agree about this, there remains the vital task of determining how best to integrate her carefully rendered critique of historicism with the other lines of criticism that I have outlined. To the extent that we disagree, it may be a question about how broadly or narrowly to construe the core problems of Frankfurt School critical theory.

THE DISPLACEMENT OF CRITIQUE

I raise these questions about the scope of the Frankfurt Schools' normative problems because I believe that they orient our approach to reformulating critique. Allen argues for a decolonization of critical theory, which she formulates as an end of backward-looking, Eurocentric progress-thinking. I wholly support this move, but see the project of decolonization as one that can take broader form based on the critique that Allen has given us. In more general terms, it can be a *double* decolonization that proceeds along both epistemic and methodological lines.

Consider, for instance, the impact of the narrow methodological approach I have just outlined. Critical theorizing has often devolved into a dispute over clashing paradigms. It often emphasizes metatheory over substantive engagements, conducting the discussion in terms quite abstract and distant from concrete problems. This has produced highly refined understandings of the relative merits of different paradigms, but ones that are also quite hypothetical. From this perspective, "I believe we should adopt paradigm X" counts as a critical insight, and the definitive establishment of paradigm X as the correct approach is all too often seen as the end of the discussion rather than its beginning.

This approach tends to leave a large gap between the highly refined critical organon and the world it is intended to comment on. We develop well-polished understandings of the merits and drawbacks of different approaches, without ever actually commenting on the world and its problems. As a result, critical theory winds up being a meta-theory that describes what critique would look like, if one were ever actually to do it. The world races by while we debate how best to think about it. We can call this a *philosophical displacement of critique*.

A second but related problem is the particular direction that the Frankfurt School has taken in its choice of paradigms. This is an emphasis on procedural approaches that are ever more refined in their ability to harness the normativity of everyday life. They become a kind of meta-apparatus, established in carefully tuned form, awaiting the actual participation of "real" citizens. Here actually existing normativity acquires a kind of primal status and presumed rectitude. On the one hand, this amounts to normative modesty on the part of critical theory, but on the other hand, it ignores the chaotic, contradictory, and tension-filled character of actual political cultures. To employ the normative commitments of everyday life as a critical resource without extensive criticism of those commitments is to misjudge their quality and character. A critical theory that withdraws into a kind of democratic proceduralism or reliance on "public reason" commits this error. Democracy and rights are worthy endeavors, but they are woefully inadequate to commenting incisively on the problems we currently face. In this light, the Frankfurt School appears increasingly uncritical to the extent that its focus on procedure is premised on a reliance on normative resources that are themselves dysfunctional, problematic, and greatly in need of critique. We can call this a *procedural displacement of critique.*

In short, I believe that Frankfurt School critical theory has become both too paradigmatic and too procedural in recent years. These are two separate problems, but they travel together. Decolonizing critical theory must take aim at both of them. Allen's discussion addresses the proceduralism of recent Frankfurt School critical theory, and it succeeds quite well in revealing some of the power investments and other problems of such an approach. It does this, however, by staging a clash of paradigms: proceduralism versus contextualism, progress-oriented historicisms versus problematizing ones, and so on. The danger is to recapitulate the kind of paradigmatic abstraction that constitutes a philosophical displacement of critique.

Allen refers to her project as a form of contextualism (Allen, 2016, pp. 34−35, 209−219). This is itself a name for a paradigmatic genre of justification, one rooted in concrete contexts. Potentially one could become absorbed in a paradigmatic discussion over contextualism versus proceduralism, or something similar, that pitches the stakes of critique as a matter of adjudicating philosophical paradigms, at the risk of displacing critique.

I think there is another way of reading Allen's discussion, however. One could see it as an immanent critique of the tendency toward a philosophical displacement of critique. Her call to rethink the normative foundations of critical theory identifies key problems of a purely paradigmatic approach. The "contextualism" it holds up as a replacement need not be seen as a stylized meta-critical paradigm, but rather as opening the door for an entire class of investigations that are innovative in normativity and methodology. This, for instance, is very much the ethos of the genealogical strand of critical theory that Allen champions so persuasively. Genealogy is of necessity about some concrete issue, archive, practice, or institution. It cannot be genuinely genealogical, however, without complex forms of theoretical self-reflection that challenge the construction of the objects of critique and the modality of historical interpretation. Here, critique is reflected upon as it is practiced.

For us to pursue this subtle blending of methodological reflection and substantive criticism, we would have to avoid inscribing Allen's ideas in the same tendency to displace critique. We would have to avoid perpetuating a discussion devoted solely to the adjudication of conflicting paradigms. Of course, we wouldn't want to give up the ability to compare the respective advantages and disadvantages of critical paradigms. The point is to avoid *displacing* critique, rather than to put such a paradigmatic discussion out of business as such. A newly experimental critical theory must aim to better integrate its metatheoretical reflections with substantive criticism. This is a challenge to readers who would feel satisfied to hear their favorite paradigm well-defended and call it a day. If the point is really to clarify the struggles and wishes of the age, critical theory must be both substantive and self-reflective at the same time.

Experiments in Critical Theory

The interpretation of Allen's project that I have described would open the door to a wide array of experiments in critical methodology and normativity. It would extend Allen's insights about problematizing critique in new directions, ones consistent with her historicism, but developing new techniques of problematization that may not be distinctively historical.

One can best see what these might look like in contrast to the prevailing emphasis on proceduralism, one often theorized as "public reason." The vast majority of our normative commitments are not generated through explicit, propositional speech acts. Rather, they are reproduced silently through practices, structured into our built environment, symbolically coded into images and representations, or ride parasitically on the "explicit" content of speech. These commitments are found in what Cornelius Castoriadis and Charles Taylor have called our shared social imaginaries: the ways that we constitute and reproduce forms of common sense that are deeply naturalized and frequently problematic (Castoriadis, 1987; Taylor, 2004). By putting so much emphasis on public reason, Frankfurt critical theory has offered a conception of normativity that turns a blind eye toward these actual normative practices. This creates a mismatch between critique and reality, and a loss of critical traction on some of the most important social, political, and cultural phenomena of recent decades.

This mismatch is the result of what Allen describes as an "applied ethics" approach to critique: one that first develops an idealized critical perspective, then holds some actual society to be lacking in reference to it (Allen, 2016, pp. 16, 90). Extending this line of thinking in Allen's work, I believe that we must find ways to operate within the horizon of actually existing norms and practices, probing the fissures in our common sense, making them palpable and visceral, and using problematization to open up new forms of thought and practice and reveal the problems inherent in present ones.

The question is how best to undertake this project? The Frankfurt School laid early claim to the name critical theory, a claim that was certainly secured by the time of Max Horkheimer's 1937 essay "Traditional and Critical Theory" (Horkheimer, 1972). Since then, many other critical modalities have arisen that have equal claim to the title: feminism, queer theory, genealogy, psychoanalysis, affect theory, and postcolonialism, to name a few. What is singular and regrettable is the extent to which this rich ferment has not been engaged by the Frankfurt School, or even worse, has been ruled out of bounds.

Here Allen's concerns about power, alterity, marginalization, and problematization can be taken up in a wide variety of ways. We can add to the list a number of techniques and modalities that do not even have a label: ones that proceed intuitively and contextually, drawing critical lessons from the material they work with. Here critique proceeds through innovative modes of interpretation, analysis, and problematization. This might include writerly and representational modes that cause tensions and contradictions to surface. It might encompass the artful juxtaposition of concepts and values in tension with one another, or the presentation of enigmas that foil one's ability to make sense of them, or turn one's critical attention back on itself. Such critical modalities need not be linguistically deployed: we must also take seriously the power of images and representations that problematize our common sense (Benjamin, 1999; Didi-Huberman, 2005, pp. 139–228). In short, problematization can take many forms. Together they constitute an open-ended exploration of points of opacity, taken-for-grantedness, and difficulty within our own normative world. They are one example of what we might envision as an improvisatory, open-ended approach to critique. In this view, the objects of critique — actually existing norms, values, and practices — are not pre-given, so the critical approach to them cannot be either. Rather, a certain amount of interpretive virtuosity and legerdemain is needed, moving within a tension-filled, often contradictory cultural landscape to reveal problems and produce insights.

Because the forms of critique I am describing are largely contingent and improvised, the proof of their success is in the pudding. One must demonstrate this through concrete and specific analyses. A great deal of exciting work in the humanities and social sciences follows this model. Many examples are currently being published in Allen's book series New Directions in Critical Theory. It is a project to which I have also devoted a great deal of thought, so I will offer some examples of my own that try to exemplify such a practice. This is not to suggest that this work is exemplary; only that I have detailed knowledge of the intentions that animate it.

A reconfigured critical theory could, for instance, take aim at the very norms underlying the current emphasis on "public reason." The impulse toward democratic proceduralism has resulted in heavier and heavier reliance on democracy to provide the normative content that critical theory is thought to lack. The idea is that a chastened, more modest critical theory can describe legitimate democratic procedures that harness the normativity of everyday life as a source of critique. That normativity is made explicit by means of rational discourse: taking yes/no positions on propositional statements, in Habermas's case, or offering justifications for binding norms, in Forst's. There are two substantial lacunae in this idea, however. First, it supposes that democracy itself has a clear, unproblematic, and rational normative basis, such that it can function as a neutral framework for channeling other normative contents. Second, it assumes that the normative contents of everyday life themselves are unproblematic. It accords a natural rectitude to these values and ideals, seeing them as the true source of critical normativity.

This notion of critique relies on democracy when it should be criticizing it. It is a mistake to assume that our political imaginaries, cultural commitments, beliefs, and points of reference are rational. This is not necessarily, exclusively, or most importantly how people form their beliefs. "Filtering" or processing the rest of our beliefs through some democratic notion of public reason presumes too much. Like the theory of progress, it presumes that a rationally assembled conception of democracy should be imposed as a critical standard on the rest of our beliefs and practices. In Allen's terms, this is another form of colonization, similar in type to the theory of progress. It is a foreign imposition on everyday normativity. That everyday normativity, including our actual, normative commitments to popular sovereignty, is a highly problematic tangle, filled with tensions, inconsistencies, and contradictory impulses. If we problematize it in the way Allen describes, we find that it was formed as a difficult, problem-laden response to historical contingencies. Democratic norms never entirely made sense, much to the frustration of the people devising them. Still, the weight of events forced them to patch together ideas whose problems and internal tensions were slowly forgotten. Those problems can be brought to the surface again through careful critique, making us realize that democracy is greatly in need of the kind of problematization that Allen describes, rather than providing a ready-made source of normativity (Olson, 2016, chapter 4).

The problematization I am describing here is partly genealogical, of the sort that Allen champions. Genealogy works as an effective tool to show how tensions internal to the democratic project surfaced over and over again, to the frustration of its practitioners. Here, genealogy problematizes by revealing internal problematics that surfaced within these practices and were eventually incorporated into them as undigested morsels, forgotten but not resolved. Other strategies of problematization are needed as well, however, setting material practices alongside discursive and conceptual ones to show how different genres of practice create tensions with one another (e.g., Olson, 2016, pp. 81–83, 128–130).

Equally valuable is an explicit reference to the postcolonial context drawn on by Allen, juxtaposing metropolitan practice to that of the colonial periphery. Here tensions implicit within European enlightenment projects create an explosive and dysfunctional mixture when they are exported to the colonies. The diaspora of French Revolutionary ideas provokes a reaction against French colonialism in terms both familiar and foreign. Juxtaposing the two contexts is a valuable technique of problematization. It causes internal contradictions to surface in what are otherwise taken for granted ideals (Olson, 2016, chapters 6–7).

One might follow these insights about postcolonialism further, in parallel to the argument that Allen draws on so effectively in this book. She uses the idea of decolonization in an epistemic sense, providing leverage for a transformation in the normative outlook of critical theory. A more far-reaching use of postcolonial theory is completely consistent with this argument, and it can take up Allen's project of problematization in unexpected ways. Such insights can reveal the epistemic chaos that was generated by material practices of colonial slaves, for instance (Olson, 2015). Unexplained practices of signification created a probing self-critique on the part of colonial elites, problematizing the Enlightenment "universalism" that was elsewhere serving as a revolutionary doctrine. In this case, silent, unexplained material practices generated a powerful form of problematization.

Such an analysis joins Allen's project by providing leverage against the overstated normativity of the Frankfurt School, while at the same time tantalizing us with broader vistas. One could imagine expanding such a decolonized critical theory further: Allen's vision of problematizing critique fused with various strands of postcolonial thinking, for instance. Such an extension of her project could open up new critical horizons: critiques of racism, the ongoing instabilities of the decolonized world, polarities between global north and south, refugee and immigrant phenomena, and so on. Here, we are imagining a nondogmatic critical theory that can collaborate constructively with projects like postcolonial theory. In so doing, it would be one invigorated by a broader array of imaginaries, issues, normative horizons, contexts, and events than those it currently entertains. The result would be new critical modalities and new ways of thinking about critical normativity.

TOTALING UP THE DAMAGE

This speculation about new modes of critique invites us to ask what we should make of the old ones. Specifically, how should we think about the performative implications of Allen's engagement with the Frankfurt School? She interprets three generations of Frankfurt thinkers with scrupulous care. How do we understand the tension between this engagement and the force of her criticism, which might seem to suggest outright rejection of those views? This leaves us wondering whether there are resources within this tradition that can be carried forward into the future, or whether it should be surpassed by Foucault, Adorno, and the well-developed literature on decolonization and postcoloniality.

To answer this question, we might ask what can be salvaged from Frankfurt School work if we bracket its teleology and normative foundationalism. Could we, for instance, imagine a Habermasian theory of the public sphere freed from the normative bounds placed on public discourse by the idea of "regulative presuppositions of speech"? A Honnethian conception of freedom not rooted in a universalistic historicism flavored by European modernity? Or a Forstian notion of public discourse not centered on the idea that we have done what is necessary toward others when we have provided a proper justification for the norms that bind them?

Habermas's work stands out in particular for its well-developed array of critical concepts that are still valuable for social critique. Notions of legitimation crisis, the public sphere, system and lifeworld, and the interconnections between different kinds of rights provide insights about issues of contemporary concern. In addition to these useful concepts, Habermas frequently provides a model as a subtle interpreter and critic of contemporary events. His occasional political writings, often published in *Die Zeit* and other German periodicals, reveal a probing, nondogmatic intellect who can also be a surprisingly vivid writer.[2] Unfortunately, these essays often circle back to the theory of communicative action that provides the normative backbone of Habermas's work, and when they do, they tend to lose their interpretative acuity and revert to a perspective that is imposed on them from elsewhere. If one reads Habermas's essays as though they were freed from the narrow strictures of this theory, however, one gets some inkling of what a more flexible, contextually appropriate mode of critique might look like on his terms.

I have tried to do something similar, using retooled Habermasian resources to explore the complex mess of norms that exist in American political culture around issues of distributive justice (Olson, 2006). Philosophers have devoted a great deal of effort to establishing various abstract norms of distribution. This, however, is an example of what Allen criticizes as "applied ethics." It evaluates society in terms of philosophically derived norms, and in so doing, it displaces critique. Habermasian ideas can provide the basis for another approach, one that interprets the actual normative commitments that circulate in contemporary societies in all of their polyvalence, tensions, and contradictions. Here, we find not only notions of freedom, autonomy, and equality, but also possessive individualism, racism, misogyny, and fear of government. Separated from the theory of communicative action, the Habermasian idea of a performative contradiction can function in a problematizing manner: it identifies the costs of chafing normative contradictions within actual political cultures. A careful, critical interpretation of these tensions and contradictions might go some way toward revealing the problematic inconsistencies in our most deeply held commitments. In this sense, it agrees with Allen's criticism of Habermas as well as her preference for problematization, sifting through what remains to develop new forms of critique.

The scrupulous care with which Allen approaches her criticism of the Frankfurt School leads me to think that she also finds much worth saving there. Her own articulation of this project is a historicism that is freed from progress-thinking, one that can thereby pursue a more open-ended problematization. To this, I would add a revised approach to critical normativity in a broader sense, one that shares Allen's well-argued preference for problematization. I can well imagine the complaints that might be raised against such a vision: that by failing to account for its normativity in a clear manner, it loses critical punch; by criticizing democratic proceduralism, it fails to tap the special normative potential of democracy. Here, I think Allen and I are very much on the same wavelength, though there may be some illuminating differences in how we would respond to such charges. That, however, is a topic for another time. For the moment, I am very pleased to be an interlocutor in this imaginative and timely discussion, and grateful to Amy Allen for initiating it.

NOTES

1. Karl Marx, letter to Arnold Ruge, September 1843, in Marx and Engels (1975, Vol. 3, p. 145) (note the differences in translation here). To my knowledge, it was Nancy Fraser who drew this phrase to our attention (Fraser, 1989, p. 113).
2. These pieces are collected as Habermas's *Kleine politische Schriften*. They currently number 12 volumes with various titles, published by Suhrkamp Verlag. The most recent is *Im Sog der Technokratie: Kleine Politische Schriften XII* (2013).

REFERENCES

Allen, A. (2016). *The end of progress: Decolonizing the normative foundations of critical theory.* New York, NY: Columbia University Press.

Benjamin, W. (1999). Little history of photography. In *Selected writings* (Vol. 2, part 2, 1931–1934, pp. 507–530). Cambridge, MA: Harvard University Press.

Castoriadis, C. (1987). *The imaginary institution of society* (K. Blamey, Trans.). Cambridge: Polity Press.

Didi-Huberman, G. (2005). *Confronting images: Questioning the ends of a certain history of art.* University Park, PA: Pennsylvania State University Press.

Dworkin, R. (1977). *Taking rights seriously.* Cambridge, MA: Harvard University Press.

Fraser, N. (1989). *Unruly practices: Power, discourse, and gender in contemporary social theory.* Minneapolis, MN: University of Minnesota Press.

Habermas, J. (2013). *Im Sog der Technokratie: Kleine Politische Schriften XII.* Frankfurt: Suhrkamp.

Horkheimer, M. (1972). Traditional and critical theory. *Critical theory: Selected essays* (M. J. O'Connell, Trans.). New York, NY: Continuum.

Marx, K., & Engels, F. (1975). *Collected works.* New York, NY: International Publishers.

Olson, K. (2006). *Reflexive democracy: Political equality and the welfare state.* Cambridge, MA: MIT Press.

Olson, K. (2015). Epistemologies of rebellion: The tricolor cockade and the problem of subaltern speech. *Political Theory, 43*(6), 730–752.

Olson, K. (2016). *Imagined sovereignties: The power of the people and other myths of the modern age.* New York, NY: Cambridge University Press.

Taylor, C. (2004). *Modern social imaginaries.* Durham, NC: Duke University Press.

PROGRESS, NORMATIVITY, AND THE "DECOLONIZATION" OF CRITICAL THEORY: REPLY TO CRITICS

Amy Allen

ABSTRACT

My response to the thoughtful and insightful critical discussions of my book, The End of Progress, *offered by Reha Kadakal, George Steinmetz, Karen Ng, and Kevin Olson, restates its motivation and rationale to defend my interpretive claims regarding Adorno, Foucault, Habermas, Honneth, and Forst by applying standards drawn from the first two theorists that are consonant with postcolonial critical theory to the perspectives, claims, and theoretical contributions of the latter three theorists. Habermas, Honneth, and Forst presume a historical present that has shaped the second, third, and fourth generations of the Frankfurt School they represent – a present that appears to be characterized by relative social and political stability – a stability that only applies in the context of Europe and the United States. Elsewhere, anti-colonial struggles, proxy wars, and even genocides were related to the persistent legacies of European colonialism and consequences of American imperialism. Yet, critical theory must expand its angle of vision and acknowledge how its own critical perspective is situated within the postcolonial present. The essays of Kadakal and Ng express concerns about my metanormative contextualism and the question of whether Adorno's work can be deployed to support it. Steinmetz challenges my "process of elimination" argument for metanormative contextualism and asks why I assume that constructivism, reconstructivism, and problematizing genealogy exhaust the available options for grounding normativity. Olson calls for a methodological decolonization to*

The Challenge of Progress: Theory Between Critique and Ideology
Current Perspectives in Social Theory, Volume 36, 73–91
ISSN: 0278-1204/doi:10.1108/S0278-120420190000036012

complement the epistemic decolonization I recommend. Critical theory should produce critical theories of actually existing societies, rather than being pre-occupied with meta-theory or disputes over clashing paradigms.

Keywords: Critical theory; progress; decolonization; Theodor W. Adorno; Michel Foucault; Jürgen Habermas; Axel Honneth; Rainer Forst; metanormative contextualism

It is an honor and a pleasure to respond to these insightful and rigorous papers on my book. I'm tremendously grateful to Reha Kadakal, George Steinmetz, Karen Ng, and Kevin Olson for their careful and challenging readings of my work and to Harry Dahms for bringing together such an impressive and inter-disciplinary group of scholars for this symposium. All four readers raise deep and difficult questions and criticisms of my work, and given the variety of disci-plines represented here – including philosophy, political theory, social theory, and postcolonial studies – those questions and criticisms cover a broad range of issues. In what follows, I fear that I will not be able to address all of the issues that have been put on the table, and in some cases the best response I can offer will be one that indicates some future directions for my research.

Let me begin by articulating what I take to be the two principal aims of *The End of Progress*. The first – critical and interpretive – aim is to demonstrate the extent to which contemporary Frankfurt School critical theorists such as Jürgen Habermas and Axel Honneth, in different ways, rely upon a conception of his-torical progress to ground their normative positions. Thus, one sense of the phrase "the end of progress" refers to an interpretive claim regarding the end that a certain notion of progress – what I call the backward-looking notion of progress as a historical "fact" – has come to serve in contemporary critical the-ory. The primary critical argument of the book is that the deployment of the notion of progress in Habermas's and Honneth's work is vulnerable to both con-ceptual and political objections. The conceptual objection turns on the question of whether a notion of progress can be used to justify or ground one's normative perspective without collapsing into conventionalism or mere self-congratulation. I should emphasize at the outset that the conceptual objection does not target the concept of progress per se, but rather is aimed more specifically at the attempt to ground one's first-order normative principles in a conception of his-torical progress – a strategy that I argue Habermas and Honneth adopt in an attempt to avoid the twin evils of foundationalism and relativism. The political objection draws on a large, rich, and wide-ranging body of work in post- and de-colonial theory that exposes the links between Eurocentric narratives of his-torical progress and the logics underpinning and justifying colonialism, imperial-ism, and the so-called civilizing mission. Again, I should emphasize here that, as I understand it, this post- or decolonial objection does not so much call into question the concept of progress simpliciter – indeed, I accept the claim that post- and decolonial critique implicitly rely on some conception of progress in the very articulation of their critique, to be spelled out in more detail later – but rather unmasks the problematic imperial logic that supports readings of

European modernity as the result of a process of progressive development whether that idea is cashed out in terms of social evolution, societal rationalization, or historical learning. Central to the argument of the book, then, is the distinction between two senses of progress: a backward-looking sense in which progress is way of reading history as a story of historical development or learning that leads up to "us" and a forward-looking sense in which progress is a moral or political goal we are striving to achieve. And this leads to a second meaning of the phrase "the end of progress," a meaning that draws inspiration from Adorno's dictum that "progress occurs where it ends" (Adorno, 2005, p. 150): namely, the idea that progress in the future is possible only if we jettison the ideologically Eurocentric narrative of historical progress as a "fact" of modernity.

Given how I have just constructed the critical-interpretive aim of the book, one might wonder why there is an entire chapter devoted to the work of Rainer Forst, who clearly adopts a different strategy for grounding normativity than that of Habermas and Honneth, one that does not rely on a conception of historical progress. Indeed, for Forst, normativity is grounded in a constructivist account of practical reason, and although he does defend a notion of progress, he understands progress as a normatively dependent concept, in the sense that it is dependent upon the right to justification that forms the normative core of his work. Although the readers for this symposium mostly sidestep my critique of Forst, it may still be worth explaining how I see it fitting into the book as a whole, as it relates to the second principal aim of the project. This second, more reconstructive aim is to defend an alternative conception of normativity for critical theory, one that does not rely on a backward-looking notion of historical progress, but that also avoids the twin evils of foundationalism and relativism. I call this conception metanormative contextualism, and I develop it in part through my readings of Michel Foucault and Theodor Adorno.

Throughout the book, the argument in favor of metanormative contextualism proceeds by the process of elimination. Starting from the methodological presupposition that critical theory resolves to draw its normative principles from within the existing social world, through a form of immanent critique, I then work through what I take to be two of the major contenders for grounding normativity in contemporary Frankfurt School critical theory: neo-Hegelian reconstructivism and neo-Kantian constructivism. Both neo-Kantian and neo-Hegelian strands of argument are combined in Habermas's work in complex ways, and, not surprisingly, given his massive influence on subsequent work in critical theory, the opposition between these two positions has structured much of the debate about normativity in Frankfurt School critical theory over the last few decades. (As those who have spent time in Frankfurt know, for many years, the end of the year soccer match organized by Axel Honneth's colloquium pitted the Kantians against the Hegelians.) But, in my view, both positions are vulnerable to conceptual and political objections. I have already indicated how these criticisms go in the case of the neo-Hegelian position; for the neo-Kantian position, the conceptual and methodological problem is that it posits a foundationalist conception of practical reason "as such" and the political problem is that it is insufficiently attentive to the ways in which power relations – including, but not limited to, neo-colonial or neo-imperial ones – shape and constitute the space of reasons.

If we are to remain within the methodological constraints of critical theory, then, this leaves a third option for grounding normativity, which is what I call metanormative contextualism. I call this version of contextualism "metanormative" because the contextualism operates at the level of the metanormative justification of our first-order normative principles. In this way, my position avoids foundationalism about justification. But it also avoids reverting to the claim that the normative principles of European modernity are the result of a process of historical progress or learning as a means of justifying them. This is the specific – and admittedly rather limited – sense in which this project could be considered a decolonizing one. Hence what I propose in the book is, as Kevin Olson notes in his paper, a kind of epistemic decolonization not of critical theory per se but rather of its primary strategies for grounding normativity. This is why the subtitle of the book is not *Decolonizing Critical Theory* per se but rather the much more modest *Decolonizing the Normative Foundations of Critical Theory* (I'll say more about this later, in reply to Steinmetz). Finally, and here admittedly is the trickier part of the argument, which I will discuss more in my reply to Kadakal, metanormative contextualism is perfectly compatible with first-order normative principles that are universal in scope; thus, it need not imply or entail normative relativism.

With this brief reconstruction of the principal aims of my argument in mind, I now turn to the specific criticisms raised by the contributors to this symposium. Reha Kadakal's paper starts with the critical-interpretive side of my argument and moves on to the reconstructive side. His first point takes aim at the claim, which he attributes to me, that there is a non-traditional philosophy of history underlying the Frankfurt School's conception of progress (p. 26). In contrast to this reading, Kadakal argues that:

> the problematic status of progress issues from precisely the lack of philosophy of history in current Frankfurt School critical theory, and that what underlies its grounding strategy is the explicit awareness that an appeal to philosophy of history in a post-metaphysical universe is no longer available. (pp. 26–27)

As Kadakal sees it, both Habermas and Honneth attempt "to arrive at 'universalizable' standards without appealing to any philosophy of history" and only attempt to defend a notion of progress "retrospectively" (p. 28). In other words, Kadakal challenges my interpretive claim that Habermas's and Honneth's strategy for grounding normativity relies on rooting the standards by which they measure forward-looking judgments about what would constitute progress in the future – the norms of discourse ethics, for Habermas, and the theory of recognition, for Honneth – in a backward-looking story about how those core normative principles are the result of a process of progressive historical development.

Fully justifying my reading of Habermas and Honneth would require repeating a great deal of material that makes up the bulk of chapters two and three of the book. Instead, I will have to settle for making two points: first, this way of reading them makes both Habermas and Honneth out to be neo-Kantians for whom claims about historical progress fall out of their universal normative principles. It seems pretty clear to me that this is not the case for Honneth, as he himself says explicitly in several places that his conception of critical theory relies if not on a philosophy of history then at least on a certain conception of historical progress (I'll come back to this distinction in a moment).[1] Matters are admittedly less clear in the case of Habermas, who is certainly open to a more neo-Kantian reading, particularly if one focuses on his discourse ethics — though here it is worth pointing out that such a reading does not make Habermas's theory more defensible against postcolonial critique, as Kadakal himself notes (p. 28), and it raises important methodological concerns as well, which are similar to the ones I have raised vis-à-vis Forst. Without recapitulating the textual arguments that I make in chapter two, I would just point out that the key issue with respect to Habermas has to do with his attempt to build normativity on, as Kadakal puts it, "quasi-transcendental foundations, that is, through postmetaphysical categories that are socio-historically specific in origin and yet can be taken to be universal in their validity" (p. 28). Implicit in this very reconstruction of Habermas's aims is the precise critical-interpretive point that I make at length in chapter two: namely, that the categories that Habermas takes as universal in their validity are rooted "socio-historically" in his rational reconstruction of the know-how of communicatively competent social actors, which means post-conventional members of post-traditional societies. Thus, however post-metaphysical this account may be, it has embedded within it a conception of the developmental superiority of this particular form of linguistic subjectivity, which is presumed to entail normative presuppositions that are universal, which is to say that at the core of Habermas's supposedly free-standing account of normativity stands an assumption about social evolution/historical progress.[2]

Second, it might be helpful to clarify that my primary concern in the book is not so much with the philosophy of history per se — and certainly not philosophy of history in its strong, speculative, metaphysical form — but rather with the notion of historical progress that although central to traditional philosophy of history can also be articulated and defended absent such a framework. Thus, even if it is true, as Kadakal argues, that "Marx's mature social theory has no philosophy of history" (p. 27), it nevertheless does operate with a notion of historical progress.[3] And even if I may perhaps not have distinguished clearly enough in the book between general claims about the philosophy of history and more specific claims about historical progress, the latter is enough, I think, as far as the argument of my book is concerned. That is to say, even if historical progress is understood not in metaphysical terms but rather as a provisional category in light of which we retrospectively have a right (or perhaps even a duty) to understand our history, the conceptual and political arguments that I make would still hold, *mutatis mutandis*, and the Foucaultian-Adornian position that I stake out would still constitute a genuine and, I think, attractive alternative.

Which brings me to Kadakal's second line of questioning, which asks how exactly genealogical problematization provides an alternative account of normativity? With respect to the former question, Kadakal argues that "problematization would be possible only if we already have a normative criteria that is fundamentally different than that which is being problematized" and that "the recognition of domination and power in the world already assumes what freedom and autonomy entails, as well as their difference from unfreedom and domination" (p. 29). As a result of these worries, he claims that "in order to serve as a method of critique [...], genealogy must already assume a theory, if not a philosophy, of history" and that:

> it is not fully clear in Allen's account how genealogy [...] could adequately serve as a method that not only offers a critique of Enlightenment ideals but also their transcendence. (p. 29)

I would not disagree with the claim that genealogy assumes some sort of theory of history; indeed, I'm interested in it precisely because it offers a theory of history that jettisons the notion of historical progress. In that sense, genealogical problematization can be understood as a determinate negation of the neo- or left-Hegelian conception of history. This is what I have in mind when I talk about the complex and doubly reflexive structure of what I call Foucault's Historical historical a priori. The historical a priori for Foucault refers to the idea that there are historically specific conditions of possibility for thought and rationality, but his immanent critique of modernity also turns on the claim that our historical a priori is also Historical − that is, it is structured through and through by History, just as the Classical historical a priori is structured by representation. Thus, if we want to get critical distance on (or negate) our historical a priori, we have to problematize that conception of History; but if we want to proceed immanently (or determinately), we have to do so *using historical means*.

This is perhaps just another way of saying that the only kind of transcendence available to us is an immanent transcendence or transcendence from within. This means nothing more − but also nothing less − than the ability to free ourselves up in relation to the historical a priori that constitutes us as thinking and acting subjects, and, in so doing, to open up the possibility of thinking and acting otherwise. In other words, immanent critique as I understand it, following Foucault, is a matter of tracing lines of fragility or fracture within the present, and using those to open up a space between ourselves and our present, in order to make the visible visible or to excavate the subsoil beneath our feet.[4] To put this in more Adornian terms, one might speak of critique as a practice of bringing elements "into changing constellations," a practice which does not reveal fixed meanings but rather interprets the present, "lights it up suddenly and momentarily."[5]

Although this conception of immanent critique remains largely implicit in my book, hopefully having spelled it out more clearly here enables me to clarify the role that Foucault's conception of unreason plays with respect to this conception of immanent critique. Kadakal is worried that I appeal to unreason as a space of pure transcendence that grounds normativity and functions as a space of freedom, and he rightly asks how and why we should think that unreason can play this role (p. 29). I share many of the concerns that Kadakal expresses here, and this is why I argue, in contrast to other readers of Foucault, that unreason should not be understood as a space of freedom that is radically outside our historical a priori.[6] In my view, this is neither the best way to read Foucault's *History of Madness* and nor is it the most promising Foucaultian conceptualization of critique. My claim, by contrast, is that unreason should be understood as a *figure* of the outside that fractures and opens up lines of fragility *within* our present and it is these lines of fragility and fracture — not the outside or exteriority of unreason — that represent the site of immanent transcendence or transcendence from within. Only in this way can unreason in Foucault serve as a model — and its value is precisely as model or exemplar, not as an articulation of *the* standpoint for critique, not least because there is no single standpoint for critique — for a kind of critical standpoint that is predicated on a form of internal exteriority that mirrors what I call the participant-observer perspective of Foucault qua archeologist.[7]

Finally, I turn to Kadakal's challenges to my distinction between the metanormative and first-order normative levels of analysis. Here, he raises two questions. First, what forms of concrete praxis are we to adopt in order to accomplish the metanormative openness to other normative horizons that I advocate? Should we here "revert back to paradigms of the rationality of linguistic communication and mutual recognition?" (p. 31). And, we might add, if that is the case, wouldn't this be surprising, and perhaps even undermining of my argument? It is true that I leave this question more or less open in the book, mainly because my primary concern is to make the metanormative point about how relying on a certain conception of progress to ground one's normative principles implicitly positions one in a position of developmental superiority and thereby undermines the goal of treating others as equals or moral contemporaries in intercultural dialogues. Given this focus, I remain more or less neutral with respect to first-order normative theories in the book. As a result, surprising though it may be to say so, I could happily admit that a form of discourse ethics underwritten with a rich account of mutual recognition and expanded to include the importance of justification could be very salutary at the first-order normative level. Since my primary concern lies at the metanormative level, I don't see this admission as causing a problem for my argument — to the contrary, it might, for example, provide another way out of the Foucault–Habermas debate, through the suggestion that we could adopt Foucault's metanormative position while maintaining some version of a Habermasian normative position.[8]

Kadakal's second question with respect to this distinction is more difficult, as it poses a central challenge to my overall argument: is it really the case that metanormative contextualism can avoid collapsing into relativism? As Kadakal puts it:

> One can perhaps conceive of metanormative contextualism as another, perhaps a more indeterminate capitulation of the fundamental historicity of our normative categories and commitments [...]. Nevertheless, historicity is not the same as relativism, and one must draw a stronger distinction between the argument for relativity and the argument for the historicity of our normative commitments than context-dependency can afford. (p. 32)

In response, I should first clarify how I understand the relationship between metanormative contextualism and individual subjectivity. To say that normative principles are justified or grounded contextually is not to say that they are justified relative to the viewpoints or perspectives of individual subjects. Rather, it is to say that they are historically embedded in forms of rationality that themselves provide the conditions of possibility for the formation of individual subjects who are capable of thought and action. In other words, the relevant "context" here is not the individual subject but rather something like the historical a priori or, if you prefer, a form of life. For this reason, I would disagree with Kadakal's claim that my contextualism "leaves our normative commitments in the precarious position of being a function of subjectivity" (p. 32). If one construes relativism as a form of subjectivism, then this is enough to show that contextualism need not collapse into relativism.[9]

Of course, this still leaves open the possibility that metanormative contextualism is nothing more than a form of conventionalism or radical historicism in which norms are ultimately relative to historical forms of life or rationality. But here I would agree with Kadakal that avowing the historicity of our normative concepts and principles — and perhaps even doing so in the case of our concept of progress — is not the same as endorsing first-order normative relativism. Hence nothing about my argument implies that we should refrain from making normative judgments about the practices of other cultures in the name of some relativist conception of tolerance. Nor does it imply that when we engage in intercultural dialogue where normative issues are at stake that we are required to undermine all of our normative assertions by relativizing them, that is, by saying "we believe in democracy, but that's just what we think" or "we think that female genital cutting is wrong, but that's just our opinion." Rather, in my view, questions of context and of historicity arise at the level of our metanormative justification of the first-order normative principles that guide our particular normative judgments. Given the way that I have developed this idea, in part by relying on work in epistemology on contextualism, I prefer to call this a metanormative contextualism. But if one insists on calling this a form of metaethical relativism, so be it. The crucial point as far as I can see is that this metanormative position neither implies nor entails any commitment to first-order moral or political relativism and the disabling political and normative consequences that follow from such a position.

Turning now to George Steinmetz's paper, let me begin with the challenge he poses to what I called earlier my process of elimination argument for metanormative contextualism. Why, he asks, do I assume that constructivism, reconstructivism, and problematizing genealogy exhaust the available options for grounding normativity? What about alternatives such as moral realism or neo-Aristotelian virtue ethics? Wouldn't these strategies provide a better alternative to the problems I diagnose in neo-Kantian and neo-Hegelian views, without the difficulties — such as the concern about relativism — generated by contextualism? Steinmetz further suggests that such positions "cannot be faulted for being biased toward western worldviews, since the precise definition of virtues varies according to the theorist" (p. 45). I'm not so sure about this last point, as it

certainly seems possible for bias to seep into the articulation of putatively universal virtues or capabilities; and, indeed, this kind of worry has inspired postcolonial critiques of, for example, Martha Nussbaum's capabilities theory.[10] With
respect to moral realism, my response would be to point to the methodological
constraint that I take to central to the project of critical social theory, specifically the idea that critical theory draws its normative content from within the
existing social world. As I see it, this means that strong forms of moral realism
are off the table for critical theory, at least insofar as they draw normativity
from the "objective" world rather than from the "social" or "intersubjective"
world — although it remains to be seen whether something like an Adornian
critical naturalism would be a compelling alternative that would be distinct from
genealogical problematization and metanormative contextualism, as Karen Ng
argues. I shall return to this question later.

To be sure, I do not argue for this methodological constraint in my book;
rather, I take it as my starting point, and then ask what strategy for grounding
the normativity of critical theory is most promising in light of this methodological constraint. If I were pressed to defend this methodological constraint, I don't
think I would have very much original to say, other than to appeal to the
broadly post-Kantian philosophical intuitions that I take to motivate it: that all
of our knowledge of the world, ourselves, and each other is mediated by the
forms of rationality that condition the possibility of our thought; that those
forms of rationality are not timeless, universal, or innate but rather are constituted in socially and historically specific ways; and that this means that those
forms of rationality are necessarily entangled with relations of power and subject
to ideological distortion. I find all of these intuitions compelling, though I admit
that defending them would be a different matter altogether, and doing so would
also have required me to write a very different book.

Two of Steinmetz's other criticisms concern the decolonizing ambitions of the
project. Steinmetz rightly challenges me to clarify what precisely I mean by
decolonizing, and he notes that this term, popular though it has become, tends
to blur important distinctions between colonialism and imperialism, and
between both of these and racism, such that using it may obscure rather than
illuminate the complex interconnections between these forms of domination.[11]
As he puts it:

> we need to ask which aspects of a given body of thought are specifically colonial or impe-
> rial, which aspects are saturated with values linked to domination other than colonial/
> imperial ones (e.g. class or gender domination), which aspects are culturally specific but not
> systematically linked to ideologies of domination, and which aspects are culturally neutral or
> universal. (p. 45)

I will admit to the kind of conceptual imprecision that Steinmetz accuses me
of in my use of the term decolonization — it is not defined as clearly as it could
or should be in the book. I have tried to spell out earlier a bit more specifically
in what sense this book can be understood as "decolonizing" something, and it
is a rather narrow sense, having to do with the attempt to wean Frankfurt
School critical theory off of a problematically progressive narrative about

European modernity — a narrative that conforms to a neo-colonial or neo-imperial logic — as a strategy for grounding its normative principles. This is why I emphasized earlier that the subtitle of the book refers specifically to decolonizing the normative foundations of critical theory, rather than to critical theory writ large. Thus, while I completely agree that all of the questions Steinmetz poses in this section of his paper are important ones that would have to be addressed in depth in any critical theory of postcolonialism or any fully "decolonized" critical theory, I do want to stress that neither of these descriptions captures what I take myself to be doing in this book. For my purposes, it is sufficient, I think, to acknowledge that the pernicious story of Euro-American modernity as the result of a process of progressive historical development that underwrites a sense of Euro-American developmental superiority runs through and serves to justify the various forms of European colonialism (in Africa and Latin America), settler colonialism in the Americas and Australia, and even contemporary informal American imperialism. As I used the term, "decolonization" refers to critically interrogating this problematic narrative of progress, excavating the role that it has played in securing the normative foundations of critical theory, and attempting to develop an alternative strategy for grounding normativity that does not rely on such a narrative.

This leads me to Steinmetz's worries about what he calls my "partial compromise with the idea of progress" (p. 44). He asks whether, by appealing to the openness and reflexivity of the Enlightenment horizon, I might not open myself up to being decolonized, in some sense of that term? I take it that Steinmetz means that by endorsing in some way the some of the values of the Enlightenment — freedom, openness, inclusivity, reflexivity — and especially by endorsing them *as* Enlightenment values, I may appear to be implicitly appealing to the superiority of the Enlightenment and its values, and thus opening myself up to the very same kind of argument that I deploy against Habermas and Honneth.

By way of a response, allow me to spell out what I see as the two senses in which my book might be said to make a partial compromise with the idea of progress. The first is insofar as I retain a forward-looking conception of progress, as a moral-political goal that we might strive to achieve. I am aware that some postcolonial critics of progress may well be unsatisfied with my attempt to break apart the pernicious backward-looking conception of progress while retaining a forward-looking sense, as they may consider the term "progress" to be so tainted by its associations with colonialism and imperialism as to be irredeemable. However, I find Rainer Forst's transcendental argument regarding progress — namely, that one can only be against progress by being for it, that is, by implicitly assuming that it would be better if we got rid of a certain understanding of progress — to be compelling, although, unlike Forst, I think that this argument goes through only with respect to what I have called the forward-looking conception of progress.[12] In this connection, it is worth clarifying that what I have in mind in preserving a forward-looking conception of progress is not some idea of civilizational progress or historical progress on a grand scale by means of which we might in the future be able to judge some cultures or forms of life to be superior to others. Rather, what I have in mind is simply the thought that when we engage in critique or, for that matter, political activism, we do so in light of some conception of if not justice or the good society then at least the less bad, less oppressive, or less unjust. Although I perhaps do not spell out fully enough in the book what this might mean, I have attempted to work out a forward-looking conception of progress in more detail in a recent paper.[13] The key points to emphasize here are the following: first, forward-looking progress is defined relative to the context of a historical a priori or form of life — thus it refers to what I call in the book "progress in history" rather than historical progress, which refers to transhistorical judgment — and second, forward-looking progress in history is understood negativistically as (following Foucault) the minimization of relations of domination or (following Adorno) the avoidance of catastrophe rather than as the progressive attainment of some positive vision of justice or the good society.

The second sense in which I make a partial compromise with progress is the one explicitly raised by Steinmetz, for it is true that I invoke the openness and reflexivity of the normative inheritance of the Enlightenment as positive features of that inheritance on which we might build. However, I do not make any claim to the developmental superiority of this normative inheritance vis-à-vis the normative positions that undergird "traditional" or "non-modern" forms of life. Rather, my point is simply that if we are to draw normativity from within our existing social world, this means that we have to start from where we are, drawing on the normative resources in our form of life. For those of us socialized and educated into Euro-American contexts, this means drawing on the legacy of Enlightenment thought (though, to be clear, I am not suggested that we draw only or exclusively on that legacy, nor am I claiming or implying that no one else is entitled to draw on it). Moreover, as I see it, I am advocating a way of taking up this normative inheritance by transforming it radically from within, precisely by radicalizing and pushing to its limits the emphasis on openness and reflexivity, until this becomes a motivation not for defending the superiority of modernity but rather, to borrow a phrase from Rolando Vazquez, for humbling modernity.[14]

Both Steinmetz and Kadakal end their papers by raising questions about what kind of sociology of knowledge production might account for the (mis)use in critical social theory of the concept of progress that I diagnose in the book. As Steinmetz puts the question succinctly, what can be said about "how and why these critical theorists fell so routinely into this trap" (p. 45)? Moreover, he asks, aren't there important differences between those who explicitly and openly defend the backward-looking conception of progress that I criticize and those for whom it is merely implicit (p. 45)? Similarly, aren't there important differences between critical theorists who subscribe to a notion of progress and, for example, "members of the imperial foreign policy establishment" or "nostalgists bemoaning the loss of the British Empire" (p. 45)? My answer to the latter two questions are yes and yes, though I'm not sure that the differences between those who explicitly endorse a conception of progress and those who are implicitly committed to one are terribly consequential. With respect to the point about distinguishing between critical theorists who defend a conception of progress and members of the imperial foreign policy establishment, I agree that there is an important difference here that we need to keep in mind: critical theorists, unlike members of the foreign policy establishment, are attempting to diagnose actually existing relations of oppression, injustice, and exploitation in contemporary globalized, multicultural, postcolonial societies and to chart paths for emancipatory transformation – which is all the more reason, I think, to point out the ways in which such theorists are implicitly or explicitly committed to a conception of progress that remains entangled with and even serves to uphold, reinforce, and legitimate relations of neo-colonial and neo-imperial domination.

As for the first question, about how and why critical theorists have fallen into this trap, I am not sure that I am equipped to answer, and would prefer to defer to the sociologists for this task, since they are in a much better position to carry it out than I am. And, helpfully, Kadakal ends his paper by offering a potential answer to Steinmetz, which suggests that the emphasis on learning, recognition, and progress in contemporary Frankfurt school critical theory can be understood as a sedimentation of a historical present defined by "a period of relative social and political stability, underlined by the welfare state as its most prominent political form, hitherto an exceptional period in European history" (p. 33). Although this is not my area of expertise, I will go out on a limb and say that this diagnosis, if correct, is telling. After all, the historical present that has shaped the second, third, and fourth generations of the Frankfurt School looks like one of relative social and political stability only if we restrict our field of vision to Europe and the United States. For the rest of the world, the post-World War II period has been characterized by anti-colonial struggles, proxy wars, and even genocides that can be directly linked to the persistent legacies of European colonialism and the ongoing effects American imperialism. But this is just another way of reiterating what I take to be one of the main points of my book: namely, that critical theory needs to widen its angle of vision by considering how its own critical perspective is situated within the postcolonial present.

Like Kadakal, Karen Ng raises some worries about my metanormative contextualism and about whether the work of Adorno can be marshaled in support of it. Specifically, Ng poses two challenges to my reading of Adorno, which she finds overly Foucaultian.[15] The first challenge concerns what Ng calls Adorno's "normative conception of truth and irrationality," while the second turns on his "critical naturalism and materialism" (p. 53). Taken together, these two challenges raise questions about whether Adorno is actually compatible either with Foucault or with my metanormative contextualism. I take it that the latter point is the more significant challenge to my argument, since, as Ng acknowledges, my aim in the reconstructive part of the book is not to argue on textual or interpretive grounds for a Foucault–Adorno synthesis but rather to draw on insights found in their work to develop my own position. So I will concentrate my efforts on the question of Adorno's compatibility with my metanormative contextualism. However, since the interpretive and reconstructive claims are closely intertwined in my argument, I will of necessity touch on both kinds of issues in my reply.

Turning to her first challenge, Ng agrees that Adorno rejects the presumption of a context-transcendent point of view, but she points out that he also maintains a normative conception of truth and irrationality (p. 5). As Ng understands it, this means that "there is a right and a wrong way to think, and this correlates with our ability to make correct and incorrect judgments about ourselves and about the world" (p. 54). On Ng's reading, then, Adorno criticizes idealism, for example, because it "takes the wrong approach to thinking, operates on false assumptions, and generates false judgments about ourselves and the world" (p. 54). Moreover, Adorno's negative dialectics is, on this view, offered as "the right approach to thinking," an approach that generates or underwrites "true judgments about ourselves and the world" (p. 54). Ng further argues that this feature of Adorno's view first of all doesn't fit very well with Foucault, insofar as Foucault and Adorno seem to draw very different conclusions from their shared rejection of the idea of context-transcendence. For Adorno, as Ng puts it, "accepting this is compatible with a normative account of truth and first-order judgments about society's wrongness and irrationality" (p. 55). Second, Ng claims that Adorno's normative view of truth is in conflict with my claim that:

> the lack of a context-transcendent point of view entails that we cannot judge the correctness or incorrectness of particular contexts or make comparative judgments in which one context is judged to be superior or inferior to another. (p. 55)

In response, I would like first to push back just a bit on Ng's interpretive point regarding Adorno and the normative criterion of truth and irrationality. I agree with Ng that Adorno claims that idealism is wrong and that negative dialectics offers a right approach to thinking, however, as I read Adorno, these claims are thoroughly indexed to history and context. In other words, idealism is wrong for Adorno because it is complicit with bourgeois rationality and it obscures the contradictions in bourgeois capitalist societies. In other words, it is not wrong or false überhaupt, but wrong given its historical mediations. Similarly, negative dialectics offers the right approach to thinking in a very specific historical and social context: namely, the context of the triumph of bourgeois rationality, the predominance of identity thinking, and the failure of idealism. Negative dialectics brings out, reflects on, and pushes to extremes the contradictions of bourgeois capitalism; as such, it is not offered as *the* right approach to thinking but as the right approach to thinking *for us*. To be sure, substantiating this reading would require more time and space than I have here, and I think it is more important to focus on the conceptual issues about the compatibility of Adorno's work with my metanormative contextualism. Still, it seems to me that, understood in this way, Adorno's emphasis on the normative criterion of truth and irrationality is perfectly compatible with a Foucaultian perspective, even if Foucault would likely prefer to talk about the antagonisms generated by power relations (in the plural) rather than the contradictions generated by capitalism.

With respect to Ng's more conceptual points, I think that these can be addressed by clarifying how I understand the relationship between first-order normative and metanormative levels of analysis. First, as I understand metanormative contextualism, it does not rule out what Ng calls "first-order judgments about society's wrongness and irrationality" precisely insofar as they are first-order judgments. In other words, what metanormative contextualism rules out is the appeal to a context-transcendent perspective from which the different contexts or forms of life or historical a priori that provide the conditions of possibility for our first-order normative judgments can be ranked or adjudicated in some final, non-contextual way. If judgments about the wrongness or irrationality of society are first-order judgments, then nothing about my metanormative approach precludes them, at least not as far as I can see. This leads me to Ng's second point. She reads me as saying that:

> the lack of a context-transcendent point of view entails that we cannot judge the correctness or incorrectness of particular contexts or make comparative judgments in which one context is judged to be superior or inferior to another. (p. 55)

Again, to clarify, I think that my claim is that we cannot make *context-transcendent* judgments about the correctness or incorrectness of particular contexts; in other words, there is no context neutral point of view from which to make such judgments in an absolute or context-transcendent way. But this does not rule out making contextually grounded judgments about the correctness or incorrectness of particular contexts, whether our own or someone else's. Indeed, this is precisely what I have in mind when I discuss Luc Boltanski's account of orders of justification in chapter four of the book.[16] Boltanski's idea is that critique can either be internal, drawing on the resources internal to a specific order of justification in order to critique that order, or external, drawing on the resources of one order of justification to critique another. But the important point is that what Boltanski calls external critique — which seems close to what Ng has in mind when she talks about cross contextual comparative judgments — neither requires nor entails reference to an overarching context of justification that transcends all contexts and enables us to assemble them into a context-neutral hierarchy.

Ng's second challenge focuses on what she takes to be the basis for Adorno's normative conception of truth, which she calls his negativistic critical naturalism or materialism. Drawing insightfully on Adorno's complex dialectical account of the relationship between history and nature, Ng argues that, for example, "the truth-content of the judgment that enlightenment has led to a new kind of barbarism is indexed to nature [...], although in a highly mediated and qualified sense" (p. 55). Ng quite rightly points out that Adorno's analysis of natural history not only holds that much of what appears to us as natural is actually historical (a thought that is central to his notion of second nature) but also that what is historical has a basis in the natural (p. 56). Thus, Adorno, she insists, is critical of unreflective or undialectical forms of historicism on the grounds that they conceal the ways in which "all history is an outgrowth of and thoroughly conditioned by nature" (p. 56). If we are to speak of historical problematization in Adorno, then, we have to acknowledge that such an idea "makes necessary reference to nature as the basis of historical truth" (p. 56).

In response, I admit that this aspect of Adorno's thought is one that I do not discuss, and that this may be a function of my attempt to read him alongside Foucault, which no doubt leads me to emphasize certain aspects of his thought and de-emphasize others. So, Ng is undoubtedly correct that I place a lot of emphasis on how and what we take to be natural is actually historical (through a discussion of Adorno's concept of second nature), without the corresponding dialectical emphasis on how the historical is rooted in the natural. However, I'm not sure that I agree when Ng makes the further claim that the rootedness of the historical in the natural constitutes a fundamental difference between Foucault and Adorno; as she puts it, "whereas natural history is a source of normativity for Adorno and a sufficient ground for critique, Foucault would reject this approach to normative grounding entirely" (p. 57). Although this is certainly a common reading of Foucault, it is worth mentioning that Foucault sometimes talks about the body in ways that could, as Ng herself notes, fit in well with Adorno's conception of natural history (p. 57). Indeed, one could perhaps even fruitfully read Foucault's famous – and controversial – appeal to bodies and pleasures rather than sex-desire as the most appropriate "rallying point for the counterattack against the deployment of sexuality" in these Adornian terms.[17] Admittedly, defending such a reading of Foucault would have to be the subject of future work. I hope to explore these issues further in my current project on psychoanalysis and critical theory. Given my interests in drive theory as central to the import of psychoanalysis for critical theory, I will have to work on reconciling my Foucaultian commitments with the conception of nature presupposed therein, and Adorno's critical naturalism may provide an interesting way to do this. In any case, I'm grateful to Ng for pushing me to think further about this issue.[18]

Finally, I turn to Kevin Olson's paper, which, perhaps because it is – at least on its face – the most sympathetic to my project of these four papers is also the most difficult to respond to. Seeking to think along with my book and to expand on some of my ideas, Olson argues that the commitment to progress in contemporary Frankfurt School critical theory is something of a red herring, and in fact should be seen not as the central problem, but rather "as symptomatic of deeper problems in their recent work" (p. 63). Those deeper problems involve deep and difficult issues of methodology and normativity, which means that decolonizing the normative foundations of contemporary critical theory "requires a somewhat wider angle of view" (p. 64). This wider angle of vision would need to encompass not only the reliance on progress narratives but also the tendency toward a "thin proceduralism" and the search for the "one right answer" (p. 64) in contemporary critical theory; the former makes critical theory reductive while the latter makes it heavy-handed.

Hence, Olson suggests, what is needed is not only the kind of epistemic decolonization that I recommend in my book but also a methodological decolonization. In particular, Olson is concerned with critical theory's problematic tendency to retreat to meta-theory or to a dispute over clashing paradigms – differing visions of how to do critical theory – rather than getting down to the work of actually producing critical theories of actually existing societies. The result of this tendency is that a huge gulf has opened up between "critical theory" and the world that they aim to critique. Olson calls this the "philosophical displacement of critique" (p. 65). The focus on procedural solutions to normative problems has also led critical theorists to overlook the extent to which the normative resources that they attempt to pull out of everyday life are themselves "dysfunctional, problematic, and greatly in need of critique" (p. 66); this leads to what Olson calls a "procedural displacement of critique" (p. 66). As Olson sees it, mainstream Frankfurt School critical social theory is not only too procedural but also too paradigmatic (i.e., too caught up in debates about whose paradigm is right); these are separate problems but they often travel together.

Olson then turns this into a subtle but incisive critique of my book when he points out that my critique of contemporary critical theory targets only the procedural displacement of critique. Not only does it not address the philosophical displacement of critique, but also it seems actually to reinforce that displacement insofar as the argument of my book takes the form of a clash of paradigms (reconstructivism versus constructivism versus contextualism) (p. 66). Thus, as Olson puts what is actually a potentially devastating criticism rather mildly: "The danger [in Allen's approach] is to recapitulate the kind of paradigmatic abstraction that constitutes a philosophical displacement of critique" (p. 66). Thankfully, Olson also offers me a potential way out, by suggesting that one could read my project differently, by seeing it "as an immanent critique of the tendency towards a philosophical displacement of critique" (p. 66). On this reading, my defense of contextualism could be understood as "opening the door for an entire class of investigations that are innovative in normativity and methodology," a class of investigations that involve a "subtle blending of methodological reflection and substantive criticism" (p. 66) — even as it does not itself constitute such an investigation. Still, Olson suggests that one could take the upshot of my argument to be that critical theory needs to "better integrate its metatheoretical reflections with substantive criticism" and should strive to be "both substantive and self-reflective at the same time" (p. 66).

I'm grateful to Olson for offering me this potential response to his charge that my book participates in a problematic philosophical displacement of critique, and I would happily agree with him that critical theory should strive to be both substantive and metatheoretically self-reflective. I also agree with his claim that problematization can take many forms, not all of which are discursive or even historical, and that what constitutes the core of problematization is "an open-ended exploration of points of opacity, taken-for-grantedness, and difficulty within our own normative world" (p. 68), which may require analysis not only of discursive but also of material practices.

Where I hesitate just a bit is with the idea that critical theory should strive to be *simultaneously* substantive and self-reflective and with the corresponding suggestion that work that proceeds by way of a clash of paradigms — as Olson is surely right to say that my book largely does — is per se problematic. I agree absolutely that it would be problematic if this was all that critical theory, understood as a collective intellectual project or enterprise, ever did, that is, if it never got around to the business of engaging in substantive forms of critique. But

I don't think that this means that individual works of critical theory that focus on metatheoretical questions are problematic as a result of that focus. To be sure, this does not mean that we should be deluded into thinking that once we have settled various metatheoretical questions (if in fact they can ever be settled), we have done all that we need to do or have produced a complete critical theory of society. I'm not sure whether Olson would disagree, but perhaps I am more willing than he is to sign on to a kind of division of labor vision of critical theory, and more comfortable than he thinks I should be with acknowledging that the aims of my book are to offer a contribution to an ongoing, interdisciplinary critical-theoretical project rather than to construct a complete critical theory of society. To be sure, that contribution is largely meta-theoretical, but I hope that the way that it addresses the meta-theoretical issues that it treats will provide support for new and different kinds of interdisciplinary and critical alliances.

In closing, let me once again thank these authors for their rich, thought-provoking, and generative readings of my book. I'm delighted to have had the opportunity to think with them about these important and complex issues surrounding progress, normativity, and the possibilities and prospects for "decolonizing" critical theory.

NOTES

1. See, for example, Honneth (2009, chapters 1 and 2) and Allen (2016, pp. 108–119).

2. Habermas himself acknowledges this rather clearly in his "A Genealogical Analysis of the Cognitive Content of Morality" (1998). This point — and the corresponding ethnocentrism to which it seems to give rise — was also acknowledged by one of Habermas's most able and knowledgeable defenders, Thomas McCarthy in his "Reason and Rationalization: Habermas's 'Overcoming' of Hermeneutics" (1991). I discuss this issue further in Allen (2016, pp. 50–61).

3. Though of course one can debate to what extent that notion of progress remains Eurocentric; on this point, see Anderson (2010).

4. For the idea that critique consists of opening up lines of fragility and fracture in the present, see Foucault, "Critical Theory/Intellectual History" (1994, pp. 126–127) and Allen (2016, pp. 183–186). For Foucault's claim that the goal of his work is making the invisible visible, see Arnold Davidson, "Structures and Strategies of Discourse: Remarks Towards a History of Foucault's Philosophy of Language" (1997, p. 2). For the idea that archaeology consists in excavating the subsoil beneath our feet, see Foucault, "The Order of Things" (1998, p. 263). I discuss these three ways of conceptualizing Foucaultian critique in further detail in Allen, "'Psychoanalysis and Ethnology' Revisited: Foucault's Historicization of History" (2017).

5. Adorno (1977, p. 127).

6. See *The End of Progress* (pp. 180–182).

7. Here, I would like to gratefully acknowledge George Steinmetz's articulation of the connections between this reading of Foucault and the work of Pierre Bourdieu. I take Steinmetz's point that Bourdieu is an important and overlooked interlocutor in my work, not only in light of his deep connections with Foucaultian method and analysis of power, but also and perhaps especially in light of his call to decolonize sociology and his critique of imperialist reason. See Steinmetz, p. 47, footnote 8. I hope to explore these connections in future work.

8. Kevin Olson raises a similar point when he asks what, if anything, can be salvaged from the contemporary Frankfurt School if we accept the argument of my book

(pp. 70–71). Presumably I think that there are some important resources there, or else why would I devote so much time to reading the work of these theorists so thoroughly? Olson suggests the possibility of borrowing certain critical and normative concepts from Habermas, Honneth, and Forst without endorsing their metatheoretical strategies for grounding those concepts. For example, Habermas's notions of the public sphere, of system and lifeworld, and of legitimation crisis could all be repurposed within the critical-theoretical framework that I develop. As my reply to Kadakal indicates, I agree with Olson on this point, and I find his suggestion of retooling the infamous idea of the performative contradiction to "function in a problematizing manner" (p. 71) to be fantastic, and very Adornian. Understood in this way, one could argue that a performative contradiction points to a problem not *with the speaker* but rather *in the world*. On this view, we should view performative contradictions as starting points for critique rather than as argumentative conversation-stopping weapons.

9. I say "need not" here because of course one could be both a contextualist about meta-normative justification and a relativist about first order normative principles. Although such a position is conceptually possible, it is not the one that I defend.

10. See, for example, Charusheela (2009).

11. To complicate things even further, we should add settler colonialism to the mix here, which would challenge Steinmetz's contention that the United States is only informally imperial, "with a minimal present-day engagement in territorial colonialism" (p. 45).

12. See Rainer Forst (2012) and Allen, *The End of Progress* (pp. 125–128, 161–162).

13. Amy Allen (2015).

14. See Rolando Vazquez (n.d.), "Relational Temporalities: From Modernity to the Decolonial," unpublished manuscript. One might see a similar impulse in Habermas's own recent work on post-secular reason, though, in my view, he does not take this far enough. See *The End of Progress* (pp. 67–77).

15. In this connection, it is worth noting that Ng echoes a point made by Kadakal, who claims that Adorno's conception of nonidentity is distinct from and, as a resource for conceptualizing critique, preferable to Foucault's notion of unreason (p. 29). I did not pursue this point above because I take issue with Kadakal's reconstruction of my discussion of unreason in Foucault.

16. See Luc Boltanski and Laurent Thévenot (2006) and *The End of Progress* (pp. 157–158).

17. See Foucault (1978, p. 157).

18. Pursuing Ng's criticism further might also help me to revisit and complicate my reply to Steinmetz's question about why I don't consider some version of realism or naturalism to be a viable alternative strategy for grounding normativity. However, I would still want to ask whether Adorno's critical naturalism could be articulated in post-metaphysical terms and, if so, whether it would constitute an *alternative* to metanormative contextualism or, rather, a complement to and further elaboration of it.

REFERENCES

Adorno, Th. W. (1977). The actuality of philosophy. *Telos*, 31, 120–133.

Adorno, Th. W. (2005). Progress. In H. W. Pickford (Ed.), *Critical models: Interventions and catchwords* (pp. 143–160). New York, NY: Columbia University Press.

Allen, A. (2015). Emancipation without Utopia: Subjection, modernity, and the normative claims of feminist critical theory. *Hypatia*, *30*(3) (Summer), 513–529.

Allen, A. (2016). *The end of progress: Decolonizing the normative foundations of critical theory*. New York, NY: Columbia University Press.

Allen, A. (2017). 'Psychoanalysis and ethnology' revisited: Foucault's historicization of history. *The Southern Journal of Philosophy*, *55*(S1), 31–46.

Anderson, K. (2010). *Marx at the margins: On nationalism, ethnicity, and non-western societies*. Chicago, IL: University of Chicago Press.

Boltanski, L., & Thévenot, L. (2006). C. Porter (Ed.). *On justification: Economies of worth*. Princeton, NJ: Princeton University Press.

Charusheela, S. (2009). Social analysis and the capabilities approach: A limit to Martha Nussbaum's universalist ethics. *Cambridge Journal of Economics, 33*(6), 1135–1152.

Davidson, A. (1997). Structures and strategies of discourse: Remarks towards a history of Foucault's philosophy of language. In A. Davidson (Ed.), *Foucault and his interlocutors* (pp. 1–22). Chicago, IL: University of Chicago Press.

Forst, R. (2012). Zum Begriff des Fortschritts. In H. Joas (Ed.), *Vielfalt der Moderne – Ansichten der Moderne*. Frankfurt: Fischer.

Foucault, M. (1978). *History of sexuality, volume 1: An introduction* (p. 157) R. Hurley (Trans.). New York, NY: Vintage.

Foucault, M. (1994). Critical theory/intellectual history. In M. Kelly (Ed.), *Critique and power: Recasting the Foucault/Habermas debate* (pp. 109–138). Cambridge, MA: MIT Press.

Foucault, M. (1998). The order of things. In J. Faubion (Ed.), *Essential works of Michel Foucault, volume 2: Aesthetics, method, and epistemology* (pp. 261–268). New York, NY: The New Press.

Habermas, J. (1998). A genealogical analysis of the cognitive content of morality. In C. Cronin & P. de Greiff (Eds.), *The inclusion of the other: Studies in political theory* (pp. 3–46). Cambridge, MA: MIT Press.

Honneth, A. (2009). *Pathologies of reason: On the legacy of critical theory* J. Ingram (Trans.). New York, NY: Columbia University Press.

McCarthy, Th. (1991). Reason and rationalization: Habermas's 'overcoming' of hermeneutics. In *Ideals and illusions: On reconstruction and deconstruction in contemporary critical theory* (pp. 127–151). Cambridge, MA: MIT Press.

Vazquez, R. (n.d.). *Relational temporalities: From modernity to the decolonial*. Unpublished manuscript.

PART II
ASSESSING THE CHALLENGE: PROGRESS, POLITICS, AND IDEOLOGY

NIETZSCHE AFTER CHARLOTTESVILLE [☆]

Robert J. Antonio

ABSTRACT

Nietzsche's texts contain diverse and sometimes contradictory themes that defy singular summations and are open to divergent interpretations. He also often deployed puzzling and contradictory statements to provoke readers' thoughts. Although not claiming to illuminate the one true Nietzsche, I contend that his sociocultural and social psychological arguments about German antisemitism and nationalism not only contradict alt right views but also theorize conditions that give rise to this distinctive type of demagoguery. Conflictive appropriations of Nietzsche have been part of the battle over capitalist crises and reactionary populist revivals for over a century, and unregulated growth and massive expansion of the global economy relative to the biosphere greatly increased material throughput and production of waste and generated a host of severe global environmental problems, including especially climate change. In this situation, the alt right contends that cosmopolitan people are deracinated, emptied of their cultural particularity, and spiritually lost. Progressives contend that cosmopolitans potentially benefit from more diverse people and perspectives, enhanced ability to empathetically play the role of the other, and consequent wider communicative capacities and refined powers of cooperation. Nietzsche too exhorted humans to "remain true to the earth" and its "garden joy," and implied a naturalist esthetics and pacification of nature, and he should be rescued from alt right by reaching beyond his legacy to envision and forge new political-economic alternatives and collective actions capable of sustaining life on the planet and

[☆] Thanks to Gary Shapiro for reading this essay and providing helpful constructive criticism.

The Challenge of Progress: Theory Between Critique and Ideology
Current Perspectives in Social Theory, Volume 36, 95–110
Copyright © 2020 Emerald Publishing Limited
All rights of reproduction in any form reserved
ISSN: 0278-1204/doi:10.1108/S0278-120420190000036014

creating and perpetuating a more just democracy that favors cosmopolitan human flourishing.

Keywords: Friedrich Nietzsche; Anthropocene; alt right; political economy; globalization; climate change

I am a *Doppelgänger*, I have a "second" face in addition to the first, *And* perhaps also a third.
                                                                    — Friedrich Nietzsche (1989)[1]

[...] Nietzsche was a precursor to the German present, and at the same time its sharpest negation — "National Socialist" and "Cultural Bolshevik" — either, depending on how he was used.
                                                                    — Karl Löwith (1986)[2]

Thirty years ago, Alan Bloom declared that the Nietzschean right had disappeared in the US and that "every Nietzschean" was a "leftist." However, Nietzsche has been on the return in ascendant American white nationalist, "alt right" circles. They have drawn inspiration and ideas from the European "new right," which originated in the late 1960s and exerted wider influence in recent years via proliferation of right-wing blogs, social media, and other online connections (Bloom, 1987, pp. 222–223; Galupo, 2017; Illing, 2017).[3] Globalization's sharply increased economic inequality within nations, much-accelerated movement of commodities, capital, ideas, images, and especially people across national borders, and consequent sociocultural clashes have spurred many new versions of racial nationalism. The intensifying legitimacy crisis of the neoliberal policy regime or "Washington Consensus" and absence of a genuine democratic alternative have contributed to Brexit, the Trump presidency, Charlottesville white supremacist protest, and other forms of neopopulism as well as to new far-right appropriations of Nietzsche. His name and words are invoked in racial nationalist screeds aimed at fomenting revolution from the right. Founder of AltRight.com and major figure at the Charlottesville Unite the Right debacle, Richard Spencer said his political transformation came after being "redpilled" by Nietzsche's *Genealogy of Morals* (Spencer, 2018; Wood, 2017). The alt right meme "redpilling" refers to shattering "politically correct" illusions about liberal democracy, illuminating realities envisioned by white nationalists, and learning to "live dangerously" as Nietzsche urged.[4] Popular on the alt right, this Nietzschean mantra, Löwith held, led in Nazi Germany "in a-round-about and yet direct way from Nietzsche to Goebbels' heroic clichés about self-sacrifice" (Löwith, 1986, p. 6).

In a now-classic study of modern European social theory 1890–1930, H. Stuart Hughes held that many thinkers who contributed substantially to this era's major transformations of social and political thought credited Nietzschean inspiration. Yet he explained that few of them addressed Nietzsche's work in depth (Hughes, 1977, pp. 34–35, 40, 51, 105–106, 171–172, 339–340). In *American Nietzsche*, Jennifer Ratner-Rosenhagen begins her analysis of intense engagements of Nietzsche by diverse writers, intellectuals, and activists with philosopher Wilber Urban's portrayal of his epiphanic all-night reading of the *Genealogy* — "the greatest single spiritual adventure" of his young life, which overturned his established beliefs, transformed his ideas "about himself and his world," and set him on a new path. Urban was "redpilled" by the same text that turned Richard Spencer's identity and world upside down. Ratner-Rosenhagen explains that many early twentieth-century American literary radicals described "reading Nietzsche as a profoundly life altering experience" — they could *"feel* his ideas" and were "enveloped" by them. She holds that the tone and style of Nietzsche's writing resonates with would-be intellectual and sociopolitical radicals. Nietzsche affirmed his "readers' feelings of radical otherness" and channeled them into revelations of "authentic selves" and reconstructed visions of the world she says. His writings' emotive transformative tone and their ambiguities, conflictive themes, and fragmentary style open them to very diverse thinkers (Ratner-Rosenhagen, 2012, pp. 29–30, 154–155, 205).

What kind of world did Richard Spencer discover via his redpilling?[5] White nationalist critiques of global capitalism, neoliberalism, corporate power, and possessive individualism converge, in part, with progressive views. However, this anticapitalism is meshed with virulent antiliberal attacks on representative democracy for deracinating, individualizing, fragmenting, detraditionalizing, and depoliticizing Western culture and on egalitarianism, feminism, multiculturalism, and multiracialism for undermining solidarity, leveling quality, and producing identical, mediocre, instrumental people. The new right and alt right contend that globalization and mass immigration universalize these declinist tendencies and undercut the distinctive cultural identities and national unity needed to forge a political will capable of defending their cultures and nations. They contend that human rights discourses liquidate cultural particularity, justify imperialism, and threaten "ethnocide." Their plans for alternative forms of governance are vague, but their vision of "participatory democracy" implies a unified political will and leaders that manifest it and act independently on behalf of the nation. White nationalists call for defense of Western culture anchored in European white identity. They advocate "the right to difference" inhering in the "biocultural" distinctiveness of each divergent nation. In their view, national, regional, or community "ethnocultural" homogeneity is necessary to preserve individual identity, cultural particularity, and global diversity or the *"pluriversum."*[6] They embrace a Schmittean "friend-enemy" distinction advocating strengthening collective identity by establishing clear public enemies — American white nationalists target Muslims, African Americans, Jews, non-European immigrants, and white-liberal and leftist racial traitors.[7] They support traditional roles for women, masculinist values, and willingness to use force. Sociopolitical and ideological iterations of these general views on the alt right depend on the group and location, but they all stress limitations on rights. outright exclusion, deportation, or elimination of the "others" (Antonio, 2000; de Benoist, 1996; de Benoist, 1998; de Benoist, 2002; O'Meara, 2004; Sunic, 2011).

The alt right sees racially mixed, culturally dispossessed Western democracies to be wastelands teetering on the edge of an abyss. Consequently, they resonate with Nietzsche's view that Western modernity is "mediocre," "insipid," "nihilist," "decadent," and near collapse. Nietzsche spoke scathingly about Europe's "sick," "reactive," "maggot" people bent out of shape by guilt's "gnawing worm" or "bad conscience" (Nietzsche, 1989, pp. 43, 75, 81, 158–159). "Everything of today," he asserted, "it is falling, it is decaying: who would support it? But I — want to push it too!" (Nietzsche, 1969, p. 226). Nietzsche said one day he would be linked to the greatest cultural crisis ever, opposed to "everything that had been believed, demanded, hallowed so far." Hoping his views would generate radical "revaluation" of Western modernity's decadent values, he declared "I am no man, I am dynamite" (Nietzsche, 1989, p. 326). His ringing plea for "preparatory human beings" to "wage wars" for new values favoring an animate "culture complex" or "order of rank" that cultivates again "higher," "noble," "aggressive," uninhibited "beasts or prey" human beings, who once flourished in the pre-Socratic West and still ruled until classical Greece and pre-Christian Rome collapsed. Nietzsche declared that people who "live dangerously" reap the most from existence. He implored:

> Build your cities on the slopes of Vesuvius! Send your ships into uncharted seas! Live at war with your peers and yourselves! Be robbers and conquerors if you cannot be rulers and possessors, you seekers of knowledge! Soon the age will be past when you could be content to live hidden in forests like shy deer.[8]

Alt right leaders, such as Richard Spencer, crave provocation and conflicts with liberals, the left, and public authorities and proudly treat their occasional bruises as costs of living dangerously in the cause of the radical "transvaluation" and a new world to come Nietzsche beckons them to.

Certain facets of Nietzsche's writing, especially when teased with strategic interpretive twists, converge with extreme right-wing populist themes. For example, his unrelenting critique of economic and political liberalism provides resources for far-right critiques of capitalism and liberal democracy. Nietzsche savaged egalitarian ideals and social movements and praised aristocratic values and hierarchy, masculinist strength, readiness to act with force, and warrior leaders such as Napoleon. Nietzsche excoriated Christian "slave morality" for celebrating the weak, pity, and piety and turning people inward and undercutting their instinctual drives and especially their "will to power." He berated the Judaic roots of Christianity and the "three Jews" — Jesus, Paul, and Peter — and "Jewess" — Mary for their ultimate responsibility for putting an end to the uninhibited, vital classical Greek and Roman ways (Nietzsche, 1989, pp. 52–53). Far-right "Nietzscheans" claim that such statements reveal Nietzsche's antisemitism, even though he emphatically rejected it.[9] Nietzsche's misogynist comments about women also have been debated intensely (Burgard, 1994; Patton, 1993; Schutte, 1986). These and other ambiguities are rife in his texts.[10] Alt right "Niezscheans" stress selectively those themes that justify their views of Nietzsche as a forerunner to their white Euronationalist positions.[11]

"There are, notoriously, many Nietzsches" says noted Nietzsche scholar Gary Shapiro (2016, p. x). Similar to Wilber Urban, Michel Foucault reported a youthful Nietzschean epiphany that helped inspire his heterodox philosophical path. Rather than the letter of the texts, Foucault declared that he took up the "challenge of Nietzsche." Describing his "fundamental Nietzscheanism," he said that he employed Nietzsche's ideas "to see" and that even his "anti-Nietzschean theses" were "nevertheless Nietzschean."[12] Addressing an interviewer's query about new right Nietzscheans, he asserted that there is more than "just *one* Nietzscheanism" and we cannot say "one is truer than the other" (Foucault, 1989, p. 247). Nietzsche's texts contain diverse and sometimes contradictory themes that defy neat singular summations and are open to divergent interpretations. He also often deployed puzzling language and contradictory sounding statements to provoke readers' thoughts. However, contrary interpretations of his arguments can often be sorted according to their veracity. Although not claiming to illuminate the one true Nietzsche, I contend that his sociocultural and social psychological arguments about German antisemitism and nationalism not only contradict alt right views but also theorize conditions that give rise to this distinctive type of demagoguery.

NIETZSCHE'S DECLINIST THEORY OF WESTERN CULTURE

My philosophy aims at an ordering of rank; not an individualistic philosophy.
— Nietzsche (1883–1888) (1968a, p. 162)[13]

Nietzsche's central interest was the "cultural complex," related "forms of domination," and types of social life that arise from them. He argued that all cultures impose an "order of rank" or hierarchy of purposes, values, ideas, and sensibilities that organize impulses and actions and provide direction and meaning to our deeds and a distinct shape to our characters and worlds. In his view, conventional moralities manifest a "herd instinct" that motivates individuals to seek security and submit and obey their cultural group's order of rank and the leaderships that create and enforce it. He saw culture to constrain the "will to power" — the "spontaneous, aggressive, expansive, form-giving" drive to create "new interpretations and directions," which he believed to be the "essence of life." Nietzsche argued that culture can channel the herd's imagination and impulses in exceptionally narrow life-denying ways. Healthy, independent people (nature's "lucky hits") and leaders of the herd, he held, abide by different orders of rank that permit much more expression of their will to power. Although contending that cultures vary in how sharply they limit this vital force, Nietzsche claimed that "all culture" transforms "beast of prey 'man' to a tame and civilized animal" who consequently suffers *ressentiment* or envy, frustration, and hatred repressed and manifested as "imaginary revenge" against "what is different" (Nietzsche, 1968a, pp. 162, 255; Nietzsche, 1989, pp. 36–37, 42–43, 78–79, 120–121; Nietzsche, 1974, pp. 36–37, 174–175). He argued that religious and philosophical elites of "ascetic priests" forge ideals that command and provide heavenly justification or other moral compensation for obedience and ascetic ways. This "slave morality," he held, has to be "burned" into memory by harsh punishment and guilty torment. In Nietzsche's view, ascetic ideals manifest a "creditor–debtor" model that originated from ancient religions in which "sacrifices" aimed to repay ancestors and ward off unfortunate future events (Nietzsche, 1989, pp. 60–67).

Nietzsche framed his cultural theory to illuminate the distinctive moralism of modern Western culture, which he contended originated with Socratic philosophy. Equating rationality with virtue and crowning conscience king, he opined, Socrates created cultural means that ended a "state of emergency" or cultural dissolution of "old Athens," which had unleashed anarchic instincts of the mob. Nietzsche argued that Socrates fashioned a new order of rank that induced obedient self-surveillance and suppression of spontaneous impulses, which ended the social crisis, but broke with vibrant pre-Socratic Athenian culture and initiated the West's downward cultural spiral. The turning inward, Nietzsche held, diminished the body and originated Western modernity's dualistic splits (e.g., subject and object, mind and body, real world and apparent world), which "say No" to reality. He portrayed Socrates as a profoundly creative ascetic priest – a "physician" or "savior" who provided purpose and direction that ultimately restored order, but at the cost of denaturalizing and weakening humanity. Socrates's last words – "Oh Crito, *life is a disease*" – typified his antinaturalist rupture and "No" to noble "living dangerously."[14] Nietzsche contended that ancient Judaic priestly culture began the Western "slave revolt in morality," which "invented sin," elevated the "poor" above the "noble," and, most importantly, bred Jesus and the Christian movement.[15] Nietzsche argued that the Christian God, who sacrificed his son for humanity's sins in a frightful, gruesome crucifixion generated "the maximum feeling of guilty indebtedness." The "creditor sacrifices himself for his debtor out of *love*" said Nietzsche. Although demanding "taking pity on the poor and helpless," "turning the other cheek" and "loving your enemies," the Christian God, Nietzsche held, is a brutal "judge" and "hangman" who condemns people to eternal misery in hell for simple disbelief or sexual pleasure.[16] He saw Christian leaders as ascetic priests extraordinaire – they demand exceptional suppression of bodily drives and generate unparalleled guilt and *ressentiment*. The suffering herd is compelled to "attribute blame" and "vent their affects" to deaden their pain, Nietzsche argued, but ascetic priests ingeniously redirect *ressentiment* entirely into self-blame. In his view, Christian ascetic priests provide meaning for human suffering, unify the herd against sinners, and control its impulses at the cost of making the herd sicker and steepening Western culture's downward arc.[17]

Nietzsche held that Christian culture "spiritualizes" and "internalizes" *ressentiment*, yet he feared that sublimated or imaginary cruelty could explode into outright violence as it did in earlier "epidemic outbreaks" of European "witch-hunt hysteria." He warned that moralistically driven and justified "orgies of feeling" violently expressed are "inscribed" unforgettably across human history and threatened again in his time.[18] Nietzsche held that epic *ressentiment* generates among some of the herd dissemblings, moralizing "souls that *squint*"– "provisionally self-deprecating, humble" yet dangerous "cellar rodents" brimming with feelings of rancor, hatred, and vengeance toward the other. "They walk among us as embodied reproaches, as warnings to us" Nietzsche declared, "how ready they themselves are at bottom to *make* one pay; how they crave to be *hangmen*."

All excused and even celebrated as "the good" doing "justice" he said.[19] Nietzsche held that the "edifice" of the Catholic Church rested on "*southern* freedom and enlightenment" and "southern suspicion" about human nature (e.g., manifested in repeated ritual forgiveness of sin and guarantees of salvation) that were swept away by the morally austere Protestant Reformation, which made everyone his or her "own priest," eliminated sacramental guarantees of redemption, and greatly intensified self-surveillance and *ressentiment* (Nietzsche, 1974, pp. 292–293, 310–313). Nietzsche also argued that extreme Protestant moralism was secularized into modern Western ideologies and social movements, which can unleash fanaticism and violence as in French Revolution (Nietzsche, 1989, pp. 52–54, 139–142).

Nietzsche stressed forcefully in the *Genealogy* and other parts of his work that Western modernity was near sociocultural collapse. He ranted about the "the repulsive, ill-smelling, mendacious, pseudo-alcoholic air everywhere" and "*comedians* of the Christian moral ideal."[20] His famous pronouncement that "God is dead" signified the collapse of faith among European churchgoers. He contended that the last stand of authentic Christian asceticism (its "latest and noblest form") ironically is specialized science's "faith in truth."[21] Nietzsche valued science's practical achievements and reclamation of nature, but attacked forcefully its "overestimation" as a substitute for religion (*a la* Comte and Spencer whom he berated emphatically). He stressed limits later eloquently expressed by Max Weber – i.e., that science cannot justify what is "worth knowing," determine "how we should live," or solve the crisis of Western "nihilism" or loss of purpose. Nietzsche thought "industrial culture" and the capitalist marketplace and workplace are prime manifestations and drivers of profound cultural hollowing out.[22] In numerous passages, he portrayed bourgeois humanity's "weakened personality" – "actors" who "confound themselves with their roles" and too readily change poses or "masks" to please others. He warned about the dangers of a combustible mix of easily preyed upon sycophantic tendencies and "historically cultivated egoism". Savaging American bourgeois culture, he decried its undue haste and continuous toil ("a string to throttle all culture and good taste") and reduction of life to a "constant chase after gain [...] in continual pretense and overreaching and anticipating others" (Nietzsche, 1974, pp. 258–260, 283–285, 302–304; Nietzsche, 1986b, pp. 83–87, 114–115).

NIETZSCHE CONTRA NATIONALISM AND ANTISEMITISM

All honor to the ascetic ideal *insofar as it is honest*! so long as it believes in itself and does not play tricks on us! Nietzsche (1887).

– Nietzsche (1989, p. 158)[23]

In paragraphs that follow the quote above, Nietzsche proclaimed the toxic combination of German antisemitism and nationalism to be the prototypical expression of such tricks and the prime manifestation of cultural exhaustion. The "cheapest of all agitator's tricks," antisemitism, Nietzsche held, manifests:

> a too exclusive diet of newspapers, politics, beer, and Wagnerian opera together with the pre-suppositions of such a diet: first national constriction and vanity, the strong but narrow principle of "Deutschland, Deutschland über alles", *and paralysis agitans* of "modern ideas."[24]

This self-declared "last *anti-political* German" warned that emergent mass politics and mass media employed "demagogic" appeals that fueled a rising tide of fanaticism. Nietzsche's self-proclaimed "immoralism" problematized moralistic reflexes or unreflective judgments based on an emotional reaction to provocative cues, especially political ones designed to inflame and manipulate *ressentiment*.[25] Nietzsche contended that genuine thinking is "slow," "patient" "mistrustful," and "resistant" − it requires reflexive "self-control" that resists impulsive moral snap judgments. His vision of a "noble culture" of intelligent, critical, independent thinkers comes in his section on "What Germans Lack" and is preceded by pungent criticism of nationalism in the Bismarckian Reich or "Europe's *flatland*." He argued that "culture and the state" are contradictory entities and that "great cultural eras" are times of "political decline" or are simply "anti-political." Nietzsche asserted earlier that wartime discipline, bravery, and obedience "have nothing to do with culture" and that nationalist fervor stirs up "systematic and oppressive philistinism." Victorious Germany was, in his view, a "un-culture" while defeated France's experienced cultural flourishing. He disparaged the "*court* historiography" of the "reichdeutsch" nationalist, anti-Semite historian and politician Heinrich von Treitschke.[26] Nietzsche said that German "nationalism and race hatred" − "national scabies of the heart and blood poisoning" − pit European nations against one another. Presciently, he warned of the mounting danger of leading "Jews to the sacrificial slaughter as scapegoats for every public or private misfortune." By contrast, Nietzsche identified with forward looking "good Europeans" who are "too manifold and mixed racially" to engage "in mendacious racial self-affirmation and racial indecency" and who aspire to an "amalgamation of nations."[27]

Nietzsche argued that socialists might create an "absolute state" that greatly exceeds the despotic powers of ancient states, but he held that this threat manifested broader dangers of later modernity's much increased "accumulations of state power" per se. He contended that nationalist and revolutionary regimes, serving impersonal moral ends, are capable of brutal regimentation and human sacrifice for "fatherland" and "national honor." Nietzsche said that the militarized state demands blind obedience, makes human life cheap, and fosters barbarism − "that profound impersonal hatred, that murderous cold-bloodedness with a good conscience, that common fire in the destruction of the enemy, that proud indifference to great losses [...]" Holding that the "modern military machine" is a "living anachronism," he dreamed of a "great day" when people would demolish the war machine.[28] However, he warned presciently that "the greatest and most terrible wars" and "temporary relapse into barbarism" lie ahead for Europe. He also speculated that Europe might forge "one will" in reaction to the Russian "menace," create a new ruling "caste" with a "long, terrible will," and compel a "fight for dominion of the Earth."[29] Nietzsche argued at many junctures that late modernity had weaker personalities, more volatile politics, and more severe regimentation. In the cultural ruins, the demagogic "great man of the masses," Nietzsche held, woos the mass by projecting their own qualities and promising to avenge their enemies. "He is violent, envious, exploitative, scheming, fawning, cringing, arrogant, all according to circumstances [...]." and thus a skilled "actor" or "shadow" adept at donning the right mask Nietzsche asserted. In this puppet play, he implies, it is unclear who pulls the strings.[30]

Although scathingly critical of the ascetic ideal, Nietzsche was highly ambivalent about ascetic priests such as Socrates. He acknowledged that their "mastery" or "art" of redirecting *ressentiment* inward and defending the herd against the healthy takes great skill, intelligence, and self-discipline. Nietzsche argued that all serious tasks require disciplining the will to power. Thus, he contended that the ascetic priest "must also be strong master of himself even more than of others" (Nietzsche, 1989, p. 126). By contrast, he warned that "the most dangerous physicians are those who as born actors, employ a perfect art of deception to imitate the born physician" or genuine ascetic priest. These "comedians" of the ascetic ideal do damage to it.[31] The great man of the masses or modern demagogue, Nietzsche held, lacks the ascetic priest's capacity for self-discipline and thus does not constrain herd *ressentiment* or direct it inward. Recall his point that the herd seeks a guilty agent real or imagined. Nietzsche saw German nationalism and antisemitism to be intertwined and Jews to serve as scapegoat and collective enemy. As in past waves of witch-hunt hysteria, demagogues of modern mass politics unify the herd by directing *ressentiment* outward toward internal and external enemies. Nietzsche anticipated Schmittean and alt right arguments that identification of clear collective enemies are moments of collective self-discovery and "high points of politics." Rather than embracing this view, however, he saw friend-enemy mass politics to be the pathology and possibly a nadir of long civilizational decline. Believing that potential true "believers" are rife and readily mobilized, he declared "the less one knows how to command, the more urgently one covets someone who commands, who commands severely – a god, prince, class, physician, father confessor, dogma, or party conscience." Hypnotizing the "senses and intellect," he held, their "fanaticism" undercuts any remains of disciplined will among the "weak and insecure" and calls "cellar rodents" to crawl out of their holes and reap their sad harvest (Nietzsche, 1974, p. 289).

Nietzsche held that ascetic self-control is benign when it serves autonomy and fruitful realization of the creative energies of the will to power, which require direction, discipline, and intense labor. He says "all great fruitful, inventive spirits" adhere to some degree to the ascetic ideal and its mantras of "poverty, humility, chastity." Speaking directly of philosopher "ascetic priests" such as himself ("we nutcrackers of the soul"), Nietzsche asserted that "no actor of the spirit could endure life" in their self-imposed, lonely "desert."[32] He argued that "spirituality" governs genuine ascetic priests' will to power – they manifest serious dedication to a cultural project beyond themselves and thus are opposite the undisciplined, other-directed, narcissistic ersatz versions. Nietzsche had aspirations of initiating transvaluation that would forge a new order of rank or post-Socratic or postmodern cultural complex. He envisioned the cultural diversity, perspectival vision, and cosmopolitan outlook of "good Europeans" (sans moralizing nationalist, antisemitic reflexes) to be immanent resources for sociocultural transformation or even manifestations of agents initiating the rupture. Nietzsche wanted to "naturalize" humanity or relocate us in nature, free us from shame and guilt about bodily drives, enrich our esthetic experiences, and nudge us to embrace *this* life fully and freely in a less workaday world. In a telling passage, he declared "we need all exuberant, floating, dancing, mocking, childish, and blissful art lest we lose our *freedom above things* that our ideal demands of us." He added that we need to need "to stand *above* morality" not anxiously or tentatively with fear of falling, but we must "*float* above it and *play*" (Nietzsche, 1974, pp. 163–164). He wanted us to learn to laugh as well as wage "war" over ideas.[33] Nietzsche's higher human being ("superman") resembles Zorba the Greek, or his female counterpart, rather than Nazi Stormtroopers or the new versions of obedient human fodder conjured up in today's white nationalist imagination or in their faux revolutionary poses.[34]

AFTER CHARLOTTESVILLE: NIETZSCHE AND BEYOND

That thirst for more of the intellectual "war and laughter" that we find Nietzsche calling us to may bring us satisfactions that optimism-haunted philosophies could never bring. Malcontentedness may be the beginning of promise. Randolph Bourne (1917).
                                                            − Bourne (1977, p. 347)[35]

Invoking Nietzsche in the essay "Twilight of the Idols," Randolph Bourne skewered his teacher John Dewey and other American liberals and progressives for supporting the US entry into World War I and for justifying war as a means to save and extend democracy. Besides the human costs, Bourne held, wartime "reactionary idealism" and patriotic "self-righteousness" undermine democratic values and preclude formulation of new democratic alternatives. As Nietzsche had done earlier, Bourne decried militarism's "poisonous mushrooms" and consequent "mob-psychology" and "spiritual apathy" precluded Dewey's hoped-for "creative intelligence." The "inexorable disease" of "mob-fanaticisms" and "hysterias," Bourne argued, forecloses critical thought and critical discourse. He eviscerated claims that opposition to the war and criticism of the wartime regime were unreasonable and that reassertion of democratic values and a free civic sphere must be set aside until after the war was won.[36] Bourne insisted that a "more skeptical, malicious, desperate, ironical mood may actually be a sign of more vivid and more stirring life fermenting in America [...]"[37] He thought that excessive wartime "optimism" among progressive intellectuals caused them to overlook realities of "American life [...] too terrible to face."[38] He was prescient about limits of progressive era reformism and a nasty, philistine sociopolitical climate that continued with post-World War I America's Red Scare, Palmer raids, anti-immigration and anti-union policies, ascendant Ku Klux Klan and racial apartheid, and plutocratic governance. Bourne's deployment of Nietzsche urged creation of new perspectives and values capable of illuminating intractable problems that required fundamental change. Richard Spencer's "Nietzschean" move aims to do the same, albeit to advance a converse reactionary politics.

Bourne's version of the Nietzschean mentality applied in our times might have stemmed the moralistic fervor that silenced mainstream media criticism and ginned up public support for the post-9/11 "Greater Middle East" wars (which persist and have caused enormous suffering and loss of life) and contested the tepid response to extraordinary rendition, grotesque torture at Abu Ghraib, and inhumane detention at Guantanamo. And such critical malcontentedness is needed to counter the virulent strain of fanaticism that looms in resurgent racial nationalism. Economic inequality, underemployment, stagnant wages, forced immigration, terrorism, war, and global environmental problems create a climate of fear. The Thatcherite mantra "there is no alternative" has been for more than three decades a fundamental presupposition of neoliberal globalization. In the vacuum, Richard Spencer and other alt right populists claim to provide *the* alternative – racial nationalism and white gentile homelands. Pitting racial friends against racial enemies, their reactionary tribalism feeds off resentment and fear. Their claims that liberal elites and media suppress and distort racial realities and the mystique of the redpilling inversion and homecoming to the banned truths and values add to lure. That the alt right addresses actual crisis tendencies of neoliberal globalization, which neoliberals deny or dismiss as necessary costs of growth or just deserts, make the conspiratorial claims and aspirations for a secure white homeland all the more seductive and dangerous. Electoral victories of Brexit and Trump gave impetus to more extreme racial nationalist versions of the global populist upsurge and helped normalize them (Streeck, 2017). The alt right celebrates Brexit as the start of a liberating deconstruction of the hybrid unified Europe of which Nietzsche dreamed and their meme for Trump – "God Emperor" – arguably manifests the Nietzschean nightmare of an ascendant "Great man of the masses."

Efforts to reclaim Nietzsche as a critic of racial nationalism must be done with cautionary points in mind mentioned at the start – his texts have contradictory themes and are open to diverse interpretations and appropriations. That he emphatically rejected racial nationalism and sociopolitical regimentation does not preclude alt right thinkers finding facets of his texts that motivate and justify their ways. Moreover, Nietzsche was a withering critic of democratic and egalitarian ideals and did not address alternative governance structures. Consequently, Bourne combined his appropriation of Nietzschean "suspicion" with egalitarian democratic ideals, which he shared with Dewey and other progressives whom he was criticizing immanently for failing in practice to affirm and live up to beliefs that they advocated in theory. Reactionary populists have brought racial nationalism from the margins into the democratic civic sphere and into electoral politics. They challenge and blur dangerously the meanings of pluralism, citizenship, and democracy. They appropriate Nietzsche's name, words, and status as a classic political outsider and forerunner critic of establishment liberalism to support political thought and collective action that he abhorred. His service as a totemic prop for the alt right should be contested strenuously. Additionally, Nietzsche's views about moralism, demagogic mass politics, racial nationalism, and especially *ressentiment* are worthy of reconsideration in wake of the global populist revival.

Conflictive appropriations of Nietzsche have been part of the battle over capitalist crises and reactionary populist revivals for over a century (Aschheim, 1992; Balakrishnan, 2017). The neoliberal U-Turn or Great Reversal toward much sharper economic inequality, Thomas Piketty argues, is giving rise to a new version of earlier static, steeply vertical, "rentier societies" in which kinship and marriage trump "study, talent, and effort."[39] Neoliberalism was framed expressly ("supply-side" economics) to enrich the investor class of so-called job creators and reduce regulatory barriers to accelerate unplanned exponential growth. The neoliberal regime ushered in the "New Gilded Age." Unregulated growth and massive expansion of the global economy relative to the biosphere greatly increased material throughput and production of waste and generated a host of severe global environmental problems (e.g., biodiversity loss, toxic waste, nitrogen pollution, freshwater loss). The most dangerous, fast moving one, climate change threatens to undermine the Holocene Epoch's unusual climatic stability and undercut the biophysical foundations of the economy, civilization, and life forms as we have known them.[40] Greatly accelerated growth in very populous newly industrialized nations and "business as usual" carbon usage and consumption in rich nations will produce major ecocatastrophes this century.[41] Because climate change adaptation and mitigation demand scuttling the growth imperative, decarbonizing society, and regulating, planning, and constricting deeply ingrained, highly profitable consumerist habits, neoliberal political elites and neoclassical economists outright deny climate change or understate its likely impacts and threats (Anderson & Bows, 2016). Publics generally support such optimism, which upholds the consumerist status quo. Consequently, the US and other wealthy nations reject *binding* international agreements to reduce carbon and methane emissions and face a fateful collision with the environmental wall.

The optimism Bourne attacked is manifested in the extreme in beliefs that unplanned, exponential growth can be sustained ad infinitum in the face of still growing meteoric economic inequality and profound threats to the biophysical bases of the global economy and civilization as we have known it. The apocalyptic struggles mentioned by Nietzsche are now on our horizon as genuine science-supported possibilities (Oreskes & Conway, 2014). The new right "identitarian" racial nationalist subject was constructed in opposition to American and European Union citizenry, arguably approximating Nietzsche's lands of racially mixed, hybrid good Europeans and the nascent universal version of the same − "cosmopolitan" human beings. The alt right contends that cosmopolitan people are deracinated, emptied of their cultural particularity, and spiritually lost. By contrast to the alt right affirmation of racial nationalist seclusion, progressives contend that cosmopolitans *potentially* benefit from more diverse people and perspectives, enhanced ability to empathetically play the role of the other, and consequent wider communicative capacities and refined powers of cooperation. Social theorist Ulrich Beck speculated that the impending eco-apocalypse could generate "anthropological shock" and "social catharsis" will give rise to a "cosmopolitan moment" and mobilization for the planet and its life forms and necessarily reduce sharply economic inequality.[42] Nietzsche too exhorted humans to "remain true to the earth" and its "garden joy," and implied a naturalist esthetics and pacification of nature.[43] Nietzsche should be rescued from alt right, but we must reach far beyond his legacy to envision and forge new political-economic alternatives and collective actions capable of sustaining life on the planet and creating and perpetuating a more just democracy that favors cosmopolitan human flourishing.[44]

NOTES

1. Nietzsche (1989, p. 225).
2. Löwith (1986, p. 83).
3. See Nietzsche commentary and links to Nietzsche essays on this white nationalist publisher site, https://www.counter-currents.com/2016/10/remembering-friedrich-nietzsche-6/; on the European New Right (Sunic, 2011).
4. Wood (2017). Being "redpilled" originates from *The Matrix* movie. The lead character, Neo, could have chosen a green pill and remained living in a comfy simulated world, shared with other enslaved post-apocalyptic humans, but he chose the red pill in order to experience the painful truth and join the life and death struggle for freedom against subjugation by the machines.
5. Spencer's "Charlottesville Statement" echoes the European new right manifesto. See Spencer (2017) and de Benoist and Charles Champetier (2012).
6. New right thinkers propose a racially unified imperial regime of semiautonomous related nations − e.g., Europe with its spatially rooted ethnic and linguistic groups sans non-Western immigrants (de Benoist, 1993−1994, pp. 81−98).
7. "The high points of politics are simultaneously the moments in which the enemy is, in concrete clarity, recognized as the enemy" (Schmitt, 1996, p. 67).
8. Although stated in this single passage, translator Kaufmann said, this "magnificent formulation" is a central motif of Nietzsche's overall thought (Nietzsche, 1974, pp. 228−229 and note 9).
9. Contradictory statements about Jews and Judaism are scattered across his works. See, e.g., Holub (2015).
10. For discussion of divergent impacts of Nietzsche, see Aschheim (1992), Ratner-Rosenhagen (2012), and Antonio (2001). For different interpretations of Nietzsche, see, e.g., Bäumler (1970), Kaufmann (1974), Love (1986), and Antonio (1995).
11. For example, Richard Spencer read Nietzsche well-enough to conduct serious interviews and engage intelligently white nationalist Nietzschean, Jonathan Bowden on the topic. Jonathan Bowden (2016a) interviewed by Richard Spencer (2017) and Bowden (2016b). See Red Ice TV's Lana Lokteff interview on Nietzsche's anti-egalitarianism with Seth Cooper and Erik Yount (2016).
12. Foucault admitted that he had "not read Nietzsche for a good many years" (Foucault, 1989, pp. 247−249, 327).
13. Nietzsche (1883–1888) (1968, p. 162).
14. Nietzsche (1968b, pp. 29−66), Nietzsche (1967), and Nietzsche (1974, p. 272).
15. Ibid., pp. 187−190, Nietzsche (1966, p. 108), and Nietzsche (1989, pp. 33−36, 52−54).
16. The break with is marked by a cessation of classical antiquity's abundant explicit artistic representations of sexuality and fertility and arrival of a God deeply concerned with the sinfulness and shamefulness of sexual pleasure and consequent relative absence of explicit sexual representations and appearance fig leaf covered genitals (Ibid., pp. 90−96).
17. Ibid., pp. 127−128.
18. Ibid., pp. 142−143.

19. Ibid., pp. 38, 44−48, 122−123.

20. Ibid., p. 159.

21. Nietzsche (1974, pp. 293, 310), Nietzsche (1989, pp. 145−156), and Weber (1946, pp. 129−156). Nietzsche's humorous passage about Zarathustra trudging through a swamp and stumbling on a scientist studying the brain of a leech was not meant to belittle science, but to stress overestimation of expertise (Nietzsche, 1969, pp. 261−264).

22. Ibid., 296−298 and Nietzsche (1974, pp. 107−109).

23. Nietzsche (1989, p. 158).

24. Ibid., pp. 158−159.

25. Ibid., p. 225; Nietzsche (1986a, p. 161); Nietzsche (1968a, p. 53).

26. Ibid., pp. 60−66; Nietzsche (1989, p. 319).

27. Nietzsche (1974, pp. 339−340); Nietzsche (1986a, p. 175).

28. Ibid., pp. 173−174, 176, 178, 378, 380−381.

29. Ibid., p. 176. Nietzsche (1966, p. 131).

30. Nietzsche (1986a, p. 168); Nietzsche held that "anyone who wants to move a crowd must be an actor who impersonates himself" (1974, p. 212).

31. Ibid., p. 160; Nietzsche (1986a, p. 137).

32. Nietszche's portrayal of an ascetic life of "voluntary obscurity," rooms in "commonplace hotels," "an occasional association with harmless cheerful beasts and birds," and "mountains for company" (punctuated by "lonely enough, believe me!") resonates with his singular wandering life (Nietzsche, 1989, pp. 108−109, passim 106−118).

33. Nietzsche imagined a possible liberated future in which all the old "power structures" would be dissolved and a "great politics" or "war of spirits" that would unleash esthetic impulses that say "Yes" to life and infuse it with meaning and purpose (Nietzsche, 1989, pp. 326−327).

34. Nobel laureate, novelist Nikos Kazantzakis wrote a doctoral dissertation on Nietzsche and likely had in mind the philosopher's conception of the higher human being when he wrote about Zorba, who manifested the qualities in the quoted passages directly above.

35. Bourne (1977, p. 347).

36. Ibid., pp. 336−347.

37. Ibid., p. 347.

38. Ibid., p. 347.

39. Piketty (2014, pp. 238−240, passim); other progressive economists have argued similarly that inequality and employment problems will continue to worsen and that populist reactions will grow. Former World Bank research economist Branko Milanovic (2016) says that we are headed toward a society of ultra-rich and those who serve them and that the US is "a 'perfect storm' of inequality."

40. The changes have been so great that scientists have proposed formal recognition of new Anthropocene Epoch in which humans drive overall ecological change (Steffen et al., 2011, pp. 739−761).

41. USGCRP (2017).

42. Compare Beck (2010, 2015) with Spencer (2017) and de Benoist and Champetier (2012).

43. Nietzsche (1969, pp. 42, 207) and Shapiro (2016).

44. The pragmatist tradition from which Bourne came converges with Nietzsche in its naturalism and anti-dualism and critique of moralism, but diverges sharply in other ways, especially in its normative emphases on deliberative democracy and justice in the distribution of the means of participation. Their egalitarian thrust and social conception of humanity stressing the capacity to play the role of the other and cooperative interdependence go beyond Nietzsche's thought. I do not suggest, however, that pragmatism provides all the analytical tools needed for today's tasks.

REFERENCES

Anderson, K., & Bows, A. (2016). A new paradigm for climate change. *Nature Climate Change*, *2*(September), 639−640.

Antonio, R. J. (1995). Nietzsche's antisociology: Subjectified culture and the end of history. *American Journal of Sociology*, *101*, 1−43.

Antonio, R. J. (2000). After postmodernism: Reactionary tribalism. *American Journal of Sociology*, *106*(2), 40−87.

Antonio, R. J. (2001). Nietzsche: Social theory in the twilight of the millennium. In G. Ritzer & B. Smart (Eds.), *Handbook of social theory* (pp. 163−178). London: Sage.

Aschheim, S. E. (1992). *The Nietzsche legacy in Germany 1890−1990*. Berkeley, CA: University of California Press.

Balakrishnan, G. (2017). Counterstrike west. *New Left Review*, *104*, 19−43.

Bäumler, A. (1970). Nietzsche and national socialism. Enda Miller (Ed., Trans.) (August 29). *Amerika*. Retrieved from http://www.amerika.org/texts/nietzsche-and-national-socialism-alfred-baeumler/. Accessed on September 3, 2017.

Beck, U. (2010). Remapping social inequalities in an age of climate change: For a cosmopolitan renewal of sociology. *Global Networks*, *10*(2), 165−181.

Beck, U. (2015). Emancipatory catastrophism: What does it mean to climate change and risk society? *Current Sociology*, *63*(1), 75−88.

de Benoist, A. (1993−1994). The idea of empire. *Telos* no. 98−99.

de Benoist, A. (1996). Confronting globalization. *Telos* no. 108: 117−137.

de Benoist, A. (1998). Hayek: A critique. *Telos* no. 110.

de Benoist, A. (2002). On politics. *Telos* no. 125 (2002), pp. 9−36.

de Benoist, A., & Champetier, C. (2012). *Manifesto for a European renaissance*. London: Arktos.

Bloom, A. (1987). *The closing of the American mind*. New York, NY: Touchstone.

Bourne, R. (1977). Twilight of the idols. In O. Hansen (Ed.), *The radical will*. New York, NY: Urizen Books.

Bowden, J. (2016a). Nietzsche's *On the genealogy of morals*. Counter-Currents Publishing. Posted June 21. Retrieved from https://www.counter-currents.com/2016/06/nietzsches-on-the-genealogy-of-morals/print/. Accessed on August 20, 2017.

Bowden, R. (2016b). *The uses & abuses of Nietzsche*. Counter-Currents Publishing. Posted April 15. Retrieved from https://www.counter-currents.com/2016/04/the-uses-and-abuses-of-nietzsche/print/. Accessed on August, 20 2017.

Burgard, P. J. (1994). *Nietzsche and the feminine*. Charlottesville: University Press of Virginia.

Cooper, S., & Yount, E. (2016). *The glorious path: Master vs. slave morality*. 3 Fourteen Radio, October 16. Retrieved from https://www.youtube.com/watch?v=EQKWvgzDi40. Accessed on October 1, 2017.

Foucault, M. (1989). How much does it cost reason to tell the truth? (Chapter 19); An aesthetics of discourse (Chapter 23). In S. Lotringer (Ed.), *Foucault live* (J. Johnson, Trans.). New York, NY: Semiotext(e).

Galupo, S. (2017). The troubling rise of Bad Nietzsche. *The Week*, May 22. Retrieved from http://the-week.com/articles/699001/troubling-rise-bad-nietzsche. Accessed on August 19, 2017.

Holub, R. C. (2015). *Nietzsche's Jewish problem*. Princeton, NJ: Princeton University Press.

Hughes, H. S. (1977). *Consciousness and society* (Rev. ed.) New York, NY: Vintage.

Illing, S. (2017). The alt right is drunk on bad readings of Nietzsche. The Nazis were too. *Vox*, August 17. Retrieved from https://www.vox.com/2017/8/17/16140846/nietzsche-richard-spen-cer-altrightt-nazism. Accessed on August 19, 2017.

Kaufmann, W. (1974). *Nietzsche* (4th ed.). Princeton, NJ: Princeton University Press.

Love, N. S. (1986). *Marx, Nietzsche, and modernity*. New York, NY: Columbia University Press.

Löwith, K. (1986). *My life in German before and after 1933*. E. King (Trans.). Urbana, IL: University of Illinois.

Milanovic, B. (2016). *Global inequality*. Cambridge, MA: Belknap Press of Harvard University Press.

Nietzsche, F. (1966). *Beyond good and evil*. W. Kaufmann (trans.). New York, NY: Vintage.

Nietzsche, F. (1967). *The birth of tragedy and the case of Wagner*. W. Kaufmann (trans.). New York, NY: Vintage.

Nietzsche, F. (1968a). *The will to power*. W. Kaufmann & R. J. Hollingdale (trans.). New York, NY: Vintage.

Nietzsche, F. (1968b). *Twilight of the idols and the anti-christ*. R. J. Hollingdale (trans.). London: Penguin Books.

Nietzsche, F. (1969). *Thus spoke Zarathustra*. R. J. Hollingdale (trans.). London: Penguin.

Nietzsche, F. (1974). *The gay science*. W. Kaufmann (trans.). New York, NY: Vintage.

Nietzsche, F. (1986a). *Human all too human*. R. J. Hollingdale (trans.). New York, NY: Cambridge University Press.

Nietzsche, F. (1986b). *Untimely meditations*. R. J. Hollingdale (trans.). New York, NY: Cambridge University Press.

Nietzsche, F. (1989). *On genealogy of morals and Ecce Homo*. W. Kaufmann & R. J. Hollingdale (trans.). New York, NY: Vintage.

O'Meara, M. (2004). *New culture, new right*. Bloomington, IN: 1ST Books.

Oreskes, N., & Conway, E. M. (2014). *The collapse of western civilization*. New York, NY: Columbia University Press.

Patton, P. (1993). *Nietzsche, feminism, and political theory*. London: Routledge.

Piketty, Th. (2014). *Capital in the twenty-first century*. A. Goldhammer (trans.). Cambridge, MA: The Belknap Press of Harvard University Press.

Ratner-Rosenhagen, J. (2012). *American Nietzsche*. Chicago, IL: University of Chicago Press.

Schmitt, C. (1996). *The concept of the political*. G. Schwab (trans.). Chicago, IL: The University of Chicago Press.

Schutte, O. (1986). *Nietzsche without masks*. Chicago, IL: University of Chicago Press.

Shapiro, G. (2016). *Nietzsche's earth*. Chicago, IL: University of Chicago Press.

Spencer, R. (2017). What it means to be alt-right. *ALTRIGHT.com*. August 11. Retrieved from https://altright.com/2017/08/11/what-it-means-to-be-alt-right/. Accessed on October 13, 2017.

Spencer, R. (2018). Politics in grand style. *Radix*, July 27. Retrieved from https://radixjournal.com/2018/07/politics-in-the-grand-style/. Accessed on September 18, 2019.

Steffen, W., Persson, Å., Deutsch, L., Zalasiewicz, J., Williams, M., Richardson, K., … Svedin, U. (2011). The Anthropocene: From global change to planetary stewardship. *Ambio*, *40*(7), 739−761.

Streeck, W. (2017). The return of the repressed. *New Left Review*, *104*, 5−18.

Sunic, T. (2011). *Against democracy and equality*. London: Arktos.

USGCRP. (2017).*Climate science special report: Fourth national climate assessment*, Volume I. D. J. Wuebbles, D. W. Fahey, K. A. Hibbard, D. J. Dokken, B. C. Stewart, & T. K. Maycock (Eds.). U.S. Global Change Research Program (Washington, DC), 470 pp, https://doi.org/10.7830/JOJ964J6

Weber, M. (1946). *From Max Weber: Essays in sociology* (H. H. Gerth & C. Wright Mills, (Eds., Trans.). New York, NY: Oxford University Press.

Wood, G. (2017). His Kampf. *The Atlantic*, June. Retrieved from https://www.theatlantic.com/magazine/archive/2017/06/his-kampf/524505/. Accessed on August 19, 2017.

"HOW CAN [WE] NOT KNOW?" *BLADE RUNNER* AS CINEMATIC LANDMARK IN CRITICAL THOUGHT [*]

Lawrence Hazelrigg

ABSTRACT

Ridley Scott's 1982 cinematic production of Blade Runner, *based loosely on a 1968 story by Philip Dick (*Do Androids Dream of Electric Sheep?*), is read within a general context of critical theory, the purpose being two-fold: first, to highlight the film's fit with, and within, several issues that have been important to critical theory and, second, to explore some questions, criticisms, and extensions of those issues – the dialectic of identity/difference most crucially – by speculations within and on the film's text. The exploration is similar in approach to studies of specific films within the context of issues of social, cultural, and political theory conducted by the late Stanley Cavell. Interrogations of dimensions of scenarios and sequences of plotline, conceptual pursuit of some implications, and assessments of the realism at work in cinematic format are combined with mainly descriptive evaluations of character portrayals and dynamics as these relate to specified thematics of the identity/difference dialectic. The film puts in relief evolving meanings of prosthetics – which is to say changes in the practical as well as conceptual-semantic boundaries of "human being": what counts as "same" versus "other"? "domestic" versus "foreign"? "integrity" versus "dissolution"? "safety" versus "danger"? And how do those polarities, understood*

[*] I would be remiss not to acknowledge the helpful perspective offered by Mary Sean Young. I thank, too, Harry Dahms for his steadfast encouragement.

The Challenge of Progress: Theory Between Critique and Ideology
Current Perspectives in Social Theory, Volume 36, 111–132
ISSN: 0278-1204/doi:10.1108/S0278-120420190000036017

*within a unity-of-opposites dialectic, change, as human beings are con-
fronted more and more stressfully by their own reproductions of "environment" – that is, the perspectival device of "what is 'text' and what is
context'?" – and variations of that device by direct and indirect effects of
human actions, as those actions have unfolded within recursive sequences of
prior versions of perspectival device, a device repeatedly engaged, albeit primarily and mainly implicitly, as a "prosthetic that could not be a
prosthetic."*

Keywords: identity/difference; unity of opposites; prosthesis; environment;
environmentalism; ecology; perspective

The plot is simple. Humans are supposed to clean up the messes left by their
productions, whether the leaving was deliberate or accidental. Having run
aground, a tanker gushes millions of gallons of oil; someone is supposed to
restore the *ex ante* balance, rescuing sea and air victims in the process. Smashed
by a tsunami following an earthquake, a nuclear power plant spews radioactivity
into soil, sea, and air; someone is supposed to clean it up, rescue victims no matter how far afield, restore the *ex ante* balance. Having stoked the wells of easy
credit in housing and other) markets into enormous overloads, despite warnings
by Robert Shiller, Richard Duncan, and William White, among other economists (and others), credit markets collapse, leaving huge numbers of debtors in
the lurch and accelerating the decline of the fabled middle class; someone is supposed to clean it up; rescue victims, restore the *ex ante* balance. This is a book
of many chapters, each of them containing lessons unheeded, damages unre-
paired, *ex ante* balances a sequence of forlorn memories echoing Kurt
Vonnegut's "So it goes."

That was yesterday. Now we are in the year 2019, faced with apparently a
new version of the same plot. The missions of Spirit, Opportunity, and
Curiosity having shown what electro-mechanical robots could accomplish on
other planets, a giant step forward in robotic political economy has planted
colonies of anthropomorphic beings–androids, some called them; others preferred "replicant"– at distant locations in what was once called "outer space,"
now called "Off World." This world, Earth, has become a rather desolate
place, an accumulation of pollutants and other problems left unsolved. As
with most films of this genre, the depicted present leaves most of its history to
a viewer's imagination–not unlike most viewers of their own passing days outside the theatre or movie house. Perhaps all of the film's bleak present is due
to nuclear devastation; or perhaps only part, the remainder an accumulation
of smaller, more gradual devastations (few viewers had yet heard of climate
change). But however dim and piecemeal the history (within the film and of
the viewer), the film's emphasis, like that of the viewer, is the here-and-now
present, plus whatever future might follow from it, and both seem rather
bleak, cluttered, used-up. Yet it is not clear that "Off World" life has been
appreciably better, even with the service of replicants in some new sort of
(though never mentioned) plantation system.

These replicants of human being possess various super-human qualities, made to order depending on the particular assignment. Outwardly they look like real men and women. Inwardly, well, who knows what the inside of another being "feels like." Each of the new editions gained at creation an implanted identity and memory. Products of the corporate world, their design was "sold" to the commonweal, to the common good, as a promise of life-saving substitutes for human beings, capable of withstanding hostile conditions, environments that would be fatal to real human beings. And if that environment should prove to be *too* hostile to one of the androids, well, at least a human life will not have been lost. Now and again a replicant malfunctions, but human specialists have been trained in skills of termination − "retirement," it is called. Between the saving of human life and the money to be made for (already abundant) corporate coffers, the existence and the uses of these replicants have seemed to most humans to be a nearly perfect optimum, truly a "win-win" bargain. Indeed, the androids have proved themselves many times over, in a sequence of improved technologies presently culminating in an extraordinary creature, the Nexus-6 edition.

But a problem has arisen. Some of the newest models have "gone off the reservation" (as one group of humans used to say of others who had been assigned their proper place). Heading back to Earth with already demonstrated lethal intent to achieve their goal, they seek more life, an adjustment to the short life-span–only four years − that was part of their creator's design for them. These revolting replicants pose another problem of pollution resulting as a by-product − or is it a side-effect? − of a proven production process. Time to call in the clean-up specialists–a team of real human beings who know how to neutralize the problem and restore the *ex ante* balance. This being America (specifically, Los Angeles), a team isn't actually needed: call in the Lone Ranger, the Palladin, the Skywalker. Here the fellow's name is Rick Deckard. His mission is simple: exterminate all the creatures who have fled the reservation and mean harm to human beings. He's done it before, reputedly was very good at putting to rest malfunctioning/misbehaving androids. But somewhere along the trail of those previous trials he fatigued, morally, it seems, as well as–more than? − physically. One can't say for sure because he's the laconic type. We don't know much about his prior life. Apparently he took early retirement some time ago–the old-fashioned sort, not the new euphemism. Today, however, he has been told bluntly (no option) that he and only he can put things right. Reluctant though he may be to return to duty, he has no choice in the matter. The decision was never his. One mere cog in the machine. Expected when called.

So we have another "action flick," the hero eventually prevailing and, at the end, riding off into the sunset, in a manner of speaking, with the girl. There are some important differences, however. To begin with, this story of action heroics has been credited − along with works by William Gibson ("The Gernsback continuum," 1981; *Neuromancer*, 1984), among others − as having inaugurated a "cyberpunk" genre of poetic art, filmic as well as print storytelling. The term "cyberpunk" seemingly less fashionable than it was ten to twenty years ago, a cribsheet definition might be useful: a melding of the whiz-bang "it's a new world" power of the cybernetic, digital, bioelectromechanical "information age," with sagas of the alienated, raw-edged loner and a generalized deep suspicion of mega-corporations (more, it seems, than of mega-governments), cyberpunk is another ratcheting up the scale of A E Housman's "world I never made."[1] It is, one might say, a next floor in the elevator ride marked by Mary Shelley's *Modern Prometheus* (1818), Nietzsche's *Zarathustra* (1883-85), Robert Musil's *Man without Qualities* (1930, 1943), and Arthur Clarke's and Stanley Kubrick's *Space Odyssey* (1968).

Another important difference is the relative quality of the production design and the cinematography, for its time a major advance in visual aids to the willing suspension of disbelief. The overall visual effect was modeled after sources such as Edward Hopper's painting, *Nighthawks*, and the illustrative arts that had featured in *Heavy Metal*, a popular graphic arts magazine. Given the budget constraints, the set work was remarkably effective for a largely "back-lot" undertaking. Most films are patchworks of script writing and rewriting, camera takes and retakes, editing cuts and splices, and so forth, with the usual result of holes here and there in the final product. This film maintains a texture of ambiguity that is vital to its thematics. But it also makes the holes harder to catch.

Third, the portrayal of life in Los Angeles 2019 is highly evocative of the eclecticism of US "American culture," its old and new threads of patchwork, as one could (and some did) during the 1970s and 80s imagine its future "picture on the wall" installations of cognitive-emotive experience. The underlying "fear and loathing" mentality was (is) evocative of a projection of the Hunter Thompson who had exposed psychotic structures of normalcy during the 1970s. Indeed, this mentality is announced at the film's beginning, with the looming presence of a large eye staring at the audience. The eye motif recurs throughout the film. In 1982 this thread from Orwell was more disturbing than today, when cameras are on nearly every street corner, in trees, lobbies, elevators, and corridors, in stores, offices, schools, subways, airplanes, and automobiles, in telephones, helmets, broaches, pens, and eyeglasses – and of course in the sky.

The film is *Blade Runner* (1982). It was based ("loosely" is the usual qualifier) on a novel by Philip K Dick, *Do Androids Dream of Electric Sheep* (1968). Dick (1928–1982) wrote obscurely for many years, contributing by one count a total of 44 novels. Obscurity lifted only enough for him to become a cult figure in "science fiction" circles until well after the film's release, when he gained more general attention for a brief time. As of 2007 his work gained something of an imprimatur with publication of four of his novels (including *Androids*) as a volume in The Library of America. Comparisons of book and film have often been made. As is often the case, there are important differences between the media. They are not of concern here. Present attention is to the film and in particular to its display of some themes of critical thought.[2]

As well, the present discussion is not a piece of filmography, though a few brief remarks of that sort will be made as orientation, in advance of the main attention.[3] Released early Summer 1982, the film enjoyed a reasonably promising first week but then lagged badly, as both popular and critical receptions were mixed at best. Complexity of storyline has been cited as one reason for the lag. More specifically, I think, the film "fell between stools" for too many viewers. Those who expected primarily an "action flick" tended to be put off by the "film noir" aspects, while those who found the latter attractive were perhaps too distracted or bored by the weight of gladiatorial contesting. The acting was more than adequate. Harrison Ford as Deckard displayed his trademark "character style" of a quizzical stoicism (somewhere between Cary Grant and Buster Keaton) to good effect. Sean Young was pitch-perfect as Rachael — in at least one respect the axial-*cum*-crucial focal point of the film. Edward James Olmos returned a superb portrayal of the sinister-seeming, steganographically mysterious Gaff, ostensibly Deckard's police partner/liaison. Rutger Hauer was equally superb as Roy Batty, leader of the lethal renegades. Other cast members also gave excellent performances. The screenplay by Hampton Fancher and David Peoples, drawing on Dick's novel directly but also on other sources some of which had been influenced by Dick's work, is a finely textured, nuanced study of ambiguities, enhanced by settings that shift obliquely between the glitzy-busy and the broken-mechanical-organic slag pile.[4] Cinematography and film editing molded the actor portrayals, sets, and sequences into an appropriately complex coherence of ambiguities. As director (plus uncredited co-producer who had a hand in writing, design, and almost everything else), Ridley Scott, just coming from his successful *Alien* (1979), made the whole of the production work very well, despite compromises with his "angels," and however difficult to work "with" he may have been.[5] The film requires careful attention, careful thought, more than one screening. It was not, still is not, an "easy read." That was by design, part of the thematic structure. Its status as "cult classic" is surely not undeserved. Beyond that, *Blade Runner* has been named one of the top ten science-fiction films of all time, indeed one of the top 100 films of any sort, by the American Film Institute.

Assumptions are always unavoidable. The largest here is that the reader has viewed *Blade Runner* at least once, gave the film careful attention, and remembers enough of it for present purposes (however elusive a definition of the latter criteria). The film exists in different versions; I refer primarily to the US "domestic cut" theatrical version, although the version first made available for in-home viewing was not much different. A still larger assumption would be about the reader's experiential context, were it not for the absurdity of it. Try as one might to shield against one's past, memories seep in. Even so, the reader should attempt to avoid anachronism, to the extent that one can, by remembering *Blade Runner* in its historical context. That was three decades ago. Bear in mind a sequence extending (e.g.) from George Lucas' *THX 1138* (1971), Michael Crichton's *Westworld* (1973), Lucas' *Star Wars* (1977), Scott's *Alien* (1979), Ken Russell's *Altered States* (1980), and Terry Gilliam's *Time Bandits* (1981; and far less ambitious than his masterpiece of four years later, *Brazil*). Thence, *Blade Runner*. All comparatives must carry the qualifier, "in/for its time," its location in a historical sequence. Moreover, that sequence is composed not only of films and printed stories, not only of artistic and aesthetic judgments; as the foregoing citations of Orwell and Thompson were meant to say, lived experiences, political-economic and other, are invested in the here-and-now of a viewing and in this here-and-now of a reading. All of that, different by reader, cannot be comprehended at each turn; and probably none of it can be comprehended *now* exactly as it was *then*. But effort to minimize anachronism will be helpful.

THEMES CRITICAL-PHILOSOPHICAL

Already the philosophical tenor has been sounded. Nearly a century ago Bertrand Russell made it clear — to the displeasure of some theologians and others who relished their incontrovertible purchase on "the facts" (of whatever kind) — that "nothing that is happening now or will happen in the future" can enable anyone or any community to "disprove the hypothesis that the world began five minutes ago, ... exactly as it was then, with a population that 'remembered' a wholly unreal past" (Russell, 1921, pp. 159−160).[6]

The notion of implanted memory is troubling in a number of registers, one of them being the question raised about boundaries and socialization. Children are told to remember certain facts — name, parents' names, address, telephone number, "beware of strangers" (or strangers of a certain kind) — but they also learn, usually more by indirection, to profess certain memories even when they cannot give reasons for them. These can include such forms/contents as details of dreams that seem to have been wakeful experiences; lies told often enough that the liar actually believes that the told event or situation did in fact occur (or, an adult variant, exaggerations in self-advertising that eventually become self-truth, the factual biography), expectations of what certain kinds of actors — that is, perpetrators of certain kinds of acts (mugging, burglary, etc.) — do generally "look like"; and legends or myths that become facts that every schoolgirl and schoolboy knows (e.g., girls are great at literature but just can't do math; George Washington could not tell a lie); and so forth. Veyne's ([1983]1988) pupils well knew that the ancient Greeks were (are) not alone. Russell was correct, of course, and a measure of our awareness of that is the rapidity and insolence with which we erect boundaries/barriers against implications. Holding purchase on "the real facts," the facts as they are in themselves, is not for the gods alone. There is, after all, money to be made, contests to be won, control to be insured. (Rachael said something about this in *Blade Runner*, indeliberately as if a child; we come to it a bit later.)

Unmistakable, too, is the theme of alienation and reification. The nineteenth century of Europe and Euro-America produced a manifold literature that developed (and to an extent introduced, one could say) this theme as part of a new population of the interiority of "mind" and "selfhood" with primarily psychologistic (though even then sociological, presuppositionally and sometimes subrosa) characters.[7] However, it has been evidently very difficult to improve on Marx' (now classic) explication of alienation and reification (e.g., Marx, [1932]1975), judging by scarcity of successful attempts (see reviews by Ollman, 1971 and Dahms, 2011, chapter 3). *Blade Runner* is replete with imagic and dialogic presentations but falls far short of a treatment that could be counted as improved insight rather than illustration. A line of poiesis that connects from Goethe's romanticist sensibility, with its insistence that "Im Anfang war die *Tat*!" (In the beginning was the *deed*!; Goethe [1808]1852, 1, 1237), to Sartre's clarification of an existentialism that bears his name, with his insistence that "Faire, et en faisant se faire et n'être rien que ce qu'on fait" (Make, and in making make yourself, and be nothing but what you have made of yourself; Sartre ([1944]1985, p. 157) runs through Marx, though is seldom attended.[8] It would probably be gratuitous to read that lesson in (i.e., "into") *Blade Runner* (or Dick's *Androids*).

The remainder of this essay is meant to focus on two other themes of critical thought. Although surely not exclusive of the foregoing considerations, these themes have different emphases. One has to do with the identity/difference and subject/object dialectic of human being. This is followed by a critical theme that is both extensive and intensive of the operation of that dialectic, using as guide the question, Whose voice has determinative authority?: Deckard's, which is both inside (as character) and outside (as narrator), with ambiguity as to whether they are one and the same? Rachael's, which lives on a Euclidean edge that might or might not be the single edge of Möbius (which means that the appearance of two surfaces dissolves into one — but also, *per contra*, that with only the slightest of twists one can be seen as two)? Or another? Surely not Batty's, chief villain. But then again…. Or perhaps none of those; instead, the center of all paranoia, the voice of the Chief Creator, head of "the System" (i.e., Dr. Eldon Tyrell, CEO of the Tyrell Corporation, maker of replicants, and Rachael's boss), working levers behind the screen, Wizard of Oz style?

TO BE HUMAN

What is the meaning of being human? This has probably been the most frequent focus of post-viewing conversations about *Blade Runner* (and the first main thread of internet blogs attending the film): what does it mean "to be human"? It is no doubt one of the oldest topics of human reflexive conversation. Various answers are on record, from Protagoras to Plato to Aristotle's *zöon politikon*, a being inherently social (i.e., relational). Augustine wrote, and lived, different answers, starting with the more sociological (avant la lettre) in his early adult years. Striving to find his balance between evidence of the senses, empirical and uncertain, and evidence of an internal rationality, a self-knowledge which, for all the certainty of that inner experience, could not be proven certain by any empirical means, Augustine's evaluation of alternative approaches included two that, by our categories, fit approximately "the psychological" and "the sociological." Beginning in the latter of the two mainly as a "naive" act of communal experience, his reading of the Stoics brought him to conviction in the superiority of the "psychological" perspective, with its pursuit of evidences of and from an inward self-knowledge (see *De Trinitate*, 10.2.6–10.3.18, 10.3.39–10.3.45).[9] But later (see Books 11–15 of *De Trinitate*) he returned to the "sociological" perspective, with its emphasis on evidence via community, via others' perceptions and convictions (including of and about oneself), though now it is the "sociological" under the aegis of theological belief. By the time he attempted to negotiate the contest between coenobitic and eremetic versions of monasticism, his view of the meaning of being human came strikingly forth in denunciation of the eremites (see *Contra Faustum*, 1.3).[10] Centuries later a meeting was convened in Valladolid, to settle disputes over another set of membership boundaries: these indigenous creatures of Europe's New World, what were they? Truly human? Or some strangely human-like beast, incapable of dreaming the dreams of angels but suitable to Aristotle's category of "natural slave"?[11] Whence, several years later and a few hundred miles north, Montaigne published some subtle yet sharp barbs against any doctrine of the meaning of being human that subordinated immanence of condition to a promise of transcendence only by privileged claim of authority.[12] And so on, through Pascal and Pope and many, many others, to the turn of the nineteenth century and Hölderlin's "heavenly Beings" — "Giebt es auf Erden ein Maass? Es giebt keines" (Is there a measure on Earth? There is none.)[13] — and on to mid-century when the interiority of human being was greatly expanded in quantity of qualia, in density of relations, and in obscurity of some, perhaps the most vital, sorts of meaning; and so to the present day.

Clearly we humans expend a lot of worry about identity-and-difference (which we tend to apprehend with the copula in place, i.e., as an analytical, not dialectical, relationship). We tend to prize difference, to the extent that we do, primarily because it helps us build a picture contrastively of who we are and what being that means. Augustine, like Socrates before him and Montaigne after him (and Pascal again after that), was a proponent of self-knowledge.[14] But he and they each made recourse to a different warrant and a different promise. *Blade Runner* did not change that conversation in any basic way. When it was fresh, however, and insofar as it retains freshness for new viewers, it does bring added value in the margin. At various times during the film the question is raised, sometimes directly, other times obliquely, and via the "difference mirror" held up by one or another android.

For instance, at the near-end of the brutal contest between Deckard and Batty (leader of the renegades, recall, and a "latest model" NEXUS-6, with high intelligence and super-human strength), it is clear for a moment that Batty has won. The hunter (Deckard) had become the hunted, and he now realizes that his chance of escape had been negligible all along, that Batty had merely been playing with him. For his part, Batty, though himself in mortal end-state because of programming, knows that he could easily send Deckard to his death. But he does not. From all appearances, he chooses a different conclusion. Not only does he not send Deckard to death, he offers a hand of rescue. Why? Has he only recognized that Deckard was/is not his real enemy, merely another flunky paid to do a job, and thus not all that different from (even though in some ways inferior to) Batty himself? Was the decision his twenty-first century update of the old code of chivalry between combatants? Or was it not really his decision but the residual effect of an implanted rule/memory (Asimov's first law) that androids only serve, do not harm, humans? Was it a self-reflexive moral decision, a choice to refuse an act so easily executable? What sign of emotive life did we then see in Batty's flickering coil?

One is left with choices of meaning, much as when one tries to infer the intents of another human being, here today — a child or parent or spouse or neighbor or employer. By eschewing obviousness, *Blade Runner* makes situations, ordinary or extreme, more "life-like." But *whose* life?

One of the strongest thematic dimensions of *Blade Runner*, equal to the best of the science fiction genre, is its emphasis on futurity, today as the beginning of tomorrow. In that regard, its update of hermeneutic thrust is less to do with the battle between Deckard and Batty and much more to do with cooperative relations between human being and its products, potential before actual. This is visible mainly in the background of the film's storyline ("mainly" because cooperation is less "dramatic," more "boring," than conflict). But think of the hermeneutic relation in *Blade Runner* as an exercise geared to potential productions undertaken in the name of cooperative benefits to human being. Already now, probably, and if not now soon, we could, for instance, produce hybrids between, say, chimpanzees and humans or between bonobos and humans; and with further development and refinement, such hybrids might have human genetic sequences enabling them with greater intelligence and the power of speech. Why would humans want to do that? A likely reason-*cum*-justification would be to clean up dangerous messes made by humans — for instance, radiation-contaminated sites such as nuclear-power plants, not only those that have undergone accidental melt-down but also those that have reached the end of the power cycle and contain materials which, without some sort of treatment, will remain highly dangerous for tens of thousands of years. Would that be different from training dogs to sniff for bombs, even though accidents happen? Or dolphins to seek explosive devices attached to ships? And what of modifying horses through selective breeding (a long-practiced form of genetic engineering) to run ever faster races, even if some of them must be "put down" because of shattered cannon bones? Each is an exercise in writing the bounds of meaning of human being. *Blade Runner* invites some thoughtful consideration ahead of the curve, so to speak, not behind.[15]

THE RELATION OF DECKARD AND RACHAEL

About 20 minutes into film, Deckard, having accepted the assignment he could not refuse, visits the Tyrell Corporation in search of information. He has taken along an interrogation machine that was designed to detect replicants by analyzing emotive contents of their answers to certain questions. The corporate CEO, Eldon Tyrell, tells Deckard he wants first to see the machine in operation on a human being and suggests that his assistant, Rachael, be the first subject. When Deckard has finished the test, Tyrell dismisses Rachael. The following exchange ensues (at about 22 minutes):

Deckard: She's a replicant, isn't she?

Tyrell: I'm impressed. How many questions does it usually take to spot them?

Deckard: I don't get it, Tyrell.

Tyrell: How many questions?

Deckard: Twenty, thirty, cross-referenced.

Tyrell: It took more than a hundred for Rachael, didn't it?

Deckard: She doesn't know?!

Tyrell: She's beginning to suspect, I think.

Deckard: Suspect? How can it not know what it is?

Deckard's query raises issues of context and condition. First of all, of course, Deckard had assumed from context that Rachael was human. That it took as long as it did to detect the difference was impressive and disconcerting. Clearly the technology had advanced quite a lot. Was there more than his machine had detected?

Second, there is the matter of the pronoun switch. Having decided Rachael was replicant she becomes an it. Probably a habit acquired from his prior service as an exterminator, referring to a neutered object much as we speak of inanimate objects, animate objects of unknown gender (i.e., the speaker is either incapable or insufficiently interested to detect gender)[16], and sometimes immature specimens of a species, including children, Deckard's question now sets up an aural-visual incongruity; for Rachael's physical presentation is decidedly feminine to a degree that exalts a timeless standard of (Western conventional) female beauty and sexuality. Is Deckard displaying a latent anxiety about boundaries, the sort that a man exhibits when he thinks, "Before having sex with a woman, I need to know what she is, a prostitute or a potential wife"? At this point, only possibilities come to mind.

But third, it also seems that Deckard's query is conditioned on the assumption that any actor having as much intelligent capability as this model of replicant has displayed surely must know what it *is*. How could it not? Considerations of the consistency of biography and history lead us the viewers to suppose that Deckard had not experienced this unsettling gap between instrumental intelligence and self-awareness in his encounters with earlier models. Will this gap complicate his job? Are there moral considerations not previously troublesome to his "blade running" occupational ethic? Again, it is too early to say where possibility sorts into potentiality, potentiality into actuality.

What we do know from Deckard's question is that we are still in the midst of riddles of self-identity, self-knowledge, and their intersections with the meaning of being human. Is there a new avenue in this terrain? We shall see.

Tyrell answers Deckard by pointing out that Rachael was given a memory bank drawn from first-person memories of Tyrell's family members. As a technical matter the answer is satisfying, even charming, to us the viewers as to Deckard. Rachael knows all she needs to know, Tyrell is saying. If she comes upon a question she cannot answer, well, the all too human response is always available: "I don't know. I don't remember, or perhaps I've never known the answer to that. But if it's important I will try to find out." Implanted thought is hardly a novel technology, Tyrell could have continued:

> Think of your childhood education. Think of that enormous populating of your young mind: beginning with images and words from sources such as Aesop's fables, Margot Austin's Peter Churchmouse, Stevenson's Child's Garden of Verses, and the like; then on to more and more complicated furnishings – Euclid and his basic geometry of lines and angles, Archimedes and his experiments of buoyancy and displacement, Pythagoras and his number lines and triangles and pyramids, Newton and his laws of motion, Kepler and his planetary orbits, Chaucer and his tales of Canterbury travelers, Shakespeare's Julius Caesar, Hamlet, and company; and on and on. Remember those times when you thought your head would burst from too many people, too many places and dates, too many thoughts being crammed into that small space?! All of it amounted to implanted thought. An immense historical, cultural, social fabric was brought into mind: typically, things and relations among things, including other people and understandings of others' memories and understandings, including their understandings of who you were at any moment, which you then used to get a picture of how others saw you; and on and on. Remember that early twentieth-century social scientist, George Herbert Mead, whose account of the *social* self indirectly interrogated the limits of what counts as "prosthetic"? What then is so difficult to understand about Rachael?

But these technical matters fall short of Deckard's concern, as he will realize more and more during the next hours (i.e., ensuing minutes of the film). In effect, he will remember Russell's cautionary lesson about the limits of *both* reason *and* experience. Upon meeting Rachael, we, as Deckard, accumulate evidence that she possesses a rather typical self-identity. She knows her name, her boss, her duties at Tyrell Corporation. She recognizes that others recognize her and maintain relevant expectations. She recognizes a newly encountered other, whether human or replicant, and knows how to negotiate mutual interpretations. She recognizes that she can apprehend herself as others see her, and she can negotiate those interpretations accordingly. She knows the difference between trust and skepticism, between credibility and gullibility, and she knows the difference is finely graded. Deckard's point is, if she has all of that capability, how can she *not* know that she is in some sense "fake" – that is, not genuinely human, not a *real* human being, only a copy of one? Physically beautiful, highly intelligent, emotionally accomplished, socially adept: all of that, but *still a fake.*

From this point the film could have proceeded in different directions. It "chose" to open a Nietzschean text. I say "chose" with a certain distancing – not of irony but of mild alienation–because I do not know with enough specificity the writers' and director's intents.[17] Naming it "Nietzschean" is consummatory without monopolizing or even claiming inventor's rights to a cultural formation, larger than Nietzsche, no doubt, who nonetheless had no equal in the moment of insight. In opening this text, let's backtrack a bit, rejoin Aristotle and Augustine, among others, in a brief review of relativity–that is, relationship as a state but not a condition of relation. Here we begin again with Aristotle (not that he was the first to venture general thoughts about what "relation" *is*; but he had much to say).

Recall Aristotle's account of human being as a *zöon politikon*. One of the most often quoted phrases to serve as a sort of definition of "man," it places great emphasis on relations: human being *is* being, to be sure; but it is an inherently *relational* being, present in interdependencies. Probably for most readers with social science and/or humanities backgrounds, that is a pleasing thought. But bear in mind that, beginning at the beginning, so to speak, with his Philosophical Lexicon in *Metaphysics*, Aristotle treats "relation" and the "relative" as secondary, because reference is inherently to something else. It is not a substance but a term of logic that describes one number to another (the double, the quarter, etc.) or some other property such as actuality vis-à-vis potency, and so forth. So if what is most distinctive about human being is its inherent relationality, human being stands inherently as a lesser sort of being. Similarly for the Stoics, from whose perspective Augustine has assembled realities that were condition to his turn to the Christian absolute: relation was understood to be only an exercise of mind, having no extra-mental existence. In short, we are well on the trail of human being as a *deficient* being. This becomes part of a heated dispute of Christian Europe's late thirteenth and fourteenth centuries at Vallodolid, and elsewhere, more than a century before the previously mentioned debate at Vallodolid (see, e.g., Suárez [1597]2006; and for an overview, Henninger, 1989). Given the "fallen nature of man" that lay at the center of Christianity's earthly genealogical account, there was little latitude for a different understanding of what *zöon politikon* could mean.[18] Human being was a *weak* (*debilis*) being. The originary state of being human, seemingly graced by the divine, had been debilitated, whether by original plan or by hubris in an exercise of free will or by residual roots of the beastly world.

From Vallodolid, metaphorically speaking, we can skip generations and come first to Königsberg and Immanuel Kant — whose apprehension of human being as deficient being ("crooked timber") was tempered by the futurity of a hope for species maturity, responsibility, and autonomy — and thence (skipping Schilling, Hegel, etc.), Friedrich Wilhelm Nietzsche, whose inheritance included the German pietism of Kant's time but whose fashioning from that inheritance made of Kant, one might say, an ironizing apotheosis of the modern era.

Almost from the beginning, of course, Nietzsche was a controversy. And so he remains. Nominative phrases of "the modern" — the modern era, modern society, modernism, and so forth — are polysemous in the extreme. One of the traits that has united the messages, however, has been the penchant for rejection via representative emblem. For George Bowling, circa 1939, it was a long list of emblems of degeneracy, ranging from celluloid to rubbery sausages to arc-lamps blazing throughout the night. For Constance Chatterley, earlier in the century, the list included tin cans, india-rubber, platinum, and (again, or already) celluloid. For Nietzsche the list boiled down to one emblem, the nihilist mentality that was left behind to occupy all of the dead space after absolutist authority had dissolved. The space remained, an empty space; memory of an authority once complete and indubitable remained; so nihilism fed, and was fed by, a desperate hunger for recovery, a quest for the grail.[19]

For many people who have some awareness of the controversy of Nietzsche the chief focus is on his stance regarding all then-received morality, the principal one being, for his time and place, Christian morality. He spoke plainly his criticism of it, that it is a sort of slave morality. In order to appreciate his argument in its own terms, one must try to view it from a less Christian-centered perspective than is normal in Christian (or, for that matter, Islamic or Jewish) cultures. My focus here is a bit different, however. My aim is not to dispute anyone's religious belief system (though I confess I was mostly in agreement with Nietzsche's critique long before I had read the first sentence of his writings, and probably before I knew his name). Further, this is not the place to expound on the body of Nietzsche's work as a whole. My aim is to use parts of his critical thought as beacons to illuminate more of the film, *Blade Runner*. There is a musical significance in Nietzsche that reaches for the beyond of tomorrow, the sound of what one's voice or one's piano keys will yet say. It is projective before it is representative, and metaphorical before speech gathers it into a self-commentary. The relation of Deckard and Rachael calls upon the representing/represented self, which (as Goffman, 1974, more recently than Nietzsche, reminded us) conventionally appears to us as/in a secondariness–representing already represented beings-in-relation–which manages to live in and, so to speak, trade on (i.e., interpret, or as that verb says, set always momentary exchange rates or prices), while resisting direct address of, a looming question: *What then is left to be first?*[20]

Now, replicants are representations of human being. There is nothing new in that: so, too, are celluloid images, characters on a stage (Sophocles' siblings Electra and Orestes, Miller's salesman) or in a poem (Housman's Shropshire lad, Eliot's hollow man); the motion of a fully embodied woman walking down stairs in a two-dimensional painting (Duchamp); and, in another sense of piece-work, various applications (appliances) of human speech, human motion, human calculation; and so forth. But replicants such as Rachael and Roy Batty are restricted neither to residency in a viewer's mind nor to bioelectromechanical form or Gestalt of an *eidos*. Here, for Deckard, an eidetic of difference seems increasingly on verge of vanishing into an eidetic of identity that repeals the relation of difference by sucking its dimensionality of being – the space between sides, so to speak – into nothingness. This is not exactly a new trope in literary creation, to be sure. Brushes with it are at least as old as Achillean angst over the distance between hero and god, and film noir renditions of the inherent uncertainty of third-party loyalty (as in Simmel's *tertius gaudens*) have served as main line of tension for countless spy thrillers, matrimonial "diaries," and so on. But some films invite us to suspend disbelief one extra step, and *Blade Runner* does just that. Deckard (Ford's stoical stylism is especially effective in this) must deal with an issue of ambiguity at the juncture of epistemology and politics, or "claim to know" and "claim of authority": how to know/determine self *prior* to representation, as an act simultaneously of politics (authority) and aesthetics (rhetoric) as well as epistemic "discovery" (invention as truth-telling), that is, as an act that will inspire a legitimacy of endorsement, not merely of compliance)? What counts as "authentic"? – and what precisely can *that* mean as a pre-representational act, as an originary presentation? Revelation is always an easy answer. But here the grounds of revelation seem to have been monopolized between the mega-corporate Tyrell and the murderous Roy Batty (who, after all, only wants more life).

Nietzsche, too, rejected revelation as answer. Revelatory answers are of a piece with slave mentality, that ironized remnant of absolutism. Nietzsche does not dispute Kant's demonstration of the rational and experiential limits of human knowledge, and he recognized the force of Kant's assertion of what he (Kant) called "the necessity" of the transcendental illusion. That is, with the death of the absolute, the human knower is left to human devices–subjective principles, interests, perspectives, and so forth – but credibility (including first of all *self*-credibility) apparently cannot be had without proceeding as if those subjective principles, interests, and perspectives were in fact objective, even though this is to mistake "a subjective necessity of a connection of our concepts" (the logical relations that render them coherent, etc.) for "an objective necessity in the determination of things in themselves" (Kant, 1787, B354/A297). Nietzsche had no time for those who claim to be, as he said in *On the Genealogy of Morals* (1887[1968], p. 539), "mouthpiece of the 'in itself' of things, a telephone from the beyond" (whether that "beyond" be the otherworldliness of a divine presence or a direct, concept-free access to object as it is supposedly in its own metier and destiny). His rejections of such claims, and claimants, were usually scathing, as when he ridiculed those who are "credited with a direct view into the essence of the world, as through a hole in the cloak of appearance, and thought able, without the toil or rigor of science, thanks to this miraculous seer's glance, to communicate something ultimate and decisive about man and the world" (Nietzsche, 1886[1984], p. 113).

Others had done as much. Nietzsche took another step.

Earlier I referred to a passage that Izenberg (1992, p. 6) quoted from Hölderlin (see note 13, above). Here I want to add Izenberg's gloss of that passage:

> the self, as the passage from Hölderlin quoted above clearly shows, *knows* its own originary superiority, knows that it is the source of the idea of an objective absolute, but does not allow its knowledge in any way to shake its belief in the externality of the absolute and its ability to rely on it (Izenberg, 1992, p. 8).

While I remain less than confident that the quoted passage (a translation) and, even more, this gloss do convey Hölderlin's intents, I think that the gloss (and to that extent the quoted passage) is closer to Nietzsche's intents.[21] Closer to but not exactly Nietzsche. To be sure, Nietzsche's argument agrees with regard to "the source of the ideas of an objective absolute": it is a thoroughly human source (and resource, e.g., of manipulations). In addition, one can say that there is a sense in which his argument agrees about knowledge of human being's "own originary superiority" (though that sense has much to do with the emphatically assertive thrust of the announcement). But the difference of Nietzsche is this: on various occasions he proclaimed, sometimes in ringing tones, his "unconquerable mistrust" (or "distrust," depending on translator choice; Nietzsche, [1886]1968, p. 414) of "the *possibility* of self-knowledge." Think of that famous inscription on the Temple at Delphi – "gnōthi seautón"; or "nosci te ipsum," the Romans said (know thyself): repeated over and over, it has long been a catchphrase of teachers, healers, counselors, clergy, and more.

What could be more fundamentally vital, we are led to believe, than the imperative to "know thyself!" But for Nietzsche? *Per contra*: it is "a recipe for ruin" ("Untergang," a having gone down, a diminishment; or, recalling the Scholastics at Valledolid, a debilitatedness; Nietzsche, 1968[1908], p. 710).

One never knows "what one is" because one's being is always *in process* — and should be when it is not, when it has been stultified, oppressed, allowed to atrophy. "To become what one is, one must not have the faintest notion of *what* one is." Reciting "almost the most certain thing I do know about myself," Nietzsche referred to "a kind of aversion in me to *believing* anything definite about myself" ([1908]1968, p. 710; [1886]1968, p. 414). To know *what* one is relegates being to a fixation, impedes, even stills, its on-goingness, its striving to be more. This is not to deny history, biography, conditionality, or anything of the sort. But those are moments of a *past* time, and to let such moments rule the question of "What shall I do now?" is to engage in self-defeat. The answer to "What shall I do now?" is, or should be, the answer to "What shall I become?" — which is to say, *becoming* what I shall be. Any being is what it is of course as a consequence of conditions, contexts, causes, its biography and its history — which themselves are known only as present productions (whether written now or read now). In going on, if one does, one proceeds in/as a certain "psychology" of projection, however heavily conditioned in/as a "sociology," a "biography," a "history," it will have (inescapably) been. What choice is there? One goes on, to make more life, to become what one is; or one stultifies in the inertia of what one is, a mere outcome of past conditions.

What does all of that have to do with Deckard, and the Deckard-Rachael relation?

At some point between Deckard's question to Tyrell and his exit with Rachael, Deckard made something of those Nietzschean realizations his own. The tenor of ambiguity disallows nomination of a specific time-place as if marked by an act of revelation, a privileged claim to know the *what* (it is) of the moment of event. At some point Deckard's question about Rachael ceased to matter because the answer could no longer make any difference. The "space," so to speak, where that difference had once had possibility no longer exists. Where that space once was is now a liberated will to "more life," the will to move on, to make more being, without any particular promise or guarantee of outcome-of-being, without the stultifying anchorage of knowing *what* one is in the moment of moving on (so that moving on, making more life, can occur).

Bukatman (1997, p. 7) began his study of *Blade Runner* by observing that it "is all about vision. Vision somehow both makes and unmakes the self in the film, creating a dynamic between a centered and autonomous subjectivity (eye/I) and the self as a manufactured, commodified object (EyeWorks [a manufacturer of eyes for androids])." Vision as both sensibility and intelligibility, as both process of a here-and-now and as project-of-future, carries a heavy burden of continuity throughout the film, a continuity that calls out ambiguities (much as Goffman did with his interstitial question, "What is it that is going on here?"; e.g., Goffman, 1974, pp. 8ff). At key junctures in the film, that "calling out" is a matter of voice. The prime instance is Deckard's somewhat incredulous cry about Rachael, 22 minutes into the film: "How can [she] not know?"

The bleating plea of Deckard's voice urges us to believe in at least this one "rock-solid fact" – that Rachael truly did not know, truly had "lived" a life of naive innocence of self – and it is that solidity that then anchors us for the seemingly final turn: just as Rachael did not know, maybe Deckard also did not, does not, know? "Is he or isn't he?" – another almost-subrosa insistence about exposing true identity, another desperation to "get the facts right," another desperate effort to "move 'through the mirror' to the other side, as we could during the golden age of transcendence" (Baudrillard, 1991, p. 312).[22]

But maybe Rachael *did* know. Who's to say? Where better to hide, if you are an all-too-human replicant, one who has been mole at the highest level, than in the plain sight of (a post-epiphany maintained posture of) "self-ignorance"? – and then, when the hunt intensifies and the need for security against exposure rapidly grows, as comely pleasing companion to that most accomplished of renegade hunters, Rick Deckard? Maybe Rachael was canniest of them all.

But, no, what man would believe it? In a story as determinedly male-centered as *Blade Runner* (as in Dick's story) that reading of Rachael would not arise.[23]

The mirror to which Baudrillard referred is reflective, of course, because of the tain which we do not see. What does Deckard see in it? What does he see in it, more especially, when thinking of Rachael? The question of Rachael's early naïveté might be as easily reflective as not. Does Deckard wonder about himself? Who he is? Or rather – to recall his revision of his question about Rachael – *what* he is?

There is no resolution. Even with the "Hollywood ending" that some producers insisted be tacked on, the film does not attempt to overcome the "dilemma" of identity/difference. Ambiguity is maintained through the last frame. Gaffe, having apparently passed an easy opportunity to kill Rachael, intones his what-difference-does-it-make verdict – Oh, well, no one lives forever – which rekindles the romantic's transcendent hope in face of the apparent fact that neither Rachael nor Deckard is evincing any course beyond resignation in a private-dyad locale. The viewer is left to imagine what might yet develop from their late actions, what self-realizing motive-as-project might yet be reflected in those last witnessed actions. Life goes on. Revolutionary it will not be. But could it be?

Revolution is a public act, as is authority, the legitimacy of a power, the credibility of a voice. The dyadic microcosm at the end leaves open Nietzsche's question of an authority of voice. If Rachael and Deckard, whatever each may be, have achieved an insight about the identity/difference dialectic, they do not attempt to speak it to anyone else. Who would believe them? As Nietzsche (1886[1968], p. 414) asked, "Will people believe me?"

A CONCLUDING THOUGHT

Shortly after the turn of the twentieth century, shortly after Nietzsche's death, Charles Péguy (1910, p. 27) observed, "Tout commence en mystique et finit en politique." (Everything begins in mystique and ends in politics.) So it has been with *Blade Runner*, and every other initial ingenuity whether cinematic, musical, or otherwise poetic. In a moment of the experience of freshness, history has been held apart, a forgotten relevance, allowing a space of enchantment; but only then to notice that the enchantment has dissolved into ordinariness, as a history has resumed. The question is, do we learn anything in the process? For the human life form, according to a writer who was popular during the middle of Péguy's (our) bloody century, "all life is six-to-five against." Actually, those odds are not so bad. They could have been, might at any moment have become, as Damon Runyon appreciated, much worse. Are they now getting better? Or worse still? *Blade Runner* leaves the question to us. The year of *Blade Runner*, its turn at an enchantment, was a long time ago.

POSTSCRIPT (NOVEMBER 2017)

The foregoing essay was written in 2012. A number of cinematic changes have occurred during the past five years. I will note only one: the sequel, *Blade Runner 2049*, recently released, offers some revision of its past, so to speak, but I have not attempted to accommodate it (as I did not with Scott's "Final Cut" version, published in 2007). Other changes could be noted as well, but I will mention only one.

Changes other than cinematic during the past five years have too often been startling, distressing, and too often both. The entanglements resist a sorting into discrete items in a list. For those of us who are or have been educators, one of the most worrisome is the growing gap between what the proverbial average adult "needs" to know, ought to know in order to maintain competencies of various kinds, and what he or she does know. This gap comes to mind repeatedly from daily news. I was reminded of it again while reading the foregoing essay once again, after a lapse of quite some time (and this time to judge its resilience against the sequel). A little more than midway into the essay I referred to "high intelligence and super-human strength," in description of the new-model being as represented by Roy Batty. It now occurred to me that whereas "super-human strength" has long been a major problem (as well as benefit) for human life – imagine, for example, being crushed in the coupling of two railway carriages; no chance of deflecting harm by grabbing *that* steer by the horns – "high" or now "super-human intelligence" has been capturing more and more attention as threat as well as benefit. Here, too, historical perspective is important. While the nominative phrase, "artificial intelligence," is of recent currency, humans have been investing machines with algorithmic intelligence for a long time (e.g., autopilot, automatic shut-down circuits, automatic alert circuits, and so forth). But that same perspective highlights a new difference. Until recent years few if any programmers worried about investing human limitations, errors, or biases in their latest progeny of intelligent machines. Then the thought dawned, and that thought spawned another: instead of instructing the machine with what we know about this and that, let's teach the machine how to learn from its own experiences. Better yet, let's give an already smart machine the freedom to learn on its own, within a few broad parameters (sometimes only one, an operational definition of the goal). The result has been a massive increase in machine intelligence. One indication of that increase is given by the following. An ancient board game called Go is at one level very simple, at another very complex. There are 10^{170} legitimate moves on the playing board. (That number is more than twice the estimate of all atoms in the known universe.) A machine has mastered the game to a level that not only surpasses all reigning expert (human) players; these very players are now learning new strategies and tactics by studying records of the machine's games against itself. This is just a beginning. Machines can teach one another. Each new generation can begin at the level attained by the prior generation. Each human each generation must begin from scratch (not quite Locke's tabula rasa but close). Mind the gap. Unless the machines can explain to us, in a logic that we can understand, the process by which it arrived at its solution, we should quarantine the solution. The unknown unknowns could be terrifying.

NOTES

1. Lawrence Person (1998) gave this account in his "postcyberpunk manifesto" (note the past tense): "Classic cyberpunk characters were marginalized, alienated loners who lived on the edge of society in generally dystopic futures where daily life was impacted by rapid technological change, an ubiquitous datasphere of computerized information, and invasive modification of the human body." My Housman reference is to Number 12 in his poem cycle, *A Shropshire Lad* (1896).

2. Other of Dick's stories also became the bases of films, most notably *Total Recall* (1990; plus the 2012 remake), *Imposter* (2002), *Minority Report* (2002), *Paycheck* (2003), *A Scanner Darkly* (2006) and *The Adjustment Bureau* (2011). Influences of Dick in *The Matrix* sequence have been noted, in particular the notion that "the world we know [is] nothing more than an information grid" (Rose, 2003) — an old notion trading on material-and-ideal (form-and-content, matter-and-energy, etc.) dualities, extending from Plato through Christian doctrines to Spinoza and Hegel, on to Claude Shannon, Talcott Parsons' evolutionism, and Niklas Luhmann's ecological communication, but with new thrust and a virtual palpability in the new era of bio-engineering. A fitting biographic study of Dick is Carrère's ([1993]2004).

3. The volume of *Blade Runner* filmography is quite large. One of the best treatments, lean and incisive, is Bukatman's (1997) entry in the British Film Institute's Modern Classics series. Frank Rose's review of *Paycheck* in *Wired* magazine (Rose, 2003) situates *Blade Runner* within Dick's filmic afterlife; see also Gopnik (2007). Sammon (1996) offers an extensive account of the process of making the film. Essays collected by Kerman (1997) are also available.

4. Some viewers and film critics, it is true, found the script to be "muddled," "confusing," "inconsistent," "hard to follow," and the like. While the multiple rewrites did introduce some mistakes, the core of the negative response seems to be the ambiguity, which is indeed core to the film by design. Perhaps mass media viewers had been experiencing too much ambiguity, undecidability, etc., in their everyday lives to be happy facing still more of it on their screens of escapism.

5. All film making is highly tedious, contentious, stressful; *Blade Runner* was exceptionally so, by most accounts (see, e.g., Sammon, 1996). Scott was demanding, it is clear; but it is also clear that he, too, was under much pressure from various quarters, including those with the financing. It was mainly the latter, for instance, who insisted on the "riding into the sunset with the girl" ending, over Scott's objections. A "director's cut" (1992) restored the original ending (or at least one version of "original ending") and removed the voice-over narration by Ford, which producers also required as an aid to viewer comprehension. According to Scott in an interview with Sammon (1996, p. 377), this director's cut "is closer to what I was originally after." Note that there have been at least a half

dozen versions of the film. The 1982 release was soon supplanted for purposes of cable TV, video, and DVD release (until 1992 and the director's cut) by the international cut, which was slightly longer and more graphic in violence.

6. Borges ([1940]1962) used the same logical impossibility as a major thread in one of his most widely read stories, "Tlön, Uqbar and Orbis Tertius." There are rich veins of insight to be gained from careful readings of literatures on "false memories" (e.g., first-person reports, witness testimony, etc.), "alien" or "implanted thought," and similar topics (e.g., Stephens & Graham, 2000), both in their own terms and in relation with, e.g., Hegel's discussion of "unhappy consciousness" (Hegel [1807]1977, §117) and Sartre's "bad faith" (e.g., Sartre, 2000, pp. 147−185, esp. 167−169; also, Beauvoir, 1947). On the prevalence (obsessive, insistent, futile) of omphaloskepsis, see Hazelrigg (1995, pp. 85−108). One should bear in mind also that ambiguity and ambivalence, stablemates though they can be, are different. Ambiguity is primarily semantical; ambivalence, syntactical, and usually indicative at least of inconsistency if not outright contradiction.

7. Castiglia (2008) has given for the US antebellum period an analytic treatment, featuring names such as Timothy Shay Arthur and Nathaniel Hawthorne, that well matches earlier treatments of corresponding European examples such as Charles Dickens and Victor Hugo. See also Dumm (2002).

8. This "motto," as Sartre termed it, he wrote in an article, "A propos de l'existentialisme: mise au point," published in the periodical *L'Action*, 29 December 1944. I agree with McCleary's translation (Sartre, [1944]1985, p. 157) and have followed it. Note, however, that the verb "faire" is complex to an extent that no one word in English captures and includes meanings of "do," "act," "be," "form," as well as "make" and is the basis of a large number of idioms. It is probably the most often used verb in French. With that range in mind, I believe "to make" is the best choice of an English substitute.

9. Chapter 14 of Book 10 contains a discussion that several readers (e.g., Blanchet, 1920) have described as an early version of the argument known as Descartes' *cogito*; something of that argument can also be read in chapter 3 (i.e., the passages from 39 to 45).

10. The Augustine texts are cited from Augustine (1991) but have been referenced by book and chapter of individual works and thus can be read in any complete edition. Caner (2002) is good especially on the regulatory aspects of the monastic movement as a project of reflexive self-fashioning.

11. Here, too, a large literature exists. Pagden (1982) provides a reasonable point of entry.

12. With regard to the events of Valladolid, for instance, see the thirtieth of the first book of Montaigne's *Essays*.

13. Hölderlin was not always consistent, however. This passage is from a late poem, "In lieblicher Bläue" (Hölderlin, 1966), and there is reason to doubt its authorship. But that doubt pertains to various texts in Hölderlin's *oeuvre*, which exists in different official versions. Izenberg (1992, p. 6) quoted this passage from *Hyperion*:I know that it is only need that urges us to bestow on nature a kinship with the immortal in us, and to believe that there is a spirit in matter, but I know that this need justifies us in doing so. I know that where the beautiful forms of nature announce to us the divine presence, we ourselves project our own souls into the world; but what, indeed, is not what it is except through us?A bit startled to read such words by Hölderlin, I sought, without success, to read the passage in context in one or another of the (German) versions of the *Hyperion* text. Perhaps it is from some of the compositional remnants that have been retained. I return to the passage later.

14. For Hölderlin, on the other hand, self-knowledge was dependent on correct apprehension (or visiting) of the Absolute (such that the passage cited by Izenberg [see prior footnote] is perhaps less than it has been made to be). This is appropriate occasion to remember one of the (mostly unsung) greats of post-World War II German philosophy, Werner Marx (1924−1994), another member of the Marx family of Trier. For a sample of his work, see Marx, 1983 (1987).

15. Currently legal theorists are deliberating once again the boundaries, for example, of where/how prosthesis begins as an "add on" to the human body. If an ocular appliance

attached to my head brings me sight, how does that differ from your use of eyeglasses to restore acuity? Are there differences in legal rights? If the ocular appliance cannot be detached but by a medical specialist under surgical conditions, am I thereby deprived of right to travel by commercial aircraft? What are the appropriate legal conditions of search and seizure? If the appliance processes light much more efficiently and precisely, such that I can develop hand-eye coordination to a degree that makes the best baseball pitcher's suite of pitches rarely successful, does that mean I lose the right to compete for a position on a major-league baseball team? If the appliance enables me to lip-read at a line-of-sight distance of one mile, does that mean I lose rights of freedom of assembly? And if my appliance is capable of processing radiant energy beyond the "ordinary" visible-light spectrum (e.g., Superman's x-ray vision), then what?

16. Cockroaches are sexually dimorphic and gendered in behavior, but the victim of our extermination efforts is usually an it, seldom a she or he, even to the professional exterminator who is technically capable of seeing the difference.

17. That one of the writers, Fancher, stoutly insisted on maintaining a crucial ambiguity resulted in a condition that makes "Nietzschean" applicable even had none of the principals ever heard the name. The point will unfold.

18. It was here, note, that what came to be called a "doctrine of internal relations" was enshrined in Stoicism's compartment of the intra-mental − that is, existing only in mind.

19. Two brief histories of this process are by Gunter Remmling (1967) and Geoffrey Hawthorn (1987). Very popular in their respective days, they retain good value as overviews and, twenty years apart, as comparative windows interesting for their differences and similarities (to each other and to one's understanding today).

20. My first sustained engagement with Nietzsche, undertaken in the 1970s, was reported in Hazelrigg (1989, pp. 126−142). The case I was arguing has received much better presentation by Pippin ([2006]2010), which I sample below. Also, regarding Nietzsche's place in the scheme of philosophy–and especially its self-understanding as a non-ideological soterial discourse–see Pippin (1999, esp. pp. 116−118). Regarding my view of Goffman's place in this, see Hazelrigg (1992). The citations of George Bowling and Constance Chatterley are to characters by George Orwell (*Coming Up for Air*) and D H Lawrence (*Lady Chatterley's Lover*). My citation of "price" with regard to the verb "interpret" draws on the Latin etymology of the latter, the root word of which, prétium, generally translates as "price" or "worth" (as in Cicero's "certum prétium constituere," to fix the price).

21. And if indeed Hölderlin's, then the early nineteenth-century author of *Hyperion* and the late nineteenth-century author of *Beyond Good and Evil*, *Genealogy of Morals*, and so forth, were much nearer one another than I have appreciated.

22. Baudrillard cites some of Dick's works as exemplifying "a gigantic hologram in three dimensions, where fictions will never again be a mirror held to the future, but rather a desperate rehallucinating of the past"; and, one might say, as an advertisement of a world lacking "mirrors or projection or utopias as means for reflection" (Baudrillard 1991, pp. 310, 312). As much could be said of works by Borges. But given Borges' place in the historical record, his works gained the library classification, "magical realism, progenitor of."

23. It would be a step too far to describe *Blade Runner* as misogynist. Strictly speaking, that is. For such would imply that women had valued status in this world of 2019. Hate is expensive. Ignorance is cheap. Ask Rachael. Especially after her filmed life. Sammon (1996, p. 383) reported from his interview of Scott the latter referring to "this patriarchal technology [that] could create artificial women" who would surely be designed as "young and sexually attractive." It should be pointed out also (as Sammon did) that the only people we see Deckard kill are women.

REFERENCES

Augustine. (1991). *The works of St. Augustine*. Hyde Park, NY: New City Press.

Baudrillard, J. (1991). Simulacra and science fiction. A. B. Evans (Ed.). *Science Fiction Studies* (Vol. *18*) (November), 309−313.

Blanchet, L. (1920). *Les antécédents historiques du "Je pense, donc je suis"*. Paris: Félix Alcan.

Borges, J. L. ([1940]1962). Tlön, Uqbar and Orbis Tertius. In J. E. Irby (Ed.), *Labyrinths* (pp. 3–18). New York: New Directions.

Bukatman, S. (1997). *Blade Runner*. London: BFI.

Caner, D. (2002). *Wandering, Begging monks*. Berkeley: University of California Press.

Carrère, E. ([1993]2004). T. Bent (Ed.), *I Am alive and you are dead*. New York: Metropolitan.

Castiglia, C. (2008). *Interior states*. Durham, NC: Duke University Press.

Dahms, H. F. (2011). *The vitality of critical theory*. Bingley, UK: Emerald.

de Beauvoir, S. (1947). *Pour une morale de l'ambiguité*. Paris: Gallimard.

Dick, Ph. K. (1968). *Do androids dream of electric sheep?* Garden City, NY: Doubleday.

Dumm, Th. (2002). *Michel Foucault and the politics of freedom*. rev. ed. Lanham, MD: Rowman & Littlefield.

Goffman, E. (1974). *Frame analysis*. Cambridge: Harvard University Press.

Gopnik, A. (2007). Blows against the empire: the return of Philip K Dick. *The New Yorker, 83* (August 20).

Hawthorn, G. (1987). *Enlightenment and despair* (2nd ed.). Cambridge: Cambridge University Press.

Hazelrigg, L. (1989). *A wilderness of mirrors*. Gainesville: University Press of Florida.

Hazelrigg, L. (1992). Reading Goffman's framing as provocation of a discipline. *Human Studies, 15*, 239–264.

Hazelrigg, L. (1995). *Cultures of nature*. Gainesville: University Press of Florida.

Hegel, G. W. F. ([1807]1977). *Phenomenology of spirit*. A. V. Miller (Ed.). Oxford: Oxford University Press.

Henninger, M. G. (1989). *Relations: Medieval theories, 1250–1325*. Oxford: Clarendon.

Hölderlin, F. (1966). *Friedrich Hölderlin: Poems and fragments*. London: Routledge & Kegan Paul.

Housman, A. E. (1896). *A Shropshire lad*. London: Kegan Paul, Trench & Treubner.

Izenberg, G. (1992). *Impossible individuality*. Princeton: Princeton University Press.

Kerman, J. B. (1997). *Retrofitting Blade Runner* (2nd ed.). BowlingGreen, OH: Bowling Green State University Popular Press.

Marx, K. ([1932]1975). Economic and philosophic manuscripts of 1844. In K. Marx & F. Engels (Eds.), *Collected works* (Vol. 3, pp. 229–346). New York: International.

Marx, W. (1987[1983]). T. J. Nelson & R. Lilly (Eds.), *Is there a measure on earth?* Chicago: University of Chicago Press.

Nietzsche, F. ([1886]1968). Beyond good and evil. In W. Kaufmann (Ed.), *idem, The Basic Writings of Nietzsche* (pp. 181–435). New York: Modern Library.

Nietzsche, F. ([1886]1984). M. Faber & S. Lehmann (Eds.), *Human, all too human*. Lincoln, NE: University of Nebraska Press.

Nietzsche, F. ([1887]1968). On the genealogy of morals. In W. Kaufmann (Ed.), *The Basic Writings of Nietzsche* (pp. 439–599). New York: Modern Library.

Nietzsche, F. ([1908]1968). Ecce homo. In W. Kaufmann (Ed.), *The Basic Writings of Nietzsche* (pp. 657–791). New York: Modern Library.

Ollman, B. (1971). *Alienation*. Cambridge: Cambridge University Press.

Pagden, A. (1982). *The fall of natural man*. Cambridge: Cambridge University Press.

Péguy, C. (1910). *Notre jeunesse*. Paris: Cahiers de la Quinzaine.

Person, L. (1998). Notes toward a postcyberpunk manifesto. *Nova Express* 16 (later posted to Slashdot). Retrieved from http://slashdot.org/story/99/10/08/2123255/notes-toward-a-postcyberpunk-manifesto. Accessed on 12 October 2008.

Pippin, R. B. (1999). *Modernism as a philosophical problem* (2nd ed.). Oxford: Blackwell.

Pippin, R. B. ([2006]2010). *Nietzsche, Psychology, and first philosophy*. Chicago: University of Chicago Press.

Remmling, G. (1967). *Road to suspicion*. New York: Appleton-Century-Croft.

Rose, F. (2003). The second coming of Philip K Dick: the inside-out story of how a hyper-paranoid, pulp-fiction hack conquered the movie world 20 years after his death. *Wired* 11 (#12; December).

Russell, B. (1921). *The analysis of mind*. London: George Allen & Unwin.

Sammon, P. M. (1996). *Future noir*. New York: itbooks.

Sartre, J.-P. ([1944]1985). A more precise characterization of existentialism. In R. McCleary, M. Rybalka, & M. Contat (Eds.), *The Writings of Jean-Paul Sartre* (Vol. 2, pp. 155–160). Evanston, IL: Northwestern University Press.

Sartre, J.-P. (2000). *Essays in existentialism*. New York: Citadel.

Stephens, G. L., & G. Graham. (2000). *When self-consciousness breaks: Alien voices and inserted thoughts*. Cambridge: MIT Press.

Suárez, F. ([1597]2006). J. P. Doyle (Ed.), *On real relation*. Milwaukee, WI: Marquette University Press.

Veyne, P. ([1983]1988). P. Wissing (Ed.), *Did the Greeks believe in their myths?* Chicago: University of Chicago Press.

von Goethe, J. W. ([1808]1952). *Faust. Part 1*. G. M. Priest (Ed.). Chicago: Great Books.

SOCIOLOGY AT THE END OF HISTORY: PROFESSION, VOCATION AND CRITICAL PRACTICE

Daniel M. Harrison

ABSTRACT

As the social scientists of modern society, sociologists find themselves in a peculiar situation. Human civilization appears on the brink of collapse; the ravages of global capitalism are turning natural and social orders upside down. Some theorists are declaring the "end of history," while others wonder if humans will soon become extinct. People find themselves increasingly shouldering burdens on their own, strangers to themselves and others. Struggles for recognition and identity are forged in harsh landscapes of social dislocation and inequality. The relationship of the individual to the state atrophies as governmental power becomes at once more remote and absolutely terrifying. How are we as sociologists expected to theorize under such circumstances? What implications result for the mission of sociology as a discipline and area of study? What political initiatives, if any, can counter these trends?

This chapter provides an immanent critique of sociology as a profession, vocation, and critical practice. Sociology today (in the US and around the globe) faces fierce social, economic, and political headwinds. The discipline continues to be a perilous choice as a vocation for independent researchers as much as the shrinking professoriate. Yet while the traditional functions of sociology are thrown into doubt, there has been an increase in critical practices on the part of some sociologists. As institutional norms, values, and traditions continue to be challenged, there will be passionate debates about the production of social worlds and the validity claims involved in such creation. Sociologists must play an active role in such discourse. Sociology is needed today as a mode of intervention as much as occupational status system or method of inquiry.

Keywords: End times; profession; vocation; praxis; sociology; critical theory

The Challenge of Progress: Theory Between Critique and Ideology
Current Perspectives in Social Theory, Volume 36, 133–155
Copyright © 2020 Emerald Publishing Limited
All rights of reproduction in any form reserved
ISSN: 0278-1204/doi:10.1108/S0278-120420190000036018

INTRODUCTION

Whither the labor of sociology in the world, here now at the "end of history"? To think that, less than a generation ago as we prepared for the new millennium, the world was celebrating globalization, international capitalist development, and all wonders technology had to offer. Today that vision of the future has all but disappeared. First came the attacks of September 11, 2001, and then the "War on Terror" followed, which continues to this day. For individuals, organizations, and societies, these are often frightening and dangerous times. Much of the world now is embracing anti-globalization, experiencing widespread inequality and warfare, and questioning the merits of the administrative/technological society. The election of the 45th President of the United States saw the emergence of social and political forces shaping contemporary US society that we are only just beginning to understand. In the sociology of knowledge, the ideology of these forces might be described as a virulent form of neo-barbarism, an authoritarian, hegemonically-masculine worldview wrapped up in white ethno-nationalism, false populism, and jingoistic conservativism. This movement and worldview, with more or less openly racist and sexist rhetoric, unadulterated chauvinism, and paranoid conspiratorial thinking, now infects a small but sizeable portion of the US population. The current President of the United States is disliked by more than half of the American electorate,[1] yet he expects 100% submission from his subjects (see Robinson, 2017). This creates significant problems for democratic governance.[2]

Just how should social theorists and sociologists try to understand this peculiar state of affairs, which impacts people not just in the United States, but all across the planet? At the macro level, there is a widespread sense of people living on the edge. Human societies appear to be spinning out of control, as they try to come to terms with complex and intractable social, economic, and cultural problems. Our worlds are increasingly catastrophic. Natural disasters (fires, tornadoes, and hurricanes) are no longer the rare events they appeared to be a few years ago, but are now regular features of the landscape. Mass shootings occur at places once considered safe, for example, in churches, hotels, and schools.[3] Risks in society are multiplying. People are dying younger and in more tragic ways (through drug overdoses, suicides, and car accidents) (Boddy, 2017). Meanwhile, the political class evades responsibility for fixing these problems and is focused much more on simply running for office (and then getting reelected) than actually governing. Economically, the stock market (at the time of writing, at least) is still flying high, but the national debt continues to accelerate and is now over US$21 trillion, up from $9 trillion just ten years ago.[4] The US social contract, once the envy of the world, lies in tatters. An authoritarian billionaire TV personality is the most powerful man on the planet. Culture has become a carnival hall of mirrors.[5]

Sociology is supposed to be the science of civilization. But how does one practice sociology when its object of study becomes more uncivilized by the day? How do we explain this turn of events to ourselves, our students, each other? "All that is solid melts to air," Marx and Engels (1978[1848], p. 476) once quipped about the revolutionary character of capitalist society. This quotation seems particularly apropos to our current situation. The sand is shifting beneath our feet. Our social institutions are wobbly, some on the verge of collapse. As the discipline that has as a central mission trying to understand the changing nature of society, just how should sociology respond to the predicament in which we find ourselves? Just what, if anything, should sociologists do?

The "Culture Wars" that Pat Buchanan and Ralf Reed championed in the 1980s have become a basic aspect of social life in the United States. Race, class and gender inequalities are increasing. Ideologues like Stephen Bannon[6] try to spin a narrative that Trump and his associates are champions for the US working class, but such a claim is laughable in light of the specifics of their agenda. Trump & Co. talk a good game when it comes to blue-collar politics,[7] but in reality, implement policies that do very little to help their constituents. The old "bait-and-switch" routine is found as often among the politicians as among the conmen. Take, for example, tax reform, Trump's signature victory during his first two years in office (Tankersley, Kaplan, & Rappeport, 2017). In their analysis of the legislation, the nonpartisan Congressional Budget Office (CBO) showed that wealthy Americans had the most to gain from the GOP tax plan (BBC News, 2017). While many families would see a small tax decrease (about US$1,300 or so) in the short run, these middle-class families would, in fact, pay more in over time. Yet tax decreases for corporations and wealthy Americans are permanent. This discrepancy does not bother advocates of the legislation who simply ignore this information (not to mention the $1.4 trillion dollars that are expected to be added to the deficit) and argue that the CBO hasn't appreciated the wonders of the trickle-down economic theory. Advocates of Trump's tax plan suggest that the average worker will be soon receiving a US$4,000 annual raise, but like the proverbial carrot on a string in front of the horse, this remains a fantasy (Lovelace, 2018). The President of the United States can claim with a straight face that the legislation will "cost me a fortune" (Tankersley, 2017), and in the same way that his followers blindly accepted his promises and assertions on the campaign trail, they continue to believe him now (see Aslan, 2017). The penchant for the Trump administration to twist the truth, constantly change the narrative, and rely on fragmentary and false information has worrying consequences across society. However, it is especially problematic for sociology since it is the discipline which is supposed to know what is really going on. How can one objectively speak of, let alone study, the social world under such bizarre social conditions?

We are stuck, or so it seems, in a Baudrillardian kind of nightmare, a *Black Mirror* episode that never ends. Perhaps it is time to dig out all those postmodernism books of the early 1980s. Even Stephen Bannon uses postmodern nomenclature as he champions the "deconstruction of the administrative state" (Rucker & Costa, 2017). Yet the absurdity and spectacular singularity of the current moment should not blind us to the pain, suffering, and social isolation affecting many in society, all of which are likely to get worse in the years ahead. The social destruction at the end of history has hit the vulnerable and disadvantaged the hardest. From the dismantling of the social safety net to the impacts of climate change, it is the poorest and the most disadvantaged, especially members of minority populations, who are always the worse off. Just who today speaks for the downtrodden and the oppressed?

According to the philosopher Slavoj Žižek, "the global capitalist system is approaching its apocalyptic zero point." Žižek claims that this apocalypse is being driven by four main factors:

> the ecological crisis, the consequences of the biogenetic revolution, imbalances within the system itself (problems with intellectual property; forthcoming struggles over raw materials, food and water), and the explosive growth of social divisions and exclusions. (Žižek, 2011, p. x)

Žižek is, of course, not the only theorist, philosopher, or writer to address these sorts of issues. Readers of Ulrich Beck (1986) might see parallels to his concept of "risk society." We could also mention Jared Diamond's (2005) work on civilizational collapse, Noam Chomsky's (2006) writing on "failed states," and George Packer's (2013) *Unwinding* of America. All of these works speak to and seek to understand the very real threats that are currently facing humanity.

Michael Hardt and Antonio Negri remind us in *Empire* (2001) how the modernist era assumed a functionality in social institutions which postmodernism calls into question. In modern societies, it was assumed that institutions such as the economy, schools, and governments, for example, could actually succeed in their attempts to solve the problems facing them. In postmodern societies, on the other hand, there is no such expectation of confidence. More often than not, it is assumed that institutions simply do not or will not work; they cannot be reformed. They are viewed as inherently dysfunctional and riddled with crisis.[8] One sees such postmodern dysfunctionality all around us today, in the media, in education, the criminal justice system, and in the government. The state as an ethical body has failed the populace. The government has been sold to the highest bidder (Associated Press, 2017). No one is minding the store.

The neo-conservative/ethno-nationalist movement of the current epoch is markedly different from the austerity conservatism of the 1970s and 1980s. Whereas Margaret Thatcher and Ronald Reagan pushed for a "starve the beast" approach when it came to the government, Trump & Co. want to kill off the beast entirely. Once this agenda is understood, many of the rather apparently murky decisions of the current administration suddenly make a lot more sense. The intention is to unmake or eliminate key state institutions that have, until very recently, been considered essential to the public good.[9] Examples can be seen in administrative changes to policies at the US State Department, the US Department of Education, the US Department of the Interior (see Siegler, 2017), the Environmental Protection Agency, and NOAA. These agencies are all undergoing massive restructuring and are facing huge budget cuts. Because of such reactionary efforts, the government as protector and guarantor of the social contract recedes further from the concrete life of people in society. The individual is left more or less to his or her own devices.[10]

However, while the Trump administration is deconstructing the administrative state, it is at the same time reconstructing or fortifying the US military state, which requires constant financial support from the taxpayer. The military and police are essentially the only governmental institutions tolerated by neo-conservative, ethno-national ideology.[11] Otherwise, the state is viewed as a bumbling, meddlesome entity that just gets in the way of business and should be destroyed (see Sebestyen, 2017). The current disinvestment and *de facto* privatization of the US government and society will likely accelerate in the years ahead. The impact of these social changes on what is left of the welfare state, civil society, the environment, public universities and colleges, and the sciences – including the social sciences and, more specifically, sociology – are chilling and consequential. In a recent interview, Francis Fukuyama (author of the *End of History and the Last Man* 2006[1992], a book once held up as an exemplar of the triumph of global neo-liberal capitalism) admitted, "Twenty-five years ago, I didn't have a sense or a theory about how democracies can go backward." Today, he says, "I think they clearly can" (Tharoor, 2017).

Given such social and political conditions facing US society, just how do we practice sociology today? These issues go to the very heart of the discipline. Indeed, as Dr Eduardo Bonilla-Silva, past president of the American Sociological Association, stated on a panel discussion at the ASA's 2017 conference: "God supposedly created the world in six days, Trump in six months has come close to destroying it" (Flaherty, 2017). Bonilla-Silva is not simply stating his personal opinion here, but is rather offering a sociological account of what the policies of the newly elected President are doing to US society. His remarks provide sociologists with an opportunity for self-reflection and social inquiry. How do we engage as sociologists when civilization itself seems at risk of being annihilated? How is it possible to teach and conduct research, let alone understand or affect change in society? How should sociologists respond, professionally, personally, and collectively to the new world we are living in? In what follows, I develop provisional answers to these questions by considering the state of sociology today in terms of profession, vocation, and critical practice. Embedded in my remarks is a heuristic, research program for doing sociology during the "end times."

SOCIOLOGY AS A PROFESSION

To use the language of the accrediting institutions, just what is our assessment of sociology as an academic profession in contemporary society? It has been a century since the death of Emile Durkheim (Lukes, 1985), a figure arguably most responsible for the intellectual enterprise known to most of us today as "sociology."[12] Just what remains of Durkheim's legacy and his conceptualization of the discipline? How fares the science of "social facts"? To borrow a quote from Bentz and Shapiro (1998, p. 1), I think it is safe to say that it is still the "best of times" and the "worst of times" for sociology as an academic discipline, as it is for much of the social sciences. On the one hand, it seems that never before has sociology had it so well. The information revolution, while not without negative unintended consequences (such as the health costs of being tethered to a computer all day), has allowed for increased efficiency and heightened productivity on the part of knowledge workers. For example, no longer do we have to trudge over to the library to find and then photocopy the journal article we are looking for — it is available in an instant. We are capable of accessing all sorts of facts, figures, and information in a similar fashion. The craft of sociology (Alford, 1998) is changing. Word processing and presentation software make it easier to write and share research. There is a vibrant methodological pluralism within sociology today, as well as openness to interdisciplinary collaboration outside the discipline. No longer must sociologists be forced to choose between rigid qualitative and quantitative research camps. For example, hermeneutics, content analysis, network analysis, visual sociology, action research, and many more methods are now rightly considered legitimate tools for studying society. Reserves of "big data" as well as the rich details found in historical archives (of say, diaries, photographs, and sound recordings) allow sociologists to probe deeply into the social landscape in ways that once seemed impossible. Conferences, webinars and academic websites allow for scholarly relationships and opportunities to grow through collaboration across the globe. In this regard, sociology seems to be doing quite well.

On the other hand, these are also dark days for sociology. The number of sociological adherents, like church attendees, is shrinking. Certainly, the percentage of tenured and tenure track teaching positions in the US academic sociology is getting smaller (McKenna, 2016). Most students who are exposed to sociology do so now in general education classes where they receive instruction from adjuncts or graduate students (Edmonds, 2015). Tenure-track lines in sociology are being cut, and then not filled or replaced with part time or nontenure track positions (Ennis, 2011). Such decisions make sense for budget-conscious institutions seeking flexibility in a tight labor market, but the consequences of replacing professorial lines with part-time contract workers are deleterious to the quality of teaching and learning, the production of research, and service commitments within and outside the academy.

As might be expected, this decline of the sociological professoriate has led to a corresponding drop-off in student interest in sociology.[13] In the 1960s and 1970s, students flocked to sociology as a major to help change the world. Students had an activist interest in reforming society and tackling persistent inequalities. Though that concern still exists, students more often today are self-interested, careerist, and apolitical. They are also paying considerable amounts of money to attend college or university. Some schools have experienced a very sharp decline in sociology majors as students enroll in what they see as more lucrative degree programs. Sociology programs are used to fighting with other disciplines on campus to keep up their enrollments. Today this competition has expanded to out-of-state schools and online institutions. It is a very competitive market for college students these days, a situation exacerbated by demographic changes (the so-called baby-bust) which have created fewer 18−22-year-olds who want to go on to pursue a college degree.[14] At the same time, degrees offered in more seemingly topical fields such as critical media studies, gender and ethnic studies, and sports management, poach students away from sociology. Sociology is also seen (wrongly, I would argue) as antithetical for students majoring in business[15] or nursing, so we lose more potential students there.

Moreover, sociology still faces its perennial problem of being viewed as an "easy" major[16] by faculty and staff on campus, as well by as parents of prospective students, and by many in society as a whole. Partially because of such factors, many sociology students come to the discipline relatively late in their educational careers and only after trying a number of other majors first.

There is of course is a productive core of high-status professional sociologists who work at elite institutions, publish their research in top journals and serve in leadership roles throughout the profession. The whole carousel (see Dahms, 1998) of academic production is thereby kept in motion, but the notion of sociology as publically relevant enterprise is disappearing.[17] Certainly, sociology has its share of stars or superheroes, such as Alice Goffman (with her 2014 book *On the Run*), Sudhir Venkatesh (especially his 2008 *Gang Leader for a Day*) or Annette Lareau (*Unequal Childhoods*, 2003). There is obviously high-level sociological work being published in places like *American Sociological Review*, *American Journal of Sociology*, *Social Forces*, and *Social Problems* (not to mention in the pages of this very journal!) Looking beyond the top tier publications, there is also a large (and growing) population of less selective journals where sociologists can also publish their work. Yet it is a bit like having 500 cable channels on television and still finding nothing worth watching. Even with all the published material at our disposable, and in spite of all the books that continue to go to press, there remains a gnawing sense that so very little of such output speaks to the core of what sociology is or could be. Not only is so much of the work published in sociology journals incomprehensible to a general reader, but the rest is also too often mediocre, uninspired, or consists simply of bad writing. The situation brings to mind one of the most biting lines in *Souls of Black Folk* where W.E.B. Du Bois writes that "while sociologists gleefully count his bastards and his prostitutes, the very soul of the toiling, sweating black man is darkened by the shadow of a vast despair" (Du Bois, 1897). Just what are sociologists (collectively and individually) doing about such despair (not just as it pertains to African-Americans, but to all people)? How is the discipline improving the human condition?

In face of all the information publically and privately accessible in the knowledge economy – on television and radio, in newspapers, journals, books, articles and reports, for example, not to mention all the blogs, tweets, and other posts on social media, the voice of the sociologist has become muted. It is likely to become even more so in the years ahead. The National Rifle Association recently declared war on academic, political and media "elites."[18] Neo-conservative ethno-nationalists have little regard for any science, let alone a social science like sociology, long considered by the right as a base for liberal (if not socialist or communist) propaganda. In many societies (such as Scandinavia and Europe) the research and perspectives of sociology are appreciated and often taken into consideration in the formulation of social and political policy. The perspective of social science is valued. Not so in the United States, where politicians cherry-pick the social science data that best supports their position and ignore the rest. "The elites don't need us," goes the unspoken adage in sociology, and it is true. Witness the brouhaha after Justice John

Roberts used the term "sociological gobbledygook" during a Supreme Court hearing (Bonilla-Silva, 2017). In today's society, there is widespread questioning of the value of academic research. As religious fundamentalism recolonizes more of US culture, the view for many is there is "nothing new under the sun"[19] to be found in the academy. In a peculiar reversal of status signifiers, many now consider ignorance a virtue, a view that is also embraced by the so-called leader of the Free World.[20] Colleges and universities will continue to play an important social role as agents of socialization and offer important rites-of-passage for students, but the knowledge gained in such spaces will continue to be diminished relative to the world outside them, as well as on the Internet.[21]

Going forward, it is possible that elites will become even more openly hostile to academics and the role of colleges and universities in society today (except of course, when they are speaking of their own alma mater). Forget the "fake news." What about "fake sociology," or "fake professors"? It is disturbing to think of a world where sociologists are considered "enemies of the people,"[22] but in many respects we are already there. Once the authorities declare war on journalists, the attacks on college professors will not be far behind. Indeed, this very story can be found in rightwing literature like Andrew McDonald's *Turner Diaries*, 1999[23] a work that at times looks frighteningly prophetic when we consider events like the "Unite the Right" march in Charlottesville, VA, in August 2017.

Even without such political obstacles confronting us, the situation would be quite difficult for sociology as a profession today. A profession normally tries to monopolize its skillset. Yet today, largely due to the Internet, sociological content has escaped the confines of the Ivory Tower and has become a part of the collective conscience of society. Who needs people to teach sociology when it is all freely available online, anyway? And just as the sociological content goes on the Internet, online content (e.g. blogs, tweets) becomes part of sociology. And why not? Of course, sociologists should be discussing Instagram photos or Facebook memes in their Social Inequality or Feminist Theory classes. Or share and discuss them with the folks at the next conference. Fifty years ago, sociologists were anxiously debating the "blurred genres" (Hazelrigg, 1989a, p. 33) of interdisciplinary boundaries. Today the lines between these genres are often effaced entirely. In some cases, there is outright poaching of sociological content. Professors of business, for example, often spend considerable time talking about power relationships and the importance of culture. They speak as if they are the rightful experts in these areas without acknowledging their intellectual debts to the social scientists, particularly anthropologists and sociologists (see Thompson, 2014).

The increasing cost of college tuition is also making things difficult for sociology as a profession. As state governments have withdrawn financial support for colleges and universities, the cost of tuition has been rising tremendously (Jamrisko & Kolet, 2014). It is likely that this is making students more instrumental in their course selection, decisions which are often are ultimately made by anxious, check-writing parents. Given the current political climate, one might predict a continuing turning away from majors that do not seem to allow a fast route to a lucrative career. Sociology would seem to be included in that group

(Strauss, 2017). With declining enrollments, many departments will increasingly have difficulty recruiting new students, which could then lead them into a kind of death spiral. With this lost revenue from tuition, departments would also be hard-pressed to find resources for faculty grants, conference travel and sabbaticals, thus decreasing the faculty's quality of life. The perquisites once associated with working as a professional sociologist now exist only for a small subset of the professoriate. For the rest, a sort of proleterianization of labor has become the norm.[24]

Overall, 100 years after his death, the luster of Durkheim's vision for sociology has faded. Durkheim was adamant that a legitimate science must have its own subject matter. In the case of sociology, Durkheim declared our subject matter to be social facts — external constraints on human action. He believed it was the sociologist's job to investigate and analyze such facts and in so doing would develop universal laws of the human condition. Yet over time, this proposed empirical study of social constraints (and the history of them) has largely devolved into a discipline that teaches assessable skills of reading comprehension, writing, critical thinking, statistics, and research. While all of this is somewhat understandable (after all such skills are much easier to measure than "sociology" writ large), there is nothing particularly sociological about them. Indeed, they are found in many different disciplines within colleges and universities, not to mention in state agencies, the private sector, and so on. Meanwhile the rich analysis of the social facts (constraints) that should be the focus of sociological inquiry in the first place is often forgotten after the fact. More often than not, genuine sociologies of the social landscape are more promised than delivered.

Ironically, while academic sociology departments might suffer from identity crises and institutional neglect, the need for sociology "on the ground" so to speak, is today more important than ever (Irwin, 2017; Smith, 2016). Even if sociology does not get completely squeezed out of academia, this will of course not mean that social facts will cease to exist or that sociological work won't be required. It will simply be practiced by nonacademics in think tanks, at nonprofits, in private institutes, and so on. At some level, professional sociology will clearly survive. Nevertheless, it will likely play a less institutionally relevant role in society than it has done in previous years. One can see glimpses of such a future in the decline of the sociologist as a public figure. For example, with the exception of luminaries such as William Julius Wilson, there are few contemporary sociologists who today serve as public intellectuals in US society. It is hard to find the American equivalent of say, an Anthony Giddens or a Pierre Bourdieu, in contemporary US society. Sociology as a discipline seems to be fading away, like philosophy, and Greek and Latin before it. While the death of sociology has been heralded before (see Gouldner, 1970), it seems we are closer now to actually putting the body in the ground. There has been a dramatic shift in the episteme undergirding academic knowledge which is beyond the control of any institutional actor or group of actors. Certainly as long as humans exist they will forever be trying to understand the social forces around them. But how much longer will people use sociology (at least as we understand it today) to do so?

SOCIOLOGY AS VOCATION

Having addressed some macro-level concerns surrounding issues of sociology as a profession in contemporary society, we now turn to more micro-level questions of sociology as a vocation. A vocation, that is, a calling to or an affinity for a career or a way of life can be seen as the interior face of a profession; these two aspects rise and fall together. How one manages to practice a vocation in the context of a profession, such as sociology, which is undergoing dramatic and rapid change, is a difficult dilemma indeed. How do individual teachers, scholars, and citizens who identify themselves as sociologists think about the direction the discipline is taking? How is the vocation of the sociologist changing?

Notwithstanding the religious connotations of the term, it seems it would be well worth investigating the presence or absence of a "calling"[25] among self-identified sociologists. Have we sociologists − you or me, for example − been *called* to do what we do? It would be an interesting empirical study to inquire into how professional sociologists first encountered the discipline. Anecdotally at least, it seems many sociologists often take a circuitous route getting there. They did not start out in sociology initially but were drawn to the discipline over time. You can see this pattern in the case of Talcott Parsons, for example, who studied biology as an undergraduate (see Dillon, 2014) or in the case of Earl Babbie (author of the best-selling research methods books), who refers to his sociological career an "accident" (Schaar, 2015). Yet when inquiring souls do eventually stumble upon sociology, they quickly know they have found their place. This is at the heart of C. Wright Mills' often cited yet little understood concept of the "sociological imagination" − that "Aha" moment of epiphany which convinces us all of a sudden that not only is the sociological perspective a powerful one, but it is one is also that right for "us." Once people discover sociology and the rewards of the sociological perspective, they quickly understand its value. They become one of the converted.[26]

Yet the duration of such sociological epiphanies remains an open question. Just what happens to the calling in the longer run? Certainly one would need to consider variations in the social-psychological makeup of individual sociologists, for example, in terms of motivation, perseverance, productive ability, creative thought, and so on, not to mention the good luck of avoiding contingencies of illness and bad health that can get in the way. But in the main, the concept of a calling, for Martin Luther as much as ourselves, is only useful in so much as it is practiced. On this issue, we can turn to sociological elder Max Weber (1958 [1922]) who says that in sociology you must work as if your very life depended on it. As Weber writes in "Science as a Vocation":

> And whoever lacks the capacity to put on blinders, so to speak, and to come up to the idea that the fate of his soul depends on whether or not he makes the correct conjecture at this passage of this manuscript as well may stay away from science.

Weber called this the "personal experience" of science, which he described as a "passion," a "strange intoxication," "ridiculed by every outsider." Weber claims that, without such passion, "you have no calling for science and should do something else. For nothing is worthy of man as man unless he can pursuit it with passionate devotion" (Weber, 1958[1922], p. 135). It would be an interesting project to survey say, professional sociologists around the world and ask them about their "passionate devotion" to the field today. Can such passion still be found among the ranks of contemporary sociologists, or is it missing in action? The mark of a true intellectual (sociologist or not) is one who reads, writes, and thinks − off-the-clock. Everyone else is just phoning it in to get a paycheck. The real scholars are the ones who were doing the work well before the paychecks began and will continue doing so long after the paychecks stop coming. And while it is certainly true that in contemporary sociology (and surely this is the case of much of the academia) that there are plenty of intelligent and creative minds doing excellent work, there are also many who spend their time gaming the system, doing the bare minimum to scrape by, counting down the seconds to the end of the workday, and so on. Moreover, persistent attacks on the profession of sociology lead to a diminution in sociology as a vocation. Rather than being perceived as an area of study that provides valuable insight into the nature of society and the body politic, sociology and the rest of the social sciences have become, for many at least, an irrelevant annoyance to be avoided.

This state of the discipline makes career prospects quite daunting for the young sociologist. Job searches with two hundred applicants are now the norm at many institutions. Even if individuals are lucky to find a full-time position, the faculty is often overworked and undercompensated. In some locales, adjunct instructors scrape together a living while spending their time driving between different institutions, or increasingly teach online. Overwork can lead to depression, burnout, and exhaustion. It is likely that such trends will continue in the age of Trump as the man and his supporters evince no value for a liberal arts education in general or for social science in particular. Sociologists must also successfully manage to work in a near perpetual state of distraction in which so many people live their lives today, and which makes it so difficult to think deeply (in a philosophical or theoretical sense), about the world around us. From Facebook, the latest tweets from the President, Words with Friends or Candy Crush (take your pick), and so on, at the level of "everyday life"[27] − thanks to the ubiquity of smartphones and other omnipresent gadgetry − we are constantly faced with the temptation of doing anything *other* than sociology. It is so much easier just to pick up a device than it is to engage a qualitatively different sort of object, let alone actually interact with other human beings (especially in real time). In such a manner, all sorts of "screen time" are making the idea of sociology as a vocation, highly problematic. One is pulled today in so many different directions (social, temporal, virtual, etc.) at once. The rewards of careful scholarship are increasingly illusory when measured against the pleasure and spectacle of the (social) media apparatus.

Of course, the identity of the sociologist today is not simply tied to the office or the classroom. It is possible that the "passionate devotion" to one's vocation described by Weber is now, for many people today, spread out over a number of distinct realms of social life. The sociologist becomes "called" to different research interests, activities, and specializations, inside and outside the class-room, and these may vary over the course of a career. While not all sociologists are political in orientation, some are "called" to practice a fusion of politics and sociology. For such individuals, the vocation of the sociologist is to be at once an activist and a scholar.[28] These intellectuals believe that the sociologist should not only understand, but also actively intervene in and, in so doing, change the world. This brings us to the topic of sociology as a form of critical practice.

SOCIOLOGY AS CRITICAL PRACTICE

This essay is a reflection on the practice of doing sociology in the "end times." So far, we have discussed sociology as a profession and as a vocation. I have suggested that sociology as a profession is atrophying. Because of this, the vocation of the sociologist has become more tenuous. These are perilous times for knowledge workers across the social sciences. However, as we will see, things may not be as bleak as they may first appear. In part because of the challenges faced by sociology as a profession and as a vocation, there are increased opportunities for using sociology to change the world for the better. Such opportunities allow us to conclude this work on a slightly more positive note.

Thanks to the work of one of our disciplinary founders, Karl Marx, sociol-ogy has never simply been just about the knowledge created about society, but it has been equally concerned about changing the material conditions in society for the better. Since Marx developed his own immanent critique of society (which evaluates the validity claims of actors and institutions by comparing them with empirical realities on the ground), sociology has contributed to criti-cal forms of practice − interventions in society to close the gap between "what is" and "what ought to be" (see Hazelrigg, 1989b, p. 283). As sociologists, we have the "expectation of living in a humane world based on mutual respect and solidarity" (Müller-Doohm, 2014, p. 31). Making this world a reality involves engaging in democratic action. Sociologists have a moral responsibility to describe other, more humane and just ways of living, counterpoised to the cur-rent order. Sociologists are among the ones who must hold society up to a higher standard. While such standards have been under attack and may con-tinue to be so in the years ahead, the story of the 45th President's first two years in office is (at the time of this writing) as much about the resistance to his rule than his accomplishments. After the 2016 election, with control of the presi-dency, the House of Representatives and the Senate, Republicans were bold in their political agenda. Yet to date, the President has had only one major legisla-tive achievement (this on taxes, right at the end of his first year). Much, if not most, of the Trump agenda has so far been blocked by the courts,[29] by Democrats or by members of Trump's own party. The discipline of sociology has also shared in this resistance.

For example, sociologist Barbara Risman (2016), a former president of the Southern Sociological Society and a leading voice in the discipline wrote an interesting blog shortly after Trump's victory entitled "How to Do Sociology in the Trump Era." She wrote:

> I see two questions that we need to address as sociologists. First, how do we move forward to inspire students to be civically engaged when they feel afraid and helpless? Second, how do we do public sociology in a "post-truth" age? (Risman, 2016)

To tackle the first question, Risman says sociologists must stress the importance of the social constructionist approach. As she says:

> The understanding that society is what we make it is empowering, and we must leave our students, in every course, with the understanding that they are not only products of their society but producers of the future. (Risman, 2016)

In response to the question about public sociology in a post-truth age, Risman (2016) counsels that:

> What we should do is focus on the culture, how do we get our ideas, research, and evidence out there [...] Here is our challenge, how to get beyond the echo chamber of urban college-educated America, and talk to those citizens who feel left behind [...] Our challenge is to help change culture and to do that we must find a way to break the glass barriers between college-educated elites (that's us) and those who voted for Trump. (Risman, 2016)

Risman has been one of a number of sociologists to give advice on how to deal with the Trump Administration. The American Sociological Association (ASA), which has never been known to be a particular political organization, also weighed in early in opposition to the President. In arguing against the proposed changes to US immigration policy, the ASA wrote in January 2017 that the organization would also combat "threats to data sharing, data collection, funding for scientific scholarship, academic freedom, and peer review, as well as policies that inhibit the exchange of ideas domestically or internationally." It said they would "defend the conditions for the exercise of our professional responsibilities, which include free speech, democracy, the rule of law, and the values of diversity and meritocracy." The organization also stated they would "take positions on public policy issues for which there is clear sociological evidence" (ASA, 2017).

In a separate statement, then ASA President Michele Lamont tried to explain the current political climate sociologically in terms of lack of social recognition and the boundaries that exist between different groups in society (Lamont, 2016). She argued:

> Social scientists should explicitly tackle this recognition gap. Just as we have provided citizens the language needed to describe realities such as "unemployment rate" and "stereotypes," it is time to mount a campaign to help people think about how to weaken group boundaries. As shapers of cultural frameworks, we need to help people understand that scarcity and group competition makes group boundaries more rigid, that group contact does not necessarily result in less stereotyping, but that inclusion benefits collective well-being for all. We also need to systematically compare the recognition gaps wherever they exist.

Lamont also offered a possible way of working through our contemporary social, cultural and political dilemmas through scholarship[30] and described recent works – by authors such as Thomas Piketty, Catherine Panter-Bricks,

Arlie Hochschild, and Ofer Sharone — which in her view demonstrate how sociology can be useful in capturing the trends of social life.

Such statements remind us that sociology is more than an academic profession and more than just a personal calling, but most importantly it is an intervention into society. As sociologists, it is our responsibility to never lose sight of gap between the "is" and the "ought," and to strive to make societies as democratic, just and equitable as possible. This requires intervention. Yet as we intervene, we must acknowledge difference. We would do well to listen the advice of Michael Walzer, who reminds us that: "There is nothing like the classic 'working class', neglected by Democratic politicians, waiting to be mobilized." He goes on:

> The people we need to reach are a radically mixed group. They are economically mixed: they include unemployed men and women, old people without adequate pensions, part-time workers, rust belt workers with new jobs that pay much less than they once earned, workers without union protection and with few benefits, and the rural poor—all of them frighteningly vulnerable, watching anxiously for the next downturn. And they are mixed in their identities: black and white, Hispanic and Asian, men and women, gay and straight. These people could form what Charles Mills [...] called "a transracial coalition of the disadvantaged." But first they must come to see that their difficulties are not theirs alone. Think of them as a class in formation—or, in the old language, a class in itself but not yet for itself. How can we advance the formation? That is the question we should be debating.[31]

More recently, Eduardo Bonilla-Silva, 2018 President of ASA, offered his own critique of society under the Trump administration. While he says it is easy to be preoccupied with President Trump on a daily level, Bonilla-Silva says it is better to take a longer view. Bonilla-Silva argues the focus of sociology should be "on the class, race and gender fronts." He suggests that the current "administration has not changed the fundamentals of American policy — although on the race and gender fronts, he's advancing morals that represent a step back" (Flaherty, 2017).

At the time of writing (September 2019), it seems that sociologists have become more accustomed to the world of Trump. Trump's bark has always been worse than his bite. Immediately after the election, individuals, groups and organizations in society were waiting to see the impact of his bite. It will be up to the social historians of the future to know with certainty just how much damage to US society and the world will ultimately be done by Trumpian politics. Much of what is happening in the US now is a rolling back of Obama policies, which were a response to Bush-era policies (which were in response to Clinton policies responding to Reagan, and him to Carter, etc.) And so it goes. In the final analysis, a neoliberal, socially conservative, militaristic government is again in control of the White House. Trump likes to believe that he is a different sort of Republican, but in fact he is exploding deficits and handing out tax breaks to the wealthy just like his predecessors. Sociologists and other social scientists have amassed considerable evidence over the last decades demonstrating that these policies do not create an equitable or sustainable society. Today, the biggest fault lines in contemporary society can be seen in the breakdown of civil society, the assault on the public sector, and in the absence of a new social contract. The President's megalomaniac tendencies, his embrace of know-nothingism and his devil-may-care attitude is appealing to his most fervent supporters, particularly those who feel aggrieved by challenges to their status and authority. There is an obvious danger in such attitudes (particularly in relation to women and minorities) becoming more widespread and normalized in the culture as a whole. However, what works for celebrity millionaires is unlikely to work for the average American lacking the President's social, economic and cultural resources. Even his most enthusiastic supporters and spokespeople disregard, play down, or otherwise ignore, much of what the President says. While darkness and chaos often loom large on the national scene, at the local level people throughout the United States are reinvigorating communities across ideological lines by solving problems together (see Fallows & Fallows, 2018).

In Weberian terms, the main sociological problem posed by Trump may well be his charismatic style of leadership (Weber 1978[1922]). Many US presidential candidates (e.g. John F. Kennedy, Barack Obama) have been charismatic leaders, but once they become president, they usually abide by the norms of rational-legal authority. Trump has not done so. He seems to realize that if he were to become a rational-legal figure, he would lose his charisma and, by extension, the support of his followers. However, charismatic authority is often very difficult to execute in a rational-legal framework.

One might argue that what we are seeing today in the "culture wars" surrounding this president is largely a result of conflict between these two different styles of leadership. Trump's supporters adore the power of his charisma, to the point of even comparing him to the Messiah, a characterization the President himself has embraced. As such, they likely believe that it is right for Trump to have complete freedom in his actions and demand total subservience from his subjects. After all, who can question the Messiah? Any attempt to limit Trump's power is seen as blasphemous, petty, and disgraceful.

Trump's detractors, on the other hand, are very worried about his charismatic side, and would much prefer that he become a legal-rational actor and adhere to all the appropriate rules and regulations. When observers complain that Trump has subverted so many norms of the US Presidency, this is essentially what they are talking about. Trump champions spectacular irrationality over bureaucratic rationality. He insists he is perfect in everything he says and does. Like Louis XIV, Trump essentially asserts, *"L'etat, c'est moi."* This is why he refuses to admit he is ever wrong, even in the face of obvious and overwhelming evidence to the contrary. As the very personification of the state, Trump knows he has a monopoly on power and can define reality any way he chooses. Witness, for example, his bizarre responses to different embarrassing incidents during his first term in office (e.g. his "cofeve" tweet, the Tim Cook "Apple" flub, "Sharpie-gate").

Such micro-events in contemporary politics might simply be viewed as hilarious were it not for the fact that such absolutist sentiments often cross into more serious terrain. Then it becomes impossible to know if Trump is being serious or not. We see this dynamic (to use just a few examples) in his suggestion that he might stay in office beyond just two terms, his attempt to muzzle the press and quash those who dare to speak out against him, his lavish affection for ruthless dictators, and (most recently) his intimation that whistleblowers be executed. Trump appears to think criticism should only be leveled at those beneath him in the social hierarchy. He is at the top of the pecking order and should therefore be free of all criticism. Since Trump believes he can do no wrong, any criticism is interpreted as a form of harassment, persecution, or perhaps even, crucifixion.

Ultimately, the main political problem for sociology may not be so much with Trump, but with his extreme supporters who really do view the man as a Supreme Being. These are the true believers in Trump's infallibility who adopt his rhetoric and worldview as their own. They have internalized the right-wing narrative that the entire world is rigged against him and that the "deep state" will stop at nothing to destroy him. As Weber pointed out almost a century ago (Weber 1978[1922]), it is extremely difficult for a charismatic social movement to survive after the demise of its leader. Whether Trumpism will outlast Trump will remain a fascinating question in the years ahead.

CONCLUSION

So where does that leave us? Perhaps, with the understanding that, while we might indeed be at the "end of history," we may also be at the beginning of a newer, open-ended historical period. The uncertainty of the present moment is palpable, not just for sociology, not just for US society, but for the entire planet. Yet despite this uncertainty, somehow we must still act, even and until the real "end of history" (Hazelrigg, 1989b).[32]

The social world is increasingly complicated and more often than not misunderstood. It needs to be properly deciphered. However, as Harrison White notes in *Identity and Control* (1992), social theory continues to be in the "doldrums" (1992, p. 3). The necessity of a new theory of society has never been greater. Many of the "theorists" discussed and taught today in contemporary social theory classes came of age fifty years ago, when society was qualitatively different. Just when will be the next paradigm shift (see Kuhn, 1962) in theory occur? Will there be productive "return to theory" in the years ahead to help us come to terms with our predicament?

On December 6, 2016, sociologist Randall Collins (one of the most senior and respected theorists in the field) published an article on the weblog of the American Sociological Association. He titled his entry: "The Real Structural Problem: The Self-destruction of Capitalism." In this piece, Collins makes the rather chilling argument that capitalism will soon collapse because of automation — the increasing number of robots out there who will soon be taking our jobs. Collins raises some salient points. After all, how can society continue to exist if people have no ability to support themselves? As he says, "Capitalism depends ultimately on having an income-earning population who can buy its products. Displacement of workers by machinery is the formula for the self-destruction of capitalism." Collins claims that "computerization and the electronic media are eliminating the middle class" (Collins, 2016). He then goes on to predict that the "collapse of capitalism will happen in the 2040s or 2050s," about 50 years prior to what he says will be the beginning of a widespread eco-logical collapse. Yet for all his pessimism, Collins nonetheless argues that, around the middle of the twenty-first century, even after the collapse of global capitalism, "there will be time for a regime that is people-oriented rather than profit-oriented to solve global warming." Let us hope he is right.

Collins' appeal for a "people-oriented regime" mirrors the call in this chapter for a reinvigoration of public sociology. This will obviously be a protracted, collective struggle, which will continue until the real "end of his-tory" (should such a day ever arrive). Such a social movement will require concerted efforts on the part of sociologists as scholars *and* citizens to act to protect truth, justice, democracy, science, and perhaps even civilization itself. Sociology is urgently needed to properly understand the dominant social, economic and political orders in society today (see Smith, 2016). Given the paucity of sociology in the public sphere, there is presently a void in conversations about society that could be exploited by sociologists, partic-ularly as they concern the articulation of race, class, and gender inequalities. Sociologists have an opportunity to prove their mettle. More than ever we need once again Marx's "ruthless criticism of everything existing" (1978 [1843], p. 12; see also Frasier, 1985). So, much in society today demands be understood, analyzed, critiqued, and changed. Let us get to work.[33]

NOTES

1. See https://news.gallup.com/poll/203207/trump-job-approval-weekly.aspx
2. See Mounk (2017). In July 2018, former Secretary of State Madeleine Albright declared Trump to be "the most undemocratic president in modern American history" (Ehrlich, 2018).
3. For a good sociological explanation of the phenomena of rampage shootings, see Newman (2005).
4. See https://www.treasurydirect.gov/govt/reports/pd/histdebt/histdebt_histo5.htm
5. For an overview of our current condition and where we may go from here, see Hazelrigg (1989a).
6. Bannon is an enigmatic character. His anti-establishment style, weather-beaten appearance, and browbeating demeanor have been embraced by the far right (despite his falling out with the President). Bannon is a keen theoretician and tactician of the contem-porary conservative movement. Ultimately, his position is untenable as he wants to have it both ways. On the one hand, he ingratiates himself to the media (Peters, 2017) and in so doing, attempts to convince the public that both he and Trump are not in fact far-right ideologues but rather political centrists. "Dude, he's Archie Bunker," Bannon claims (Peters & Haberman, 2017). The "Access Hollywood" tape (the veracity of which, inci-dentally, Trump questioned over a year after he apologized for it) is in Bannon's view simply "locker room talk" (Alemany & Watson, 2017). Bannon asserts that Trump sup-ports all Americans with his economic nationalist program. Yet in reality, Bannon is still wedded to symbolic politics. One saw this, for example, in his advice to the President in terms of the "Muslim Ban," canceling televised White House press briefings, waiting to comment on Charlottesville, rolling back transgendered troops in the military, remilitariz-ing police forces across the country, and so on. Bannon also campaigned with right-wing zealots such as Judge Roy Moore, who is fiercely Christian, anti-Muslim and anti-gay rights. Moore is apparently what Bannon (and Trump) thought of as the future of the country. It is also interesting to point out some ways in which Bannon and Trump dis-agree. For example, on the issue of tax reform, Trump did not support initiatives

(proposed by Bannon) to increase taxes on America's top earners. As Lynch and Paletta (2017) report, Bannon believed that "raising the top rate paid by the wealthiest Americans was a way to follow through on the populist principles Trump invoked in his campaign." Trump was happy to renege this campaign pledge. The extent of all the other broken promises the 45th President has made to America will be revealed in due course.

7. At a speech in St. Louis, MO, in late November, President Trump claimed solidarity with the US working class. As he said: "But really, the people that like me best are those people, the workers. They're the people I understand the best. Those are the people I grew up with. Those are the people I worked on construction sites with" (Tankersley, 2017).

8. As Baudrillard once said, the apocalypse "has already happened [...] All that remains to be done is to play with the pieces" (Gane, 1993, pp. 43, 95).

9. For a more systematic view on these issues, see Wright and Rogers (2015).

10. For an in-depth examination of such processes, see Daniel M. Harrison, *Making Sense of Marshall Ledbetter* (2014).

11. See Isaac and Harrison (2006). In late November 2017, it was reported that the Trump administration was considering a proposal to privatize some of the functions of the CIA (Roston, 2017).

12. For a foundational critique of Durkheimian sociology (especially its neo-Kantian) roots, with glimpses at an alternate style of inquiry, see Rose (1981).

13. According to the ASA, in 1970, sociology had a "4 percent share of bachelor degree recipients." By 2015, this had "declined to less than a 2 percent share." See http://www.asa-net.org/your-sociology-program-thriving-consider-changing-popularity-your-major

14. See Cook (2014). But there continues to be huge variation in terms of race, ethnicity and gender. At my current institution, approximately 65% of the student body is female. It seems that men (particularly white men) are increasingly less likely to attend college, while rates are increasing for members of other groups (e.g. African-American women). My sense also is that sociology is an increasingly attractive major among African-American students in general and African-American female students in particular. Properly understanding such trends goes beyond the purpose of this chapter. However, the interest could partially be explained by more African-American students attending college and university in general, the explicit attention that sociology as a discipline gives to the issues of race and ethnicity (in both teaching and research), and the fact that towering figures in the African-American community (for instance, Martin Luther King Jr. and Michelle Obama) were sociology majors.

15. As Harrison White says, "I have been doing my best for some years now to get sociologists — students as well as faculty — into the business schools [...] Business schools are natural places for sociologists to be, and sociology is the natural intellectual base in social science for business schools" (in Swedborg, 1991, p. 90).

16. Popular culture does not always help the case for sociology. As an example, consider this scene from *Dirty Harry*: "Sociology? Oh, you'll go far - that's if you live [...] Just don't let your college degree get you killed 'cause I'm liable to get killed along with ya." See: https://www.youtube.com/watch?v=RitnM9n0jTY. The idea of sociology as an "easy" major usually vanishes after the individual in question takes a class in it (particularly if it is a theory and or a methods course). Monty Python gets a dig in at sociology in their "Hell's Grannies" Skit: "Reporter: The whole problem of these senile delinquents lies in their complete rejection of the values of contemporary society. They've seen their children grow up and become accountants, stockbrokers and even sociologists, and they begin to wonder if it is all really [...] *(disappears downwards rapidly)* arggh!" See http://www.montypython.net/scripts/hellgran.php

17. It would be interesting to address whether this apparent decline in sociology in the United States is universal, or if and to what extent sociology is facing happier futures elsewhere in the world.

18. https://www.c-span.org/video/?c4667607/nras-lapierre-greatest-domestic-threats-academic-political-media-elites. See also https://www.apnews.com/c8cfcc9f96de439ca0d7d7c338f97949

19. Ecclesiastes 1:9.

20. "I love the poorly educated," exclaimed Donald Trump in February 2016 after winning the Nevada Primary (Hafner, 2016). See also Graham (2017).

21. As Hazelrigg (1989a, p. 30) put it almost three decades ago, "we have witnessed the death of the disciplines of social science in all aspects but the occupational."

22. For a very disturbing harbinger of things to come, see http://professorwatchlist.org. See also htttp://www.campusreform.org for right-wing efforts to root out liberals on the Faculty.

23. This book was found in the possession of Timothy McVeigh after he blew up the Murrah Federal Building in Oklahoma in 1995.

24. "The lower strata of the middle class — the small tradespeople, shopkeepers, and retired tradesmen generally, the handicraftsmen and peasants — all these sink gradually into the proletariat, partly because their diminutive capital does not suffice for the scale on which Modern Industry is carried on, and is swamped in the competition with the large capitalists, partly because their specialised skill is rendered worthless by new methods of production. Thus the proletariat is recruited from all classes of the population" (Marx & Engels, 1978[1848], pp. 479–480).

25. For the classic sociological statement on the calling, see Weber (2001[1904]).

26. Of course, there are also social processes through which people lose their affection for sociology, become de-converted, and eventually stop being sociologists altogether. But that is the subject for another chapter.

27. See Smith (1989).

28. Cornel West is a figure who perhaps best exemplifies such an intellectual position.

29. Trump earned another victory recently with the Supreme Court ruling 5:4 in his favor regarding his ban on people traveling to the US from certain predominantly Muslim countries (Reuters, 2018). However, it should be noted that the court only ruled on the constitutionality of the President's action. As Chief Justice John Roberts stated, "We express no view on the soundness of the policy" (Reuters, 2018).

30. There might be a greater likelihood of this happening if the political class actually read and consulted sociological work when making decisions, but this unfortunately does not seem to happen much in the United States. Whereas the elected officials might rely on sociologists in other societies, in the United States the practice is that legislators use their own analysts and legislative aides when researching social issues. As sociologist Herbert Gans notes, "When no one asks us for advice, there's no incentive to become a policy field" (in Irwin, 2017). Because of such non-communication, the perception that sociology has nothing to offer the conversation continues.

31. Walzer (2017). See also recent remarks by Chantel Mouffe where she argues "Movements cannot be left just to the streets." She continues:

> I am very critical of the idea of politics as fomenting a moment of total rupture with the existing status quo. This is not how revolutions work. At some point, mobilizations will lose steam. You cannot change things only on the horizontal level of social movements. You have to develop what Podemos calls "an electoral war machine." You need to try to come to real power in the institutions and government. (in Shahid, 2016)

32. As Hazelrigg (1989b, p. 265) puts it, "If we are committed to act (and short of the end of history we *will* act), we are always committed to act where we stand."

33. For additional leads, see Burrowoy (2004).

ACKNOWLEDGMENTS

I would like the thank the helpful comments of Harry Dahms, Lawrence Hazelrigg, Daniel Kavish, and attendees at the "Sociology between a Profession and Vocation" session of the annual Southern Sociological Society in Greenville, SC (March 30–April 1, 2017), where an earlier draft of this chapter was presented.

REFERENCES

Alemany, J., & Watson, K. (2017). Bannon compares Moore report to access Hollywood tape. *CBS News*. November 9. Retrieved from https://www.cbsnews.com/news/steve-bannon-speaks-in-new-hampshire/

Alford, R. R. (1998). *The craft of inquiry*. New York, NY: Oxford University Press.

American Sociological Association. (2017). Statement of the American Sociological Association concerning the new administration's recent and future activities. January 30. Retrieved from http://www.asanet.org/news-events/asa-news/statement-american-sociological-association-concerning-new-administrations-recent-and-future

Aslan, R. (2017). The dangerous cult of Donald Trump. *Los Angeles Times*. November 6. Retrieved from http://www.latimes.com/opinion/op-ed/la-oe-aslan-trump-cultists-20171106-story.html

Associated Press (AP). (2017). Sanders in Pennsylvania warns the US is approaching 'oligarchy.' *The Inquirer*. Retrieved from http://www.philly.com/philly/news/politics/presidential/20171203_ap_44fd9a0152fe47b1aaece48147644806.html

BBC News. (2017). Tax bill: Trump victory as Senate backs tax overhaul. *BBC News*. December 2. Retrieved from http://www.bbc.com/news/world-us-canada-42205181

Beck, U. (1986). *Risk society*. Thousand Oaks, CA: Sage.

Bentz, M., & Shapiro, J. (1998). *Mindful inquiry in social research*. Thousand Oaks, CA: Sage.

Boddy, J. (2017). The forces driving middle-aged white people's 'death of despair.' *National Public Radio*. March 23. Retrieved from https://www.npr.org/sections/health-shots/2017/03/23/521083335/the-forces-driving-middle-aged-white-peoples-deaths-of-despair

Bonilla-Silva, E. (2017). ASA President Eduardo Bonilla-Silva responds to Chief Justice John Roberts. October 10. Retrieved from http://www.asanet.org/news-events/asa-news/asa-president-eduardo-bonilla-silva-responds-chief-justice-john-roberts

Burrowoy, M. (2004). Presidential address: For public sociology. Retrieved from http://burawoy.berkeley.edu/PS/ASA%20Presidential%20Address.pdf

Chomsky, N. (2006). *Failed states*. New York, NY: Henry Holt.

Collins, R. (2016). The real structural problem: the self-destruction of capitalism. December 17. Retrieved from http://speak4sociology.org/2016/12/07/the-real-structural-problem-the-self-destruction-of-capitalism/

Cook, L. (2014). Is the college admissions bubble about to burst? *US News & World Report*. September 22. https://www.usnews.com/news/blogs/data-mine/2014/09/22/is-the-college-admissions-bubble-about-to-burst

Dahms, H. (1998). Beyond the carousel of reification: Critical social theory after Luckács, Adorno and Habermas. *Current Perspectives in Social Theory, 18*, 3–62.

Diamond, J. (2005). *Collapse: How societies choose to fail or succeed*. New York, NY: Penguin.

Dillon, M. (2014). *Introduction to sociological theory*. New York, NY: Wiley-Blackwell.

Du Bois, W. E. B. (1897). The veil of self-consciousness. *The Atlantic*. August. Retrieved from https://www.theatlantic.com/ideastour/civil-rights/dubois-full.html

Edmonds, D. (2015). More than half of college faculty are adjuncts: Should you care? *Forbes*. May 28. Retrieved from https://www.forbes.com/sites/noodleeducation/2015/05/28/more-than-half-of-college-faculty-are-adjuncts-should-you-care/#7fda08381600

Ehrlich, J. (2018). Madeleine Albright calls Trump 'most undemocratic president in modern American history.' *CNN*. July 2. Retrieved from https://www.cnn.com/2018/07/02/politics/madeleine-albright-donald-trump-undemocratic-president/index.html

Ennis, D. J. (2011). The last of the tenure track. *The Chronicle of Higher Education*. July 1. Retrieved from https://www.chronicle.com/article/The-Last-of-the-Tenure-Track/128076

Fallows, J., & Fallows, D. (2018). *Our towns: A 100,000 mile journey into the heart of America*. New York, NY: Pantheon.

Flaherty, C. (2017). Teaching sociology in 2017. Retrieved from https://www.insidehighered.com/news/2017/08/15/sociologists-talk-about-teaching-political-now-emphasis-charlottesville

Frasier, N. (1985). What's critical about critical theory? *New German Critique*, Spring/Summer, 97–131.

Fukuyama, F. (2006[1992]). *The end of history and the last man*. New York, NY: Free Press.

Gane, M. (1993). *Baudrillard live*. New York, NY: Routledge.

Goffman, A. (2014). *On the run: American life in a fugitive city*. Chicago, IL: University of Chicago Press.

Gouldner, A. (1970). *The coming crisis of western sociology*. New York, NY: Basic Books.

Graham, D. A. (2017). Why do Republicans suddenly hate college so much? *The Atlantic*. July 13. Retrieved from https://www.theatlantic.com/politics/archive/2017/07/why-do-republicans-suddenly-hate-colleges-so-much/533130/

Hafner, J. (2016). Donald Trump loves the 'poorly educated' – And they love him. *USA Today*. February 24. Retrieved from https://www.usatoday.com/story/news/politics/onpolitics/2016/02/24/donald-trump-nevada-poorly-educated/80860078/

Hardt, M., & Negri, A. (2001). *Empire*. New York, NY: Harvard University Press.

Harrison, D. (2014). *Making sense of Marshall Ledbetter: The dark side of political protest*. Gainesville, FL: University Press of Florida.

Hazelrigg, L. (1989a). *A wilderness of mirrors: On practices of theory in a gray age*. Tallahassee, FL: The Florida State University Press.

Hazelrigg, L. (1989b). *Claims of knowledge: On the labor of making found worlds*. Tallahassee, FL: The Florida State University Press.

Irwin, N. (2017). What if sociologists had as much influence as economists? *New York Times*. March 17. Retrieved from https://mobile.nytimes.com/comments/2017/03/17/upshot/what-if-sociologists-had-as-much-influence-as-economists.html

Isaac, L., & Harrison, D. (2006). Corporate warriors: The state and changing forms of private armed force in America. *Current Perspectives in Social Theory*, 24, 153–188.

Jamrisko, M., & Kolet, I. (2014). College tuition costs soar. *Bloomberg*. August 18. Retrieved from https://www.bloomberg.com/news/articles/2014-08-18/college-tuition-costs-soar-chart-of-the-day

Kuhn, T. (1962). *The structure of scientific revolutions*. Chicago, IL: University of Chicago Press.

Lamont, M. (2016). Trump's triumph and social science adrift...What is to be done? Retrieved from http://www.asanet.org/trumps-triumph-and-social-science-adrift-what-be-done

Lareau, A. (2003). *Unequal childhoods: Class, race and family life*. Berkeley, CA: University of California Press.

Lovelace, B., Jr. (2018). Tax overhaul means a $4,000-a-year pay raise for the average family, Trump advisor says. *CNBC*. January 29. Retrieved from https://www.cnbc.com/2018/01/29/tax-overhaul-means-4000-a-year-pay-hike-for-average-family-hassett.html

Lukes, S. (1985). *Emile Durkheim: His life and work*. Stanford, CA: Stanford University Press.

Lynch, D. J., & Paletta, D. (2017). Hours after GOP passes tax bill, Trump says he'll consider raising tax rate. *The Washington Post*. December 2. Retrieved from https://www.washingtonpost.com/news/business/wp/2017/12/02/trump-waffles-on-corporate-tax-rate-demand-central-plank-of-gop-tax-plan/?utm_term=.a75094e2f5d7

Marx, K. (1978[1843]). For a ruthless criticism of everything existing. In R. Tucker (Ed). *The Marx-Engels reader*. New York, NY: W.W. Norton.

Marx, K., & Engels, F. (1978[1848]). The communist manifesto. In R. Tucker (Ed). *The Marx-Engels reader*. New York, NY: W. W. Norton.

McDonald, A. (1999). *The Turner diaries*. (2nd ed.). Charlottesville, VA: National Vanguard Press.

McKenna, K. (2016). The ever-tightening job market for Ph.Ds. *The Atlantic*. April 21. Retrieved from https://www.theatlantic.com/education/archive/2016/04/bad-job-market-phds/479205/

Mounk, Y. (2017). The past week proves that Trump is destroying our democracy. *The New York Times*. August 1. Retrieved from https://www.nytimes.com/2017/08/01/opinion/trump-democracy-institutions-destroyed.html

Müller-Doohm, S. (2014). *Adorno: A biography*. New York, NY: Polity.

Newman, K. S. (2005). *Rampage: The social roots of school shootings*. New York, NY: Basic Books.

Packer, G. (2013). *The unwinding*. New York, NY: Farrar, Strauss, & Giroux.

Peters, J. W. (2017). Key takeaways from Steve Bannon's interview with the Times. *New York Times*. November 10. Retrieved from https://www.nytimes.com/2017/11/10/us/politics/steve-bannon.html

Peters, J. W., & Haberman, M. (2017). Bannon was set for a graceful exit. Then came Charlottesville. *New York Times*. August 20. Retrieved from https://www.nytimes.com/2017/08/20/us/politics/steve-bannon-fired-trump-departure.html

Reuters. (2018). U.S. top court upholds Trump travel ban targeting Muslim-majority nations. *New York Times*. June 26. Retrieved from https://www.nytimes.com/reuters/2018/06/26/world/26reuters-usa-court-immigration.html

Risman, B. 2016. How to do sociology in the Trump era. *American Sociological Association*. December 12. Retrieved from http://www.asanet.org/news-events/speak-sociology/how-do-sociology-trump-era

Robinson, E. (2017). Loyalty to Trump isn't enough. *The Washington Post*. October 5. Retrieved from https://www.washingtonpost.com/opinions/loyalty-to-trump-isnt-enough/2017/10/05/297a9d30-a9fb-11e7-850e-2bdd1236be5d_story.html?utm_term=.3a93d3a6d309

Rose, G. (1981). *Hegel contra sociology*. New York, NY: Verso.

Roston, A. (2017). The Trump administration is mulling a pitch for a private 'rendition' and spy network. *Buzzfeed News*. November 30. Retrieved from https://www.buzzfeed.com/aramroston/trump-administration-mulls-private-rendition?bftwnews&utm_term=.nork66X17#.rjzMVV2N3

Rucker, P., & Costa, R. 2017. Bannon vows a daily fight for the 'deconstruction of the administrative state.' *Washington Post*. February 23. Retrieved from https://www.washingtonpost.com/politics/top-wh-strategist-vows-a-daily-fight-for-deconstruction-of-the-administrative-state/2017/02/23/03f6b8da-f9ea-11e6-bf01-d47f8cf9b643_story.html?utm_term=.568008bee529

Schaar, C. (2015). Emeritus profile: Earl Babbie. *ASA Footnotes*, November. *43*(7), 1, 4.

Sebestyen, V. (2017). Bannon says he's a Leninist: that could explain the White House's new tactics. *The Guardian*. February 6. Retrieved from https://www.theguardian.com/commentisfree/2017/feb/06/lenin-white-house-steve-bannon

Shahid, W. (2016). America in populist times: An interview with Chantal Mouffe. December 15. Retrieved from https://www.thenation.com/article/america-in-populist-times-an-interview-with-chantal-mouffe/

Siegler, K. (2017). Trump to take aim at Utah's national monuments, reversing predecessors' legacies. *National Public Radio*. December 4. Retrieved from https://www.npr.org/sections/thetwo-way/2017/12/04/567803476/trump-to-take-aim-at-utahs-national-monuments-reversing-predecessors-legacies

Smith, D. (1989). *The everyday world as problematic*. Boston, MA: Northeastern University Press.

Smith, N. (2016). Calling all sociologists: America needs you. *Bloomberg View*. August 31. Retrieved from https://www.bloomberg.com/view/articles/2016-08-31/calling-all-sociologists-america-needs-you

Strauss, K. (2017). College degrees with the highest (and lowest) starting salaries in 2017. *Forbes*. June 28. Retrieved from https://www.forbes.com/sites/karstenstrauss/2017/06/28/college-degrees-with-the-highest-and-lowest-starting-salaries-in-2017/#7f1bf4a82343

Swedborg, R. (1991). *Economics and sociology*. Princeton, NJ: Princeton University Press.

Tankersley, J. (2017). A 'main street' tax speech becomes a riff on the rich. *New York Times*. November 29. Retrieved from https://www.nytimes.com/2017/11/29/us/politics/a-main-street-tax-speech-becomes-a-trump-riff-on-the-rich.html

Tankersley, J., Kaplan, T., & Rappeport, A. (2017). Senate Republicans pass sweeping tax bill. *New York Times*. December 1. Retrieved from https://www.nytimes.com/2017/12/01/us/politics/senate-tax-bill.html

Tharoor, I. (2017). The man who declared the 'end of history' fears for democracy's future. *Washington Post*. February 9. Retrieved from https://www.washingtonpost.com/news/worldviews/wp/2017/02/09/the-man-who-declared-the-end-of-history-fears-for-democracys-future/?utm_term=.5898359b4085

Thompson, D. (2014). Turning customers into cultists: Why many companies now take their cues from religious sects. *The Atlantic*. December. Retrieved from https://www.theatlantic.com/magazine/archive/2014/12/turning-customers-into-cultists/382248/

Venkatesh, S. (2008). *Gang leader for a day*. New York, NY: Penguin.

Walzer, M. (2017). The historical task of the left in the current period. *Dissent*. January 2. Retrieved from https://www.dissentmagazine.org/online_articles/historical-task-of-left-present-period-trump

Weber, M. (1958[1922]). Science as a vocation. In H. Gerth & C. W. Mills (Eds.). *From Max Weber*. New York, NY: Oxford University Press.

Weber, M. (1978[1922]). *Economy and society*. Berkeley, CA: University of California Press.

Weber, M. (2001[1904]). *The Protestant ethic & the spirit of capitalism*. New York, NY: Routledge.

White, H. C. (1992). *Identity and control: A structural theory of social action*. Princeton, NJ: Princeton University Press.

Wright, E. O., & Rogers, J. (2015). *American society: How it really works*. New York, NY: W. W. Norton.

Žižek, S. (2011). *Living in the end times*. New York, NY: Verso.

PART III
CONFRONTING THE CHALLENGE:
THE DYNAMICS OF PROGRESS IN
THE MODERN AGE

LAS VEGAS AS THE ANTHROPOCENE: THE NEOLIBERAL CITY AS DESERTIFICATION ALL THE WAY DOWN

Timothy W. Luke

ABSTRACT

This survey of Las Vegas, Nevada, as a benchmark for the transformations of the Anthropocene, is a provisional exercise in applied social theory. Like multiple processes of desertification that are accelerating in and around Las Vegas, this study is provisional, as it follows Las Vegas as a discrete place whose desertifying qualities are spreading far beyond Nevada, regionally, nationally, globally, and virulently so. Las Vegas, Las Vegas Valley, Mohave Desert, and Colorado River Basin are biopolitical spaces and geophysical places that iteratively replicate the psycho-social contradictions of people in search of sustainable lifestyles in global spaces rocked by ecological catastrophe, and which is open to critical scrutiny. The study more closely examines how systems of organized growth tied to commercial degradation, urban demography, military development, and nuclear devastation drive desertification in this region as well as elsewhere. Like the planet's other sprawling cities, Las Vegas is an integral component in the globalizing neoliberal omnipolitanization of the Earth's surface. The neoliberal logic of "winner takes all" also is reflected in the metrometabolic exchanges of these extraordinary urban formations. The rampant overdevelopment of a vast urban simulation, featuring multiple ruinations of its own built and natural

The Challenge of Progress: Theory Between Critique and Ideology
Current Perspectives in Social Theory, Volume 36, 159–178
Copyright © 2020 Emerald Publishing Limited
All rights of reproduction in any form reserved
ISSN: 0278-1204/doi:10.1108/S0278-120420190000036020

landscapes, may give many Las Vegans, and probably most Vegas visitors, their most fundamental sense of place.

Keywords: Anthropocene; metrometabolism; omnipolitanization; neoliberalism; desertification; Las Vegas; applied social theory

Las Vegas, Nevada is an exemplary case for exploring the Anthropocene through critical social theory. This analysis, then, how human factors in historical time are now regarded as equal to "the forces of Nature" in geological time (Zalaisewicz, Steffen, & Crutzen, 2010), which are turning more aspects of Clark County, Nevada into an even more wasted desert. As these wastelands are evolving, especially over the last century, such moments of desertification are also being both multiplied, and amplified, by the "economic and social forces of neoliberalism" (Harvey, 2011; Luke, 2005). Aridity, barrenness, and emptiness are growing in and around the hills and valleys encircling Las Vegas city as well as within its unique built environments. Moreover, the second-, third-, and fourth-order instances of this despoliation fully eclipse those first inflicted on this region by Europeanized explorers and settlers as they traversed this complex high desert ecosystem in what is now Southern Nevada during the nineteenth century.

Hence, this study more closely examines how systems of organized growth tied to commercial degradation, urban demography, military development, and nuclear devastation drive desertification in this region as well as elsewhere. Since these vectors of desertification are integral to the Anthropocene, as it is interpreted today (Chakrabartty, 2009), they merit close examination (Monastersky, 2015, pp. 144–147). If the Earth's Anthropocene period has rendered concretely timeless "the planet we made" (Vince, 2014), then Las Vegas as "the heart of the American dream" (Thompson, 1998) well typifies how the planet is being, and has been, remade (Carlson, 2009).

According to the Clark County local government "Highlights" page, tourism was a US$45.2 billion industry in 2013 (in the same general range of the national GDP of countries like Costa Rica, Ethiopia, Ghana, Lebanon, Panama, Serbia, or Slovenia), including US$9.7 billion for gambling alone in Clark County. With 162,662 hotel and motel rooms, a lot can happen in Vegas for "the average visitor." He or she is 46 years old, stays 3.3 nights on average paying on average US$111 per night room bill, laying out US$141 on shopping per visit, blowing US$38 per visit on shows, while gambling 2.9 hours a day. Typically, 15% are first-timers, 20% come from abroad, and 20% visit from Southern California. With two million people, Clark County is the most populated in Nevada's counties and supports 70% of the state's population. Yet, these two million typically will host another 35–40 million a year on these average 3.3 night visits.

Founded in 1905, Las Vegas bears the demographic distinction of being the largest city (population-wise) founded during the twentieth century in the USA. Chicago holds that place for the USA during the nineteenth century. And, just as Chicago was, in many ways, the most innovative capital of dynamic change for nineteenth-century America, one can argue this quality has been true of Las Vegas during the twentieth century. On many levels, America and the world are still "learning from Las Vegas" (Venturi, Izenour, & Brown, 1977).

Rapid climate change in the late twentieth and early twenty-first centuries mainly is attributed to the profligate use of fossil fuels by human beings. As an extraordinary urban formation hundreds of miles from many others of comparable size, and an area first settled in the 1850s when America's modern oil industry began, Las Vegas is one the world's most oil-dependent cities in the world. Its economy depends on millions of fossil-fueled visitors coming and going every month. Even though this consumption of hydrocarbon energy worldwide has different uneven and discontinuous patterns to it, many intellectuals find themselves fabricating a new historical metanarrative tied to this one trend: modern humans' increasing combustion of the planet's mineralized biotic prehistory as the fossil fuel energy powering modernization.

As the fossilized carbon of antediluvian organic matter is burned to light homes, run factories, and propel vehicles, the economy and sociology of the present produce new symbolic universals, namely, the material markers of exhausted hydrocarbon energy released into the soot, smog, and smoke in the skies today. These markers are so prevalent that they weigh heavily enough on the planet to mark a new era in geological time: the Anthropocene (Schwägerl, 2014). What happens in Vegas might stay in Vegas, but what exhausted energy it takes to move millions there and back every year disperses everywhere and lingers for decades as greenhouse gases in the air, water, soil, and biota of the planet.

Unintentionally, these noxious by-products of human production and consumption have become the crown of commodified creation. For the average consumer after the end of history, his or her supreme historical goals, as Fukuyama (1992) asserts, are "endless accumulation." Little did he know, this attribute of modernity also would entail the radical accumulation of greenhouse gases that aggravate rapid climate change, which now has captured the spotlight in crisis narratives framing the Anthropocene concept. Mitchell's analysis (2013) of "carbon democracy" can be pushed beyond his nuanced ethnography of the strategic ties between modern democratic governance, organized labor in the hydrocarbon industries, and the increasing exploitation of fossil fuels: it becomes a universal history for the Anthropocene.

Modern urban industrial society itself, as other scholars (McNeill, 2001; Mumford, 2010; Virilio, 1995) have argued, rests upon commercial modes of economy, new cultural values, and "a form of politics whose mechanisms on multiple levels involve the processes of producing and using carbon energy" (Mitchell, 2013, p. 9). Whether they are consumers or producers, the leading industrialized, affluent, and urban countries today are all "oil states" that are each "living oil" (LeMenager, 2014). Without the energy they derive from petroleum, their current forms of political and economic life would not exist. Their citizens have developed "ways of eating, traveling, housing themselves and consuming other goods and services that require very large amounts of energy from oil and other fossil fuels" (Mitchell, 2013, p. 6). Ecologically, the Anthropocene is the Age of Petroleum, and the oil-fueled mobility of metropolitan Las Vegas – ratified by its "Welcome to Fabulous Las Vegas" on entry heading north on the Strip and "Drive Carefully" on exit headed south on Las Vegas Boulevard – is emblematic of its excesses.

Two interlocked questions are associated with these historic changes. First, are the supplies of oil, gas, and coal sustainable? This question has fascinated ecologists, economists, and ethicists for decades. Predictions of "peak oil" have been made and revised many times over the past 150 years. Current consensus models suggest the most easily accessible oil could be exhausted in a few decades, natural gas in a few more decades beyond oil, but coal could maybe last for centuries. Nevertheless, the world's hydrocarbon burn rate is accelerating, since over half of all oil ever brought to the market has been consumed from 1980 through 2010.

The second larger question is not a surprise, since early measurements of rising levels of carbon dioxide in the atmosphere were first detected, and then tracked, during the initial years of "the space race" between the US and USSR. These carbon dioxide concentrations have risen 40% since the 1760s, and not surprisingly, about half of that increase has happened since around 1980. As the President's Science Advisory Committee in the United States wondered over 50 years ago, how soon might these changes prove "deleterious from the point of view of human beings" (Revelle, Broecker, Craig, Leeling, & Smagoronsky, 1965, pp. 126–127)? Some of the best indicators of those negative effects can be found in the pernicious desertification trends that characterize the development of Las Vegas, Nevada. Even so, the unending gamble on greater gains and lower losses, which are the essence of neoliberalism and its participants' entrapment in high-stakes risk, keep them coming year after year to The Strip.

Like desertification, environmentality (Luke, 1995) is a cluster of complex changes. And, in the context of a layered accumulation of different desertifying trends in Las Vegas, environmentality practices are continuously shaped and steered in specific directions to harmonize individual and collective human behavior. The government of the self and others in Las Vegas has required a series of disciplinary projects, first, to observe and, then, to organize these desert locales in a manner that systematically can serve as "the space of movement" in which governing the self and others has aimed at "broadening and organizing that space, methods of power and knowledge" in so many ways that "methods of power and knowledge assumed responsibility for the life processes and undertook to control and modify them" (Foucault, 1980, p. 143).

Taming "The West" in the Las Vegas Valley has been a complex and demanding task. The new geopowers implied by controlling land, water, food, labor, and other resources to sustain the biopower of human and nonhuman life has involved propounding new logics, interconnections, and operations to settle and civilize this desert domain (Luke, 1995, pp. 57–58). Yet, its civilization has been one in which the citification process has unfolded as a series of intra- and extra-urban desertification. As an urban formation, Las Vegas is but one node in a network of networks, which continuously restructures everything artificial and natural to extract matter, generate energy, assemble labor, and apply information (Al, 2017). And, in so doing, these formations work to more rightly dispose of things and more conveniently arrange the ends of people seeking to coexist, among a governmentalizing disposition of things (Foucault, 1991).

Even though it is only one urbanized node, Las Vegas also carries unique normative weight in styling the regimens of citified living. Environmentality in Las Vegas — the Entertainment Capital of the World — is impossible to comprehend without tracing out its imbrication with "entertainmentality" (Luke, 2006, pp. 2–4, 151–164). In laying claim to serving as "The Entertainment Capital of the World," Las Vegas puts another spin on its place within the current neoliberal urban landscape. As one experiences with many concepts, current usages of "entertainment" occlude meanings force its origins that reveal more about its significance in the present than one might first guess. Coming into Middle English as *entertene*, this contemporary term derives from the Old French *entretenir*, and all three indicate "to entertain" means "to hold" or "to keep among." Entertainment, then, brings with it an essentially carceral significance and indicates essentially practices that are confining, containing, or capturing by nature. Consequently, "entertainment" is an activity, arrangement, or apparatus intended to keep one occupied, maintaining confined conditions or engaging one in a contained fashion — like the slot machine rows in a casino, countless stale floor shows off The Strip, or the high roller giant Ferris wheel with its LED light show.

Entertainments might well be intriguing diversions, amusing engagements or agreeable occupation. At the bottom line, however, entertainment is any occupation that curtails its charges with particular tactics of containment that keep both people apart, and together, all at the same time and place. If nothing else, such conditions of confinement for the city's more permanent tenants and barely lingering tourists enable Las Vegans to guarantee "the only rules in town," which gonzo journalists like Hunter Thompson have been known to break are very simple: "burning the locals, abusing the tourists, and terrifying the help" (Thompson, 1998, p. 173). When speaking of territory, population, and sovereignty, the basis of new desertified modalities for the governance of the self and others in this extraordinary city emerges here. That is, one can explore how "entertainmentality" coevolves with "environmentality" in Las Vegas by keeping local residents, eager tourists, the help, and gaming industrialists all in the most convenient place in this desertified order of people and things to command their conduct of conduct.

Las Vegas as an urban formation shines very brightly here: its goal as the world's entertainment capital is to hold its residents and visitors apart but together at the same time. Being "held in place" and "kept among" the Strip's spectacular diversions, fresh cycles of "entertainmentality" emerge out of the multiplex of desertifications in Las Vegas that show where, how, why, and when each individual "in his being, can be concerned with the things he knows, and know the things that, in positivity, determine his mode of being" (Foucault, 1973, p. 354).

As sites of otherwise or elsewhere illicit carnal knowledge, monetary risk, vicarious power, and bacchanalian excess, Las Vegas is the perfect carceral operation that gently detains millions daily in a stifling asphalt and concrete desert by deploying the delights of the flesh, flights of fantasy, and mechanically reproduced fun strung out with the allure of high-stakes individually calculated risk at the heart of the American Dream. Ultimately, the house always wins, everyone says they had a good time, and then "what happened in Vegas stays in Vegas." As Raoul Duke asked on arrival at his Vegas hotel:

> Who *are* these people? These faces! Where do they come from? They look like caricatures of used-car dealers from Dallas. But they're *real*. And, sweet Jesus, there are a hell of a *lot* of them — still screaming around these desert-city crap tables at four-thirty on a Sunday morning. Still humping the American Dream, the pre-dawn chaos of a stale Vegas casino. (Thompson, 1998, p. 57)

These degrading delusions, nonetheless, revalorize world entertainment capital anywhere Las Vegas is imitated, while at the same time sustainably degrading this desert region by systematically extracting through entertaining voluntary excess the money of millions here in the Mohave. By servicing the psychosocial desperation of its residents, visitors, and workers in the Entertainment Capital of the World, the magic of compound interest, fat profits, and high traffic deliver year after year the strong margins that "the gaming industry" seeks at these machinery sites (Luke, 2012).

This devious dialectic of environmentality and entertainmentality continuously modulates the desertification of everyday life, which the Las Vegas Strip exemplifies *in extremis* as its vendors inexorably strip everything, everyplace, and everyone down to endure their most delighting debasement in Vegas. The desertification of this arid place, then, mediates the desolations of global space as despoiled entertainments begin to shape-shift again in these desert environments. Entertainment often fabricates an environment; and, in Las Vegas, all environments are valorized as entertainments. Nonetheless, the Anthropocene is not at all tame (Wuerthner, Crist, & Butler, 2014). Elvis did not sing "Viva Las Vegas" for nothing: the dense layering of desertification in this city is all about constantly creating the anticipation Hunter Thompson (1998, p. 158) felt, namely, "that something wild and evil is about to happen; and it's going to involve you." As Raoul Duke and Dr Gonzo learn, this wildness suffuses everything in Las Vegas, but it proved not to be a great town for psychedelic drugs — reality itself is too twisted there (Thompson, 1998, pp. 169–175).

Since Las Vegas during the 1940s was the only place in America, for example, where gambling was legal, then why would it be shocking that "organized crime" showed up to corner the action. After all, as Moe Dalitz told the US Senate Committee on Organized Crime, "'Who else knew how to run games except gangsters'" (Nies, 2014, p. 48), so the liberal Democratic state easily could easily look away from the daily take in Paradise, NV as the Mob made the inexorable realities of Mr and Ms America losing millions of dollars a day at gaming into a legitimate new mass-market entertainment. And, if one refuses the roll the dice on the table out on the town, then he or she can test his or her luck by hopping into a helicopter to buzz Zion National Park, the Grand Canyon, and/or Hoover Dam, trying the Sky Jump at the Stratosphere Hotel &

Casino tower or doing 10 high-speed laps around Las Vegas Motor Speedway in a Lamborghini.

DESERTIFICATION AND DEVELOPMENT

Desertification is action — whether anthropogenic or autochthonous. Its effects transform arable, habitable, or viable land through destructive biophysical changes; degraded land use or despoiling environmental changes into infertile, uninhabitable, or nonviable places. What once could have been, or indeed was, somewhat bountiful instead is rendered barren. In some ways, the deserts of the Las Vegas Valley (encircled by the Spring Mountains in the west, McCullough Mountain to the south and Sheep and Las Vegas Mountains to the north) have experienced remarkable waves of anthropogenic desertification since 1905 when Las Vegas was founded. This ongoing desertification by an urban formation unfolds through the nexus of multiple processes of destruction at a distance as its citified metrometabolic systems (Luke, 2014, pp. 39–53) extract more and more resources from far and wide to fuel its accelerating degradation as a site for human and nonhuman habitation. The now-ended nightmare of Black Mesa's waters, coal seams, and people on the Navajo reservation being chewed up from 1971 to 2005 to light up (from the massive coal slurry-line that supplied the Mohave Power Station in Laughlin, Nevada) the suburban sprawl of Clark County is only one case in point (Nies, 2014).

Las Vegas was not always in a desert. From the end of Pleistocene into the early Holocene (Roberts, 1998), much of Las Vegas Valley was submerged in a large prehistoric lake. Southern Nevada is outside of the Great Basin area and its ancient seas in the north, but this smaller ancient lake of glacial ice and snow run-off from the surrounding mountains drained down Las Vegas Wash into the Colorado River Basin along with the Virgin and Muddy Rivers (http://www.onlinenevada.org/articles/nevadas-physical-setting). The state's namesake, then, has always shaped its biogeography. The colder wetter climate in the Valley then supported juniper-pinyon scrub woodlands with a diverse population of ancient megafauna, including many mammoths, sloths, horses, camels, and bison.

Fire pits and rock flakes at a few sites suggest small Paleo-Indian communities found this area to be a hunter-gatherers' paradise, as they also inhabited the region. Many archeologists and paleontologists have documented aspects of this prehistoric biome, and one can find accounts of these ancient days at the Tule Springs National Monument (www.tulespringslv.com) north of the city as well as Clark County Wetlands Park (www.clarkcountynv.gov/wetlandspark), Floyd Lamb Park at Tule Springs (www.vegas.com/attractions/off-the-strip/floyd-lamb-park), and the Las Vegas Natural History Museum (www.lvnhm.org). The latter site actually is located not that far from North Las Vegas Boulevard around the I-15 and I-515 intersection just above the Mob Museum, the Neon Museum, and the Old Downtown district.

To see Las Vegas now as a growing desert is not difficult. It is situated in what historically had been a largely uninhabited and uncultivated place. When initially surveyed by a Mexican scout, Rafael Rivera, in 1829, there were still enough small springs and streams to feed a cluster of wet meadowlands amid the Mohave Desert that surrounds the valley, which gave the site, and later the city its name, "Las Vegas." Much of the wider region around Las Vegas, however, is nearly devoid of vegetation due to a lack of rainfall. Encircled by mountains to the west, north, and southeast, much of the valley is sandy sedimentary soil or volcanic rock. With arid hard-baked playas here and there, patches of creosote-bursage flats survive, and contemporary variants of its earlier Holocene flora are found now 2,000−3,000 feet higher up in the nearby mountains' pinyon-juniper woodlands.

In many ways, the entire metropolitan area in modern times remained dominated by desert — barren, desolate, and infertile. What little riparian wetland still existed in the nineteenth century did attract John C. Fremont to the valley in 1844. Mormon homesteaders and ranchers also moved into the area after 1855. Until 1866, what is Clark County was part of the Arizona Territory, but then Congressional action extended the State of Nevada down to the junction of the California−Arizona Border near what then was Fort Mohave, Arizona. But, there were only a few dozen inhabitants in Las Vegas when the San Pedro, Los Angeles, and Salt Lake railroad punched through the valley from Salt Lake City to Los Angeles in 1905. As the biggest city in America founded during the twentieth century, Las Vegas has made the hard-core engineering problem of imploding old high rise buildings into a high art and public spectacle. Yet, it also ironically has kept intact its original building first begun in 1855 along Las Vegas Creek. The Old Mormon Fort is located in downtown Las Vegas Boulevard North and Washington Avenue (www.parks.nv.gov/parks/old-las-vegas-mormon-fort/), and its grounds cradle with the lore of frontier life along the Old Spanish Trail.

When William Clark of the railroad platted out and then helped incorporate the city in 1905, its population was less than 500, which represented extraordinary growth from its population of 22 in 1900. In 1906, the Overland Hotel and Hotel Nevada opened at Fremont and Main Street in downtown Las Vegas, and they would develop into today's still standing Las Vegas Club and the Golden Gate casinos. The 1910 census records Clark County as having 3,321 people with 800 residing in Las Vegas. It is during these times in the waning hours of the Old West that the city's sustaining myths take hold. Indeed:

> the founding myth of Las Vegas is that is a place for a fresh start, a place in the sun where a person is not burdened by failures in other locales,

so a new metropolis rises "on the story of an ordinary individual with great gambler's luck who hits the jackpot and changes his or her life" (Nies, 2014, p. 45).

In the grip of such faith in random good fortune, the city also gives free rein to liberal abandon and avoids as much regulation and oversight as possible. Much of what is regarded as Las Vegas, or the Strip, actually lies outside of the city itself in the unincorporated communities of Paradise (population roughly 223,000 in 2010) and Winchester (roughly 28,000 in 2010). These census-designated places began their existences in 1950 as "Paradise B" and "Paradise A" to prevent city annexation of just then beginning to boom new casinos outside of downtown. At 46.7 square miles, Paradise ("B") was founded in April 1951 with Winchester (Paradise A) formed in January 1952 with 4.3 square miles. Paradise contains not only most of The Strip but also the grounds of McCarran International Airport, the University of Nevada-Las Vegas, and now equals in population the state's capital city, Reno, to the far north.

Despite years of considerable growth during the Great Depression and World War II, the population of Las Vegas in 1950 still was only 24,624. Yet, the "leisure industry" began to burgeon during the 1940s — with the opening of the El Rancho Vegas Hotel and Casino in 1941, the Last Frontier in 1942, the Flamingo in 1946, and Thunderbird in 1948 on The Strip. During the 1950s, the Desert Inn in 1950, Sahara and Sands in 1952, Tropicana in 1957, and Stardust in 1958 — all on The Strip, matched this growth. Fremont Street downtown with its "Glitter Gulch" was remade after 1992 as the "Fremont Street Experience" with a canopy-covered pedestrian mall of neon excess. Once dubbed Glitter Gulch by the Las Vegas Chamber of Commerce, it earlier featured a considerable growth in the number of iconic hotels and gaming venues — El Cortez in 1941, Pioneer Club in 1942, Monte Carlo in 1945, Golden Nugget in 1946, Eldorado in 1946, and Westerner in 1947. Along with those establishments, 1950s-era growth brought into the same area downtown — the Horseshoe Club in 1951, Lucky Strike Club in 1954, Birdcage Casino in 1956, Fremont in 1956, and Silver Palace in 1957. With such attractions, the city's population by 1960 was 64,405, 125,787 by 1970, and 164,674 by 1980.

DESERTIFYING AN ARID PLACE ALL THE WAY DOWN

Even though it was founded in one of North America's most arid deserts, Las Vegas has proven to be a very robust and strange attractor. With no comparative advantage for competing in open legal markets, Las Vegans treated the desert as their ace in the hole. If nothing else would work, they exerted the will to endure recurring waves of even greater desiccation of body and soul amid the dry expanses of the Mohave all around them. While not associated directly with aridity, the acceptance of providing the deep desolation for profit stressed that whatever material gains there were to be had when "something happened in Vegas," then it would stay in Vegas. To recognize such barren emptiness, riotous excess, or painful duress as opportunity is significant. The city creatively has asked its inhabitants to embrace annihilation, debasement, and implosion as their ultimate growth strategy (Zizek, 2010). Sin is not a violation of the good; it simply celebrates another dirty secret of capitalism — private vices fulfilled are not a loss; they each additively compound into public virtue. The allure of pleasure-filled reification in human relations might seem contradictory, but attracting more deviants and misfits to produce diverting delights and deep devastation along with the already established citizens has been a formula for success. Still, their proliferation also adds to the metro region's uninhabitability by pulling millions more curious risk-takers into these wastelands with myths of fame and fortune to be found through the pursuit of vice. In this fashion, Las Vegas is truly a "working landscape" (Cannavo, 2007) for some of the dirtiest of today's "dirty jobs."

Degradation as Desertification

Las Vegas Valley had been an oasis for Native Americans during their centuries of inhabitation in the Mohave Desert, but it became a fortified site for Mormon settlers and wagon trains moving between Utah to California in the 1850s. Its opening to the railroad, however, turned Las Vegas into a growing node in national networks of distribution for materials, energy, and people being pushed and pulled through the logistical flows of nineteenth and twentieth-century America. Sensing increases in traffic, the residents of this desert valley went on alert to be "as hospitable as possible in any manner imaginable" to many wayfarers.

Seeing easy money in crooked card games, loose women, cheap liquor, bad entertainment, and easy family services, the city fathers decided gradually from 1910 to 1931 (with off-and-on again moral panics about such legislative edicts) to solidify their state's unique niche — with the support of Reno and the boom-ing metropolis of Los Angeles only a few hours away — in "the sin business," e.g. licensed gambling, no-wait marriage, legal prostitution, and short-wait divorce. Arguably, these policies could be treated as part of the industrialization of immorality, but they gave Las Vegas a unique twist to its desertification by ignoring strict moral and legal strictures against these practices elsewhere (Luke, 2012).

In this enterprising small city, the casinos, wedding chapels, bordellos, and courtrooms fully accommodated these pressing human needs elsewhere. For years, a unique type of tourism flourished at a number of "divorce ranches" (each one part women's retreat, part water park, part desert sanatorium, part dude ranch) to afford "The Reno Cure." Discontented wives could stay for the very short 42-day (reduced from 120 days in 1927, and then 90 days by 1931 to spur heavier traffic) waiting period for divorce (Brean, 2014). Here, once again, environmentality blended with entertainmentality as the shifting subjectivity of these resource-intensive leisure visitors was intensified and/or protracted by the diversionary detentions of special entertainments, keeping mostly female visitors in these designated zones of domestic deconstruction. Whether it was personal, moral, family, ethical, or cultural degradation, many capitalized on these moments of individual crisis to boost business for decades.

Such degrading trends in the overall cultural ethos of Las Vegas, NV still lin-ger, as confirmed by a blog entry at www.city-data.com. In answer to the ques-tion, "Been in Las Vegas for about six months […] my thoughts […]," LV10101 notes "A couple of quick pluses" about the town:

- the weather (during winter);
- the number of restaurants; and
- unlimited entertainment.

Here, a slightly disgruntled new Las Vegan still touts the town's reputation as "The Entertainment Capital of the World," and that distinction remains the anchor of its innovative casinopolitan mode of urbanism.

Again, as LV10101 observes, the pull of Vegas for many is simple:

> pseudo-possibilities. I have to say that so harsh but I think a lot of people including myself see Las Vegas a place of possibilities. Maybe too many trips here as a tourist and not getting off the Strip seeing the real Las Vegas didn't help. <www.city-date.com/forum/Las-Vegas/ 2295351-been-las-vegas-about-six-months-html#ixzz3UUSKad8L>

Without saying as much, this city in the desert is, in fact, a vast desert of a city:

> Las Vegas is not a city, it's a place built on gambling and lack what most cities have to offer. We have one main entertainment source in Las Vegas hotels/casinos. Most of the entertainment options in Las Vegas are provided by hotels/casinos and that I believe is a minus as well. Most cities have a more rounded atmosphere, we in Las Vegas have a central core of atmosphere, gambling. When you leave the Las Vegas Strip you realize this "city" is filled with nothing but strip malls and is lacking a real community feel in many ways [...] people seem to work more part-time jobs and have less time to just take it all in. That relates to the lower pay Las Vegas provides compared to other cities similar sized. Pay, poor schools, lack of community, lack of reinvestment into the local community and you might as well prepare for another Atlantic City. <www.city.data.com/forum/las-vegas/2295351-been-las-vegas-about-six-months-html#ixzz3UUSKad8L>

The Strip radiates these waves of casinopolitan devastation as the city's most distinctive influence at many sites around the world (Luke, 2012) from Macau to Moscow. It is arguably another integral component unfolding under "the open sky" of "the world-city" (Virilio, 1997, p. 75) hosting what some regard as "Earth, Inc." (Gore, 2013, pp. 4–24). Atlantic City once aspired to be Vegas in the 1970s and succeeded for a few years with its own Vegas-styled excitements. After successive recessions and competition from scores of closer venues than Vegas, it also is largely burdened with Vegas-like blight, revealing the true desertification of the sin business *ab absurdum* (Johnson, 2010; Simon, 2004).

Fortunately, this open acceptance of going bust, imploding to regroup, and tearing apart what *is* to attain what *should be* in Vegas is this implosive-readiness in "the entertainment capital of the world." This distinction, however, follows more from its capability to swerve around "the limits to capital" (Harvey, 2007) by transmuting entertainment endlessly into capital and retain its powerful position in "the world of entertainment capital." Unlike the city's most famous slogan, "What happens in Vegas, Stays in Vegas," the relentless realities of entertainment capital's feeble sense of decorum never let up. Indeed, they almost guarantee that actually "what happens [only] in Vegas, spreads [always] from Vegas." Guarantees that whatever is imagined only to stay in Vegas is what rapidly despoils what most people elsewhere would regard as the essence of a stable spiritual, natural, or ethical life anywhere (Gragg, 2013).

Development as Desertification

The desertification of development has pushed the growing uninhabitability of the high and dry Las Vegas Valley to its outer limits of unsustainability by maintaining illusions of a wet, mild, green, and comfortable paradise of lawns, trees, lakes, and gardens. Yet, the entire metropolitan area's explosive demographic growth since 1905, and disruptively rapid development since 1990 have taxed the city's water supplies beyond their sustainability.

Those waters that drew European settlers to Las Vegas in the 1850s were barely adequate for the town when the railroad arrived. The construction of a maintenance yard for the San Pedro, Los Angeles and Salt Lake railroad in 1911 nearly doubled the city's population by 1915, which only gained 24-hour electricity from the railroad's shops the same year. However, when the Union Pacific bought out this smaller rail company, it also ratcheted down the water supplies the railroad had provided to the residents of Las Vegas, thereby stifling population growth. Only the filling of Lake Mead behind Hoover Dam during the 1930s alleviated the city's water supply issue, but it was at best a patch that lasted barely two generations. By the 1990s, a second pumping station had to be built, and now a third one (Intake No. 3 Low-level Pumping Station) is under construction. Even though Lake Mead is the largest man-made lake in North America, Las Vegas is desertifying nearby regions by desiccating its watershed, groundwater reserves, and surface water supplies to meet the daily needs of 2.1 metro area residents and 3.4 million visitors a month (www.lvcva.com/includes/content/images/docs/ES-Jan-2015paf).

Las Vegas, along with Phoenix and Tucson in Arizona, are the three major concentrations with nearly 13 million people, who occupy very arid sites in the Colorado River Basin's 246,000 square miles sprawling across large parts of California, Wyoming, Colorado, Utah, Nevada, New Mexico, and Arizona. Yet, another 25−30 million people are dependent on the Colorado River Basin's waters for agricultural, domestic, industrial, and recreational needs. It has 29 major dams, hundreds of miles of aqueducts, scores of canals, and multiple managers to extract the maximum efficiency for water use. An analysis in the 1990s argued that every drop of water in the basin is used 17 times a year (Reisner, 1993, p. 120) after being stored in man-made reservoirs that hold four times the river's annual flow. That economy of use is now long gone.

In 1937, Las Vegas dug its first pipeline to Lake Mead as it filled to a full pond, believing this water supply could sustain its needs for the foreseeable long-run future. Yet, the town had only 24,624 residents in 1950, while the city alone had nearly two million people in 2010, and that was up radically from 741,459 in 1990. Moreover, the number of foreign visitors a month to Las Vegas in 2010 was 2.5 million in 2010 (US Department of Commerce, 2011). In 2000, Las Vegas ran its second pipeline to Lake Mead for water intake, and the third one will draw water from the lake at 870 feet above sea level even though its "dead pool" level is 900 feet (Brean, 2014, p. 5B). Since 2000, the lake has dropped 130 feet on average and sat at 1,078 feet above sea level in November 2018 (http://mead.uslakes.info/level.asp). The two existing pipelines were laid when no one expected the lake to drop to 1,000 feet, so if it drops another 85 feet about 90% of the Las Vegas Valley's water would be essentially inaccessible (Brean, 2014, p. 5B). Fearing Colorado River water soon will not be enough; the Southern Nevada Water Authority is proposing to draw groundwater from within a 300-mile arc of rural territory in rural eastern Nevada to sustain the city in the prolonged drought that the entire Southwest appears to be facing for decades (Brean, 2014, pp. 1B, 5B).

While most people are only passing through, Las Vegas still unsustainably must provide for a demographic tide of nearly 37–42 million people passing through and staying awhile every year. How much jet fuel, gasoline, diesel fuel, and electricity is used to move, feed, house, entertain, and clean up after a city this size in the Mohave Desert is also accelerating desertification that reaches all around the USA and across the world. The first railroad train came in 1905, the first commercial air flight land in 1926, automobile and bus traffic also became significant in the 1920s and 1930s: for over a century, Las Vegas has been an electrifying destination. Its neon fantasias, and leisure wonderlands, are alluring, but it is also a carbon capitalist city made possible only by millions of fossil-fueled lines of flight in today's desentifying "hypercarbon reality" (Murphy, 2014, pp. 317–338).

Destruction as Desertification

The rise of the military economy and warfare state in the USA was launched in the late 1930s. With millions of square miles of vast empty spaces, the entire American West is a well-known "national sacrifice zone." And, Nevada is one of the places most easily and often sacrificed to any great act of horrendous despoliation the American republic may require. Las Vegas Army Air Field, now Nellis Air Force Base, for example, trained tens of thousands of aerial gunners during World War II. The city's spatial isolation allowed thousands of men, hundreds of aircraft, and scores of towed targets to fly around Las Vegas for years while firing millions of rounds of live 0.30 and 0.50 caliber machine gun ammunition into the Western Skies of the Colorado basin states. From Korea and Vietnam through today's wars against terror, live-fire practice runs continue around the region with strafing and bombing drills as well.

Likewise, the city of Henderson on Las Vegas' eastern boundaries began growing, for example, before Pearl Harbor, but it only had around 3,000 residents. Once World War II began, it served through most of the 1940s as the main location for Basic Magnesium, whose huge industrial plant supplied about 25% of all magnesium components for incendiary munitions, engine parts, and airframe components purchased by the War Department. Employing 14,000 people and using a quarter of all Hoover Dam's electricity output, the plant closed and was transferred to the state after 1945. During the Cold War, the PEPCON and Kerr-McGee companies produced ammonium perchlorate for ballistic missiles, the Space Shuttle, and NASA, but they closed down after the May 4, 1988, PEPCON disaster when that factory exploded. Kerr-McGee continues production in nearby Cedar City, UT, and it also is a major producer of nuclear fuels and other materials for the DOE. Severe perchlorate contamination has been draining 8.7 million gallons of water and 20.4 pounds of perchlorate into Las Vegas Wash, however, since the 1990s, but those high levels of fairly serious contamination in the Colorado River itself were dropping by the mid-2000s (https://www.dtsc.ca.gov/LawRessPolicies/Regs/upload/HWMP_WS_ dPerch-Sec9.pdf). Despite this record, a considerable spectrum of munitions and defense goods still are part of the Las Vegas Valley's economy.

More pertinently, during the twenty-first century, Clark County and Las Vegas emerged as major sites of the nation's drone warfare forces working with Nellis and Creech Air Force Bases in the key operational and training roles for the USA's RPV reconnaissance and attack drone aircraft units. These aspects of desertification in this region now reach through the rarified extremes of cyberspace to deliver drone-fired decimation by Hellfire missiles all around the world. Such destructive ecologies have not begun to equal the desertification of nuclear devastation advanced during the Cold War, but those devastations were foreshadowed in the 1940s by the training of the 509th Composite Group, mostly in the Wendover, Utah, and Nevada areas around Wendover Air Force Base. This unit was composed of the specially selected, trained, and deployed detachment of B-29 Superfortress heavy bombers and their crews that delivered the two atomic bombs on Japan during August 1945. Nonetheless, the decades of devotion to delivering death from the air also suffuse their cultural effects on the city's residents. It is a hard-earned distinction for this desert place, but this reputation casts a certain shadow. And, these shades of gray lend little glory to the servicemen and women deployed to operate such machineries of remotely piloted destruction from above today.

Devastation as Desertification

The desertification of Las Vegas that is undoubtedly the darkest and deepest also came to it through the US Army Air Force nexus with the Atomic Energy Commission (AEC). Because of its well-tested isolation, the range of the Las Vegas Gunnery School 65 miles northwest of the city was prepared for an incredible use in 1950. The Pentagon formally established the Nevada Test Site (NTS) on January 11, 1951, and then detonated the first airburst nuclear bomb test on January 27, 1951 (1-kiloton device) on Frenchman Flat. Most of the USA's 858 nuclear tests at the NTS were conducted underground after 1963, but 122 were aboveground events from 1951 to 1963 (when the 1962 Nuclear Test Ban Treaty ruled that all future American and Soviet atomic tests would be conducted underground). Like Kazakhstan in the USSR, Nevada in the USA served as one of the Earth's single most frequently targeted sites for repeated nuclear bomb blasts. Most citizens remember Hiroshima and Nagasaki in Japan. Yet, few Americans know that their own national soil has served as the first, and most extensively, devastated places on the planet thanks to the AEC, and then Department of Energy, setting off nuclear explosions across the USA from Alaska to New Mexico and Colorado. Nevada, however, ended up experiencing the greatest number of aboveground atomic bombs detonated in America during peace with over 60 times as many explosions than Japan experienced in war.

The desertification from this devastation will endure for millennia. The government of the United States of America has now survived over 225 years, but each nuclear weapon's test blast was a devastating act of diplomatic bluster, military spectacle, and scientific experimentation that has left severe toxic effects across this region for ages. Radioactive isotopes rained down across the Southwest intensely for nearly once a month during a dozen years in the mid-twentieth century, but the half-lives of their most noxious radioactive isotopes can be dangerous for up to 24,000 years – well over 1,000 times the duration of the America republic. The flora, fauna, soils, waters, and humans, which are left to live in Nevada, the Colorado River Basin, and much of the USA downwind of the Nevada Test Range, must inhabit this radioactive desert for millennia.

The desertification of nuclear devastation at a distance – tied to Las Vegas in this instance – triggered many serious seismic events in Clark County, mushroom clouds were visible from nearly 100 miles away in any direction, and decades of intense nuclear contamination caused an extraordinary rise in the incidence of bone cancer, brain cancer, gastrointestinal cancers, leukemia, lymphoma, melanoma, and thyroid cancer. The greatest impact was documented from the early 1950s to 1980 (Falk, 1982, p. 134; Johnson, 1984, p. 230), but the mortality rates from these afflictions remain high in the 17 most-affected counties immediately surrounding the test site. Air, soil, and water contamination occurred during the aboveground tests, but about a third of the subterranean tests were detonated near aquifers in which water-borne plutonium and uranium isotopes also will pose risks to water supplies for thousands of years (Rogers, 2014, p. 5B).

ENVIRONMENTALITY/ENTERTAINMENTALITY AS URBAN ECOLOGY

Las Vegas, as a site of continuously re-engineering cultural valorization, is a key nexus in the worldwide circulation of symbolic codes, operation of machinic collectives, and consumption of corporate commodities that lace together the material logistics of everyday life as global urbanization (Al, 2017). In 1900, Las Vegas had 22 residents; but, by 2000, it had grown into one of 800 cities in the world with a population of at least 500,000. Moreover, the loosely coupled "systems of objects" (Baudrillard, 2006) and "cultivation of subjects" (Foucault, 2010) at work in this one city have experienced its Las Vegas Strip experience openly being adopted as a prized normative benchmark for urban design and cosmopolitan culture in many of the other 799 cities around the world of comparable size thanks to global mass media, world tourism, and architectural style. As one of stronger anchors of "a new social system beyond classical capitalism," Las Vegas generates a continuously evolving business by continuously restyling professional conventions, grand hotels, trade shows, entertainment productions, food services, shopping venues, and esthetic fashions that spread quickly through "the world space of multinational capital" (Jameson, 1992, pp. 59, 54).

Out west of town, in Red Rock Canyon, it is easy "to think like a mountain," as Aldo Leopold (1949) has asked all ecologists to do for decades. In a clever alliterative leap of logic, Steven Vogel (2014) flips around Leopold's injunction,

but instead bids ecologists "to think like a mall." Las Vegas real estate developers were way ahead of him in the 1980s, but his point is worth considering.

At times, Vogel's "thinking like a mall" essentially accedes with feeble liberal
faith to ignoring Marx's outraged refusal to accept reification. That is, built
environments, such as malls, are features in "second nature," like mountains in
"first nature." Hence, "to think like a mall would be to see that it, too, might
know something that we do not, and realize that the social world too, can be
autonomous of us, just as beyond our understanding, and beyond wishes, as a
mountain" (Vogel, 2014, p. 187). Is Vogel's essay perhaps mistitled, because he
ultimately does not seem to think like the mall he and his neighbors have lost in
Columbus, Ohio? Instead he moves to caress, cradle, if not kiss, the hidden hand
of the market at work in all malls as milieux.

For Vogel, malls do not fail, as David Harvey (2009) would argue, because
of the continuous churn of spatial valorization and devalorization of commodified space in an endless artificial and venal search for personal profit, which
pushed City Center down, while pulling the Mall at Tuttle Crossing, Easton
Tower Center, and Polaris Fashion Center up (Vogel, 2014, p. 176). Harvey
maintains the tumult of such volatile urban landscapes is the compound result
of all the careful planning, shrewd investment, and creative destruction behind
capital valorization. Vogel gets lost instead in the mysterious mists of mystified
money: City Center's demise "was not knowable or predictable by anyone ahead
of time: It occurred *autonomously*, independently of the choices and desires of
any person or any corporation. This is of the essence of a capitalist economy
[…] the invisible hand. If anything controlled the malls' fate, it was the hand −
but that hand is not the hand of any one of us or any group of us, so the mall's
fate was not in *our* hands. Other to every one of us, it was autonomous" (Vogel,
2014, p. 186).

The naturalization of human choices by "good capitalists" (Vogel, 2014,
p. 186) appears to almost magically create more up-scale competition in more
modern, wealthier areas of Columbus, Ohio. Such spells of "discontinuous
growth" guarantee urban decay "always just happens." That new malls opened
larger, more modern shops, with free parking, and better marketing to Vogel
was merely the dynamic outcome of other, autonomous, inexorable changes −
far beyond anyone's control. The invisible hand let go that "set of forces," which
no human being could fully predict or control (Vogel, 2014, p. 186), because
any built environment, urban market, or human artifact has "the autonomy it
always possesses, an autonomy we neither can nor would wish to remove"
(Vogel, 2014, p. 187).

Vogel's interesting effort, however, to draw an analogy by asking us to "think
like a mall" instead of "a mountain," like Leopold, actually is somewhat old news
by the imaginative lights of urban planners working across Las Vegas. Evidence
of their pioneering advances is particularly apparent in the increasingly elaborate
and interconnected megastructure on the Las Vegas Strip (or Las Vegas
Boulevard). The malignant expansion of this vision sprawls from Sahara Avenue
in the north to Russell Road to the south, although Tropicana Avenue was once
the southern boundary until Mandalay Bay was built slightly north of Russell

Road in 1999. Today, I-15 often is seen as this new metropolitan hub's western boundary, while Paradise Road marks its eastern border. Ever expanding, this faux "Monte Carlo in the Mohave" has been rising from the flames of capitalism's creative destruction as the mega-mall of all earthly delights for over 35 years.

One of the prime movers for this direction of thinking was Steve Wynn. Since 1980, Wynn has been all about "thinking like a mall." He planned, organized, constructed, and then opened his property, "The Mirage," in November 1989. Using Wall Street investment capital raised with junk bonds, the Mirage was the first from-the-ground-up project opened in Vegas since the mid-1960s. He soon followed that first massive hotel (3,044 rooms) with the nearby Treasure Island Hotel and Casino in 1993 (2,664 rooms and 220 suites). Joined together by a tram to Mirage, both hotels are tied to the Fashion Show Mall (opened in 1981 by the Rouse Company). With nearly 2 million square feet of space, 250 plus stores, and seven anchor stores, these megastructures were joined by Wynn's Bellagio project in 1993 after he and company purchased and demolished the 1950s-era Dunes Hotel.

The Bellagio opened in 1998. Unlike the legendary Dunes property, which always struggled financially at that site throughout its history due to its once considerable distance from old Las Vegas' downtown, the Bellagio has been a tremendous success for over 20 years. Wynn followed this same strategic plan in 2000 when he purchased the more famous and successful Desert Inn, and then began demolishing its structures in 2001 to make way for his Wynn Las Vegas resort that opened in 2005. Wynn integrated the old Desert Inn Country Club and Golf Course into the resort and, still devoted to thinking like a mall, set up the Wynn Esplanade Shoppes with an elite mix of boutiques, featuring the ultimate up-market names like Cartier, Chanel, Christian Dior, Givenchy, Hermes, Louis Vuitton, Oscar de la Renta, and a full-blown Ferrari-Maserati and Lamborghini dealership to tempt any impulse buyers who might hit it really big in the casino. Is Vogel really asking one to think like a mall, or only pleading not to see how his ruminations might culminate in experiencing only the Wynn mega-mall milieux?

CONCLUSIONS

Like the planet's other sprawling cities, Las Vegas is an integral component in the globalizing neoliberal omnipolitanization of the Earth's surface, or the "world-city, the city to end all cities," in which the technical, social, organizational, and cultural realities of commercial spatiality that index individual, regional, and national wealth largely now accumulate in cities "in which the interaction of exchanges" increasingly does not differ "from the – automatic – interconnection of financial markets today" (Virilio, 1997, p. 75). The neoliberal logic of "winner takes all" also is reflected in the metrometabolic exchanges of these extraordinary urban formations, which Las Vegas has helped so many others "to learn" all about (Venturi et al., 1977) along the Strip. While taking up around only 2% of the planet's surface, cities have now for nearly a generation sheltered over 50% of its population, used 75% of its natural resources, and generated 75% of its wastes (Smith, 2001, p. A16).

All of these trends accentuate "the crisis of place facing the United States," because the rampant developments behind such unsustainable urban metabolisms are "ruining built and natural landscapes, disconnecting people from their surroundings, and threatening individuals' fundamental sense of place" (Cannavo, 2007, p. xi). Las Vegas, however, might constitute the exception to Cannavo's important thoughts about ecologies of place as working landscapes. In this case, maybe it is the rampant overdevelopment of a vast urban simulation, featuring multiple ruinations of its own built and natural landscapes, which actually gives many Las Vegans, and probably most Vegas visitors, their most fundamental sense of place?

One in a thousand people may feel more grounded out on the rocky creosote flats of the Mohave Desert surrounding Las Vegas, but the other 999 are tightly plugged into the casinopolitan culture of this Entertainment Capital of the World whose essence floats on the dynamics of desertification (Stierli, 2013). Ironically, then, the most material crises of place for Las Vegas would have to be linked to the tremendous financial crises shaking the commercial stability of the Strip from 2000 to 2015. For all these resident or transient souls, the most dearly valued places in Las Vegas are, in fact, despoiled sites of chaotic excess, which anchor them to their casinopolitan life here.

Cruising around Las Vegas on their road trip, Raoul Duke and his attorney, Dr Gonzo, stopped at Terry's Taco Stand, USA on Paradise Road in northeast Las Vegas, and told the waitress:

> We're looking for "the American Dream," and we were told it was somewhere in this area [...] All we were told was, go till you find the American Dream. Take this white Cadillac and go find the American Dream. It's somewhere in the Las Vegas area. (Thompson, 1998, pp. 164, 165)

The waitress and the cook, Lou, thought that it was indeed up ahead and quite close. Neither one could remember if you turned left or right to get there. Yet, it maybe was "the old Psychiatrist's Club [...] big black building, right on Paradise: twenty-four hours a day violence, drugs [...]" (Thompson, 1998, p. 167). When they arrived there two hours later, Duke and Dr Gonzo located "[...] a huge slab of cracked, scorched concrete in a vacant lot full of tall weeds. The owner of a gas station across the place had 'burned down about three years ago'" (Thompson, 1998, p. 168).

Today's migrants, residents, and visitors experience far less misdirection. Steve Wynn and other casino developers have built the American Dream, and millions are coming to where it thrives – places like The Mirage Hotel & Casino, where all are invited to "Live Your Dreams Out Loud," twirling around in the delirium of environmentality and entertainmentality. As for the Anthropocene, the climatic, biophysical, hydrological, chemical, and radiological traces of what may well be a new era in geological time are repeatedly registering themselves in desertification, which clearly makes this fabulous neoliberal city – both up close and at a distance – "the heart of the planet we made."

REFERENCES

Al, S. (2017). *The strip: Las Vegas and the architecture of the American dream.* Cambridge, MA: MIT Press.

Baudrillard, J. (2006). *The system of objects.* London: Verso.

Brean, H. (2014). Pumping station recommended. *Las Vegas Review-Journal* (November 22–23): 1B, 5B.

Cannavo, P. (2007). *The working landscape: Founding, preservation, and the politics of place.* Cambridge, MA: MIT Press.

Carlson, A. (2009). *Nature & landscape: An introduction to environmental aesthetics.* New York, NY: Columbia University Press.

Chakrabartty, D. (2009). The climate of history: Four theses. *Critical Enquiry, 35*(2), 197–222.

Falk, J. (1982). *The battle over nuclear power.* New York, NY: Oxford University Press.

Foucault, M. (1973). *The order of things: An archaeology of the human sciences.* New York, NY: Vintage.

Foucault, M. (1980). *History of sexuality* (Vol. I). New York, NY: Vintage.

Foucault, M. (1991). Governmentality. In G. Burchell, C. Gordon, & P. Miller (Eds.), *The Foucault effect: Studies in governmentality.* Chicago, IL: University of Chicago Press.

Foucault, M. (2010). *The birth of biopolitics: Lectures at the Collège de France, 1978–1979.* New York, NY: Palgrave Macmillan.

Fukuyama, F. (1992). 1990. *The end of history or the last man.* New York, NY: Free Press.

Gore, A., Jr. (2013). *The future: Six drivers of global change.* New York, NY: Random House.

Gragg, L. (2013). *Bright light city: Las Vegas in popular culture.* Lawrence, KS: University Press of Kansas.

Harvey, D. (2007). *The limits to capital.* London: Verso.

Harvey, D. (2009). *Social justice and the city.* Athens: University of Georgia Press.

Harvey, D. (2011). *The enigma of capital.* New York, NY: Profile.

Jameson, F. (1992). *Postmodernism, or the cultural logic of late capitalism.* Durham, NC: Duke University Press.

Johnson, C. J. (1984). Cancer incidence in an area of radioactive fallout downwind from the Nevada test site. *Journal of the American Medical Association, 251*(2), 230–236.

Johnson, N. (2010). *Boardwalk empire: The birth, high times, and corruption of Atlantic city.* Medford, NJ: Nexus Publishing.

LeMenager, S. (2014). *Living oil: Petroleum culture in the American century.* New York, NY: Oxford University Press.

Leopold, A. (1949). *A sand County Almanac.* New York, NY: Oxford University Press.

Luke, T. W. (1995). On environmentality: Geo-power and knowledge in the discourses of contemporary environmentalism. *Cultural Critique, 31*(Fall), 57–58.

Luke, T. W. (2005). Scanning fast capitalism: Quasipolitan order and new social flowmations. *Fast Capitalism*, 1.1 (August). Retrieved from http://www.fastcapitalism.com

Luke, T. W. (2006). *Museum politics: Power plays at the exhibition.* Minneapolis, MN: University of Minnesota Press.

Luke, T. W. (2012). Casinopolitanism. In G. Ritzer (Ed.), *The Wiley-Blackwell encyclopedia of globalization* (Vol. 1). New York, NY: John Wiley & Sons.

Luke, T. W. (2014). Urbanism as cyborganicity: Tracking the materialities of the Anthropocene. *New Geographies: Grounding Urban Metabolism, 06*, August, 39–53.

McNeill, J. R. (2001). *Something new under the sun: An environmental history of the twentieth-century world* (the global century series). New York, NY: W. W. Norton & Company.

Mitchell, T. J. (2013). *Carbon democracy: Political power in the age of oil.* London: Verso.

Monastersky, R. (2015). The human age. *Nature, 519*(March 12), 144–147.

Mumford, L. (2010). *Technics and civilization.* Chicago, IL: University of Chicago Press.

Murphy, R. (2014). The emerging hypercarbon reality, technological and post-carbon utopias, and social innovation to low-carbon societies. *Current Sociology, 63*(3), 317–338.

Nies, J. (2014). *Unreal city: Las Vegas, Black Mesa, and the Fate of the West.* New York, NY: Nation Books.

Reisner, M. (1993). *Cadillac desert.* New York, NY: Penguin.

Revelle, R., Broecker, W., Craig, H., Leeling, C. D., & Smagoronsky, J. (1965). Restoring the quality of our environment: Report of the environmental pollution panel. *Atmospheric carbon dioxide* (pp. 111–133). Washington, DC: The President's Science Advisory Committee.

Roberts, N. (1998). *The Holocene: An environmental history*. Oxford: Buckwell.

Rogers, K. (2014). Nuclear testing remnants move underground at slow pace. *Las Vegas Review-Journal*, (November 22–23), 5B.

Schwägerl, C. (2014). *The Anthropocene: The human era and how it shapes our planet*. Santa Fe, NM: Synergetic Press.

Simon, B. (2004). *Boardwalk of dreams: Atlantic city and the fate of urban America*. Oxford: Oxford University Press.

Smith, D. (2001). What on earth? *Washington Post*, (February 3), A16.

Stierli, M. (2013). *Las Vegas in the rearview mirror: The city in theory, photography, and film*. Los Angeles, CA: The Getty Institute.

Thompson, H. S. (1998). *Fear and loathing in Las Vegas: A strange journey to the heart of the American dream*. New York, NY: Vintage Books.

U.S. Department of Commerce. (2011). *Overseas visitation estimates for U.S. states, cites, and census regions: 2011*. Washington, DC: International Trade Administration/U.S. Department of Commerce. Retrieved from http://tinet.ita.roc.gov

Venturi, R., Izenour, S., & Brown, D. S. (1977). *Learning from Las Vegas: The forgotten symbolism of architectural firm* (Rev. ed.). Cambridge, MA: MIT Press.

Vince, G. (2014). *Adventures in the Anthropocene: A journey to the heart of the planet we made*. Minneapolis, MN: Milkweed Editions.

Virilio, P. (1995). *The art of the motor*. Minneapolis, MN: University of Minnesota Press.

Virilio, P. (1997). *Open sky*. London: Verso.

Vogel, S. (2014). Thinking like a mall. M. Drenthen & J. Kevlartz (Eds.), *Environmental aesthetics: Crossing divides and breaking ground*. New York, NY: Fordham University Press.

Wuerthner, G., Crist, E., & Butler, T. (Eds.). (2014). *Keeping the wild: Against the domestication of the earth*. Washington, DC: Island Press.

Zalaisewicz, W., Steffen, M., & Crutzen, P. (2010). The new world of the Anthropocene. *Environmental Science and Technology*, *44*, 2228–2231.

Zizek, S. (2010). *Living in the end times*. London: Verso.

EXCHANGING SOCIAL CHANGE FOR SOCIAL CLASS: TRADITIONAL MARRIAGE PROPOSALS AS STATUS AND SCRIP

Patricia Arend and Katherine Comeau

ABSTRACT

This chapter studies the social reproduction of the traditional heterosexual engagement ritual in which men propose marriage to women, even as many women now occupy positions of power, surpass men in educational attainment, and provide their own incomes. We draw from 37 semi-structured interviews with middle-class, heterosexual women in which they discussed their marriage proposals. We argue that three related types of socioeconomic incentives encourage women to participate in traditional proposals: (1) the social status of being chosen to marry, (2) the value of gifts, especially an engagement ring, which also reflects the fiancé's implied taste, and (3) the proposal story itself as scrip for inclusion in heterosexual women's social groups. By considering social factors that mediate relationships among women, we show that economic and status incentives are important explanations for the perpetuation of the traditional engagement ritual. Specifically, the middle-class, heterosexual women in our study exchange socioeconomic status in their female-centered reference groups for their participation in gender-normative relations with their male partners.

Keywords: Consumer society; gender; proposal; scrip; stalled revolution; status

The Challenge of Progress: Theory Between Critique and Ideology
Current Perspectives in Social Theory, Volume 36, 179–198
Copyright © 2020 Emerald Publishing Limited
All rights of reproduction in any form reserved
ISSN: 0278-1204/doi:10.1108/S0278-120420190000036021

What power resides in the object given that causes its recipient to pay it back?
                                                    — Marcel Mauss (1990, p. 3)

I remember one occasion after a long negotiating session with a publisher for whom Goffman and I are both editors. I turned to Goffman and said with some disgust, "These fellows are treating us like commodities." Goffman's reply was, "That's all right, Al, so long as they treat us as expensive commodities."
                                                    — Alvin W. Gouldner (1970, p. 383)

The publication of materialist feminist Chrys Ingraham's *White Weddings: Romancing Heterosexuality in Popular Culture* (1999) marks the advent of a growing body of scholarship on the meaning and persistence of these traditionally gendered marriage rituals, despite significant social change since their inception. Her work is important for drawing attention to the wedding-industrial complex, those relationships between business and culture that facilitate the interpellation of heterosexual couples as feminine brides and masculine grooms. She and other cultural critics argue that wedding media maintain the relevance of the white wedding by constructing it as a logical outcome of heterosexual romantic love or by changing the meaning of specific ritual elements to keep it current, such as a white dress signifying bride instead of purity (Ingraham, 1999, 2008; Jellison, 2008). Still other scholars suggest that the white wedding remains popular due to its structural characteristics such as flexibility that makes possible the representation of the individuality of the couples who participate (Dunak, 2013). However, scholars have barely begun to address the paradox from the demand side of the equation.

Arend (2016) previously argued that social ties, especially between female friends, relatives, and colleagues in homosocial contexts, play a significant role in reproducing (or challenging, in limited ways) the white wedding. The social relationships between women that form the fabric of everyday life iteratively cultivate gendered cultural capital, that knowledge of what desires are appropriate for female members of a class-based group as well as the skills to realize them properly (Bourdieu, 1984; Butler, 1993, 1990). In doing so, they also facilitate how individuals encounter white weddings in mass media, such as girlfriends watching a film together, which further informs their practice of appropriate femininity. In this chapter, we delve deeper into explaining the reproduction of one part of the white wedding, the traditional marriage proposal.

This chapter argues: (1) the traditional proposal persists in heterosexual contexts at least in part because of middle-class women's investment in the status it conveys to their peers in relation to a marriage market; (2) the status derives from being chosen by a man for marriage and the particular gifts and experiences he provides during the proposal, which also reflect his taste. We further argue: (3) that the most important outcome of the proposal, other than the engagement, is the *proposal story*, which not only announces the engagement but (4) acts as scrip for entrance into homosocial contexts and (5) distinguishes newly engaged women in their reference groups. Taken together, we assert that: (6) these incentives lead some heterosexual, middle-class women to exchange social and economic status in their female-centered reference groups for their participation in gender-normative relations with their male partners.

This study is part of a larger qualitative research project that uses semi-structured interviews and participant observation to examine the persistence of the white wedding. White weddings are culturally dominant marriage rituals that, historically, involve a bride in a white gown and a tuxedoed groom reciting vows in front of friends and family, and a celebration marked by material goods and practices such as invitations, flowers, a cake, and dancing. Same-gender couples also now practice white weddings. Preliminary observations from the larger study indicate the importance of examining the ritual that kicks off the white wedding process, the traditional marriage proposal, and its economy and meaning.

While some elements of the white wedding began centuries prior, it ultimately coalesced into the dominant marriage ritual in the United States in the postwar prosperity of the late 1940s and 1950s, an era of historically high marriage rates and when the average age of first marriage was at an all-time low (Dunak, 2013). It was also a period dominated by a conservative ethos that promoted a rigid gender division of labor in households (Friedan, 1963). The ritual solidified in this era includes the tradition of men proposing to women with a diamond ring (Howard, 2006). Recently, however, the economy is struggling, marriage rates are declining, and the average age of first marriage is at an all-time high. Scholars agree that weddings and marriage for US couples now mark their social and economic achievement, rather than launch their lives together (Cherlin, 2004). Many individuals who cannot find a "marriageable" spouse, afford to finish their education, or find a well-paying job simply do not participate (Edin & Kefalas, 2005; Gibson-Davis, Edin, & McClanahan, 2005; Smock, Manning, & Porter, 2005). Not only do couples want to be economically stable before they marry, many wait until they can afford what they understand to be "real" weddings complete with a reception that includes food, music, and dancing (Gibson-Davis et al., 2005; Sassler & Miller, 2011; Smock et al., 2005). While the US Supreme Court recently legalized marriage for same-gender couples in the United States, the wedding is still exclusive to the extent that it is primarily a white, middle-class (and higher) ritual practice (Banks, 2011). This state means that we construct our analysis of the traditional proposal in a period in which marriage rituals are often connected to class and race privilege.

Our analysis rests on a central assumption. If coverture — the ownership of women's political and economic personhood by their fathers and then husbands that originated in British common law — is indeed over, then the traditions that reflect that set of laws would cease to exist in that women would not be objects unveiled at white weddings or marked with their husbands' names and would be free to initiate relationships, including marriage, to the same extent as men.

The dismantling of coverture was the major goal and achievement of the first and second waves of the women's movement in the United States. Women can now control their own votes and property, while husbands cannot rape wives with impunity, prevent them from working for wages, or force them to have unwanted children. Of course the need for social change remains, especially for the rights of women who are not white, affluent, and heterosexual, in such areas as equal pay, citizenship, representation in formal politics, organizations, mass media, and much more. If the legal control of fathers and husbands over daughters and wives is over, why do the marriage rituals that reflect that era persist? From brides being unveiled as beautiful objects to the majority of heterosexual women taking their husbands' last names, dominant culture keeps the spirit of coverture alive. What accounts for the reproduction of coverture-related marriage rituals as they relate to the culture of contemporary gender relations? How should we understand women who adhere to traditional gender norms, including those who otherwise embrace social equality? How might we define progress in the fight against sexist oppression and patriarchal social relations under these conditions?

This chapter is organized as follows. First, we present the state of the research on marriage proposals as it pertains to the question of why the traditional version persists. Second, given the centrality of the diamond engagement ring and other features of the ritual practice, we contextualize marriage proposals with reflection on their place in contemporary consumer society. Third, we present a full accounting of the research methods, recruiting, and participants of the study. Fourth, we report our findings on the status and socioeconomic incentives to participate in traditional proposals as well as the importance of the proposal story. Our concluding discussion reflects on the implications of the persistence of the traditional marriage proposal for progress in sexist gender relations.

THE PERSISTENCE OF TRADITIONAL MARRIAGE PROPOSALS

A proposal is a cultural and sometimes religious ritual that socially confirms the commitment to marry for a couple who often informally already agreed to do so. A period of engagement in a couple's relationship has existed for centuries in North America (Otnes & Pleck, 2003). Historically, heterosexual couples exclusively practiced engagement rituals, given restrictions on same-gender marriage until recently. The proposal can be understood as a rite of passage that ends the period of dating (Otnes & Pleck, 2003) and initiates a "liminal state" in the transition between childhood and adulthood or being a single person to a husband or wife (Turner, 1969). Schweingruber, Anahita, and Berns call it one link in a "chain of romantic rites of passage" that also includes prom, vow renewal ceremonies, and more (2004, p. 144). No doubt, some women still experience proposals this way. However, with a historically older average age of first marriage and with more than two-thirds of couples living together before they get married, few now experience engagement as the process of becoming an adult. Other scholars conceptualize more recent marriage proposals as consumer rituals, given the attention to romantic consumption. Otnes and Pleck (2003) emphasize the feeling of magic that proposals can convey. Historians invariably point to the jewelry industry's role in the modern ritual's popularity, especially the "Diamond Is Forever" campaign for De Beers, dubbed the "slogan of the [twentieth] century" by *Advertising Age* (Howard, 2006). Indeed, proposals may be growing extravagant to keep up with the ring's lavish nature (Otnes & Pleck, 2003; Vannini, 2004).

The contemporary proposal's particular elements formed within the past century, with the public taking the dominant proposal script to be "traditional" by mid-century (Howard, 2006). It includes: (1) a surprise, usually as part of a special occasion; (2) a man asking a woman to marry him or "be his wife;" and (3) a man giving a woman a ring, a diamond if affordable. The script usually includes the man proposing while on bended knee, though some researchers claim it is not a necessary component (Otnes & Pleck, 2003; Schweingruber, Cast, & Anahita, 2008). Some couples also like it when the man secures the woman's father's (or parents') permission or consent, though evidence suggests this practice has waned since the women's movement's second wave (Schweingruber et al., 2004). Couples often call or visit their families and friends soon after the proposal to announce their engagement, which advice books encourage them to do (Geller, 2001).

Few sociologists have examined contemporary proposals empirically with brides- and/or grooms-to-be. The first studies employed a dramaturgical perspective, arguing that traditional elements do not change because they communicate clearly to the woman and her family and friends that the engagement is real and serious (Schweingruber et al., 2004; Vannini, 2004). Lamont (2014) finds that some middle class, heterosexual women remain invested in the traditional proposal due to essentialist beliefs about men. To these women, sexual desire drives men's interest in relationships more than for women. Therefore, women must wait for a man to propose to make sure that his intentions to marry are genuine. Talking to the bride's family, buying her a suitable ring and planning a thoughtful surprise display his romantic and socioeconomic potential (Vannini, 2004). From this perspective, traditional proposals persist to confirm whether the man is marriage material or not.

Other relevant scholarly work examines the white wedding's reproduction. Most of this research focuses on the wedding-industrial complex's power to foster a hegemonic sensibility about heteronormative white weddings (Engstrom, 2012; Ingraham, 1999; Jellison, 2008). Representations in popular culture encourage women to take the white wedding for granted as *the real wedding* and hence the "natural" or "logical thing" one should plan when getting married. Part of this process has been to invent elements *as traditional*. For example, brides no longer wear white to represent that they are sexually inexperienced, but rather because white signifies "bride" (Hobsbawm, 1983; Jellison, 2008; Otnes & Pleck, 2003). As stated earlier, Arend (2016) argues that it is not the mere dominance of weddings in mass media that explains the white wedding's reproduction, but the *social* consumption of this media among family members and friends. Indeed, relations among women are as important in driving the traditional wedding as the relationships between brides and grooms; mothers and daughters shop for bridal gowns together and the bride's friends plan showers and bachelorette parties (Freeman, 2002; Mead, 2007; Montemurro, 2006, 2002). This chapter is the first study of which we are aware that addresses these relationships among women in relation to the traditional proposal.

PROPOSAL STORIES IN CONSUMER SOCIETY

Our analysis links feminist scholarship on gender and heterosexual marriage to the consumer society literature on consumption and socioeconomic status. In his classic indictment of the Gilded Age nouveau riche, Thorstein Veblen (1899/1994) pointed to a husband/wife relationship as a marker of class status, especially when men consume vicariously through their wives' displays of wealth, such as wearing a diamond engagement ring. For Veblen, this also marked the woman as the husband's property and so the status benefits were primarily his. However, women — especially white, affluent, heterosexual, cisgender women — did and do gain socially and economically through their marriages to men and by the acquisition of such objects as a ring. Those women who do not marry face social stigma.

Even in the twenty-first century, older, unmarried women face criticism that men do not; there is no masculine word that carries the negative connotation of "spinster" or "old maid." Popular culture abounds with women who fear no man will ever marry them (e.g. *He's Just Not That Into You*, directed by Kwapis, 2009), while portraying men as more concerned about their sexual prowess than whether or not they will marry (e.g. *The 40-Year-Old Virgin,* directed by Apatow, 2005). Women on the economic margins of society face even greater disapprobation. Poor women — disproportionately single, heterosexual, unmarried women of color with children — often describe how they hope to be married someday, but that finding an economically and socially stable man (nonviolent, employed, and non-incarcerated) can be difficult (Edin & Kefalas, 2005). Yet politicians and media pundits criticize them for having "poor judgment" and passing on poverty to their kids. Thus, status, as one factor among many, promotes heterosexual women's investment in marriage. We also argue that status, in part, keeps many interested in traditional marriage *proposals* as well.

In further conceptualizing the dynamic between economic and intimate relations, we agree with Zelizer's (2005) influential "connected lives" perspective. She asserts that the boundaries of most social relationships are marked in significant, symbolic ways, often through economic exchange; this includes the relationship of an engaged couple (p. 33). That she does not conceptualize individuals as intentionally calculating how best to advance their own interests does not mean that rewards for normative social actions have no impact. On the contrary, we assert that engagement-related gifts reinforce behavior precisely that way. French anthropologist Marcel Mauss (1990[1925]) famously extended Veblenian analysis to gift exchange, arguing that all gifts come with an expectation of reciprocity. In our contemporary analysis, some heterosexual, middle-class women quite clearly accept the status that comes with a marriage proposal in exchange for perpetuating traditional gender norms.

As stated earlier, some scholars consider traditional marriage proposals to be consumer rituals due to their emphasis on romantic commodities such as flowers, dinners at special restaurants, and especially a ring (Illouz, 1997). Schweingruber et al. (2008) found that the size of the ring did not matter to student research participants in their appraisal of engagement rituals, so long as the woman received one. Yet these items can be valuable and convey the engagement's status as well as the proposer's social class. All of his choices display his cultural capital, or taste, from the ring's size and quality (if he presents one at all) to the type of flowers or other gifts chosen to the atmosphere of the venue (Bourdieu, 1984). In his analysis of over 300 proposal narratives, Vannini (2004) also unpacked contemporary proposals as spectacle. They increasingly occur in front of large audiences, such as on a Jumbotron at professional sporting events. Most of the bride's social network will not be privy to this display. Even if there is a recording to share on social media, women will still need to narrate their experiences to those who view it, either in person or in the comments. The bride communicates the status that comes from the proposal through the telling of the *proposal story*, arguably the most important outcome of the proposal event.

Here, like Allison Pugh (2009), we draw on the long theoretical tradition that examines consumption as a form of communication in consumer society from "Veblen to Baudrillard to Bourdieu [...] and Lamont" (p. 51). In her research on children, Pugh demonstrates that consumer goods, such as toys, can operate as *scrip*, or "meaningful tokens," a kind of currency that grants kids entrance into their social worlds not regulated by parents (p. 52). Vacations, video games, and other goods and experiences provide the content of conversation and exchange in everyday lives embedded in consumer society. Absent those items, individuals must work to make those connections in other ways, a process she calls "bridging labor" (p. 66). Analogously, we argue that a ring or proposal story can function as scrip among adult women. In other words, a proposal story can give women access to certain social groups, where they then participate in the daily round of conversation among female friends, family members, and colleagues. Going beyond Pugh, that participation is also an opportunity to convey the status signified in the story and display their ring, sometimes comparing the size of the diamond to the rings of other women. We would expect engaged heterosexual women without a ring or a good story to bridge the gap between themselves and their peers in other ways.

The social science literature on the relationships between women's social groups, consumption, and gender inequality is surprisingly small. The empirical scholarship on reference groups, competitive consumption, and consumer desire (such as the fashion cycle in apparel) rarely addresses women in their peer networks, pink-collar workplaces, social clubs, etc. There are, however, several important exceptions. Peiss's (1999) social history of the development of beauty culture in the United States shows how women sought advice on cosmetics from friends and neighbors over advertisers on the belief that local knowledge trumps advertising copy. This work directs our attention to how women might influence each other's participation in the traditional ritual, over and above the directives communicated by the jewelry industry.

Obligation is another factor. Research on direct sales companies such as Tupperware suggests that while house parties can be fun for some women they put pressure on friends, neighbors, and co-workers to buy something they may not want (Williams & Bemiller, 2010). Montemurro (2002) finds that obligation is a factor in women's participation at bridal showers where some "go because [they feel they] have to." Further, Storr (2003) examines "female homosociality" at Ann Summers (sex toy and lingerie) parties. Here attendees' interactions with each other and with the products for sale produce or reinforce essentialized beliefs about heterosexuality and women's subordination to men. Products also indicate class positions through taste. Taken together, this scholarship instructs us to consider proposal stories as status indicators and scrip for social inclusion that reinforce traditionally gendered relationship norms.

METHODS

Thirty-seven interviews with mostly engaged or newly married, heterosexual women ages 21–33 form the key narrative data on which we base this chapter. Three years of participant observation in various sites of the wedding industry also inform this research, including wedding expos, a bridal salon, and a support group for women planning their weddings. Arend conducted both the participant observation and the interviews, which took place in the greater metropolitan Boston area. Comeau was, at the time of proposal data analysis, a student research assistant whose work consisted primarily of coding interviews and writing theoretical memos.

Arend interviewed participants using free association narrative interviewing (FANI) (2000) (Hollway & Jefferson, 2000). This method, rooted in part in Kleinian psychoanalysis, is on the unstructured end of the semi-structured continuum and is designed as such to elicit information that might help the researcher better understand desires, fears, and other emotions unconscious to the participant. Arend employed this method with the aim of learning more about the wedding-related consumer desires of a diverse group of women. Like ethnography and other research methods, FANI can also produce unexpected material. In this case, while we did not set out to study proposal narratives, it became apparent that they provide an important lens on some women's investment in white weddings that calls for scholarly attention.

The larger study includes women in romantic relationships with women; however, we address their narratives in other writing, since this piece concerns the question of the reproduction of the traditional proposal among self-identified heterosexuals. No participant acknowledged herself to us as transgender. So, we assume, with caution, that this is a group of cisgender women, though it may include trans women who are in stealth (Schilt, 2006, p. 473). One of the interviewees ended her engagement and was unattached at the time of the interview. We recorded and transcribed the interviews before two types of data analysis: (1) the "pen portraits" (intact analytic memos) of the FANI method and (2) traditional coding using Dedoose qualitative data analysis software. A constructivist, grounded theory orientation informed the refining of codes and the writing of theoretical memos throughout the analysis process (Charmaz, 2003). Participants' names and identifying information have been changed to protect their identities. A pilot study for the larger project found very few men who met that study's criteria of thinking or talking about weddings in everyday life (beyond their own impending marriage) and therefore we excluded them.

Arend recruited participants through social networks, the volunteer page of the online community bulletin board craigslist, and a mailing to couples who had announced their engagement on Boston.com or *The Jewish Advocate*. They were also found through flyers distributed at a hair salon frequented by African American women, at bridal expos in working-class and middle-class communities in the greater Boston area, at the Filene's Basement "running of the brides" gown sale and at a support group for women planning their weddings. At these events, the brides rarely attended alone, but often had their friends, sisters, or mothers with them.

The group of participants does not comprise a random sample and therefore results are not representative of a larger population. Note, however, that the proposals described by the women in this study are very similar to those documented by other researchers. Twenty-seven women, or 73%, were White. Four, or 11%, were Black (African American and Caribbean American). Five, or 13.5%, were Asian American (Korean, Chinese, and Filipino American) and one identified as both Latina and Lebanese American, having been adopted from South America into a Lebanese American family. Efforts to recruit more women of color are ongoing in the larger study.

Based on participants' and their parents' education and occupation, most of the group interviewed are middle class. All completed high school and at least some college, with most having a bachelor's degree. Some worked in pink-collar occupations, including childcare and retail, while other occupations included social work, high school teaching, physical therapy, business management, software development, law, and medicine. Several were graduate students at the time of the interview.

We did not recruit participants through religious institutions such as churches, temples, and mosques but plan to do so in future research. Fifteen of the 37 participants said that they had no religion, including one who considered herself agnostic. Three also identified as "ex" or non-practicing Catholics. Among those who described themselves as religious, one was Jewish, one was Unitarian Universalist, 12 espoused a denomination of Protestant Christianity, and five were Catholic.

EXCHANGING GENDER-NORMATIVE RELATIONS FOR SOCIOECONOMIC STATUS: MARITAL STATUS AND SOCIAL STIGMA

The social stigma attached to being unmarried remains a powerful, gendered incentive for many heterosexual women to desire marriage as they age. In telling the story of how her fiancé proposed, Sandra, a 24-year-old, white, middle-class woman from the Midwest, described him as her soulmate who was lost and then found. They dated in high school for four years, but then broke up during her first year of college and did not communicate for another four years. Unhappy, she casually dated a few men and he married someone else and had a child. Eventually he divorced, and they reconnected. She reflected:

> It was awful, especially because I knew he was married at the time. So I'm picturing, you know, him and his wife and his baby and their little white picket fence and everyone's happy. And here's raggedy old Sandra who's never going to get married, who's going to die this old maid with a bunch of cats.

Sandra laughed and poked fun at herself. However, the sentiments she expressed are serious and meaningful. She felt a stigma attached to being a single woman and wanted to find a mate.

Some participants described how fears of not marrying came up in their interactions with other women and pointed to the subtle ways that having it easy on the marriage market is a source of status among them. For example, Barbara, who is white, upper-middle-class, and Jewish, met her fiancé on the online dating website JDate.com, which she joined at the behest of her friend. The friend:

> was approaching thirty and for some reason it was making her freak out that she was going to enter spinsterhood shortly. It was like, "oh you have to sign up on this site with me, you know, I can't do it by myself." I think that she felt [...] embarrassed or she felt like it was a little pathetic that she had to resort to internet dating to find a guy because she couldn't find a guy through [...] more traditional socially accepted ways.

Barbara made it clear that *she* did not need internet dating and even thought of male participants as "weirdos." Yet, she did join JDate.com, and soon after met a man who eventually proposed, whereupon relations with the friend grew strained. In a related example, Madeline also communicated worries about the marriage market in her peer group. She stated:

> I have friends who agonize over will they ever get married or not. And I never agonized over it. I never thought about it. I sort of assumed it would happen [...] like they agonize over whether anybody will ever want to marry them. I agonized over whether or not I would ever actually be [...] able to be married, which I think is different.

Through her facial expressions and cadence, Madeline carefully communicated both that she understood the stigma attached to unmarried women and that her type of concern with being married distinguished her among her group of friends. While they struggled with fears of never getting married, she − a tall, model-esque, blonde − was more concerned about whether she could give up the attention she received from men, implying that the more attractive a woman is, the more options she will have on the marriage market. This sentiment matches messages from popular culture where the prettiest women, such as Kim Kardashian, Beyoncé, and Jennifer Aniston, score the largest engagement rings from wealthy men who seek *them* out, with status gained all around.

In a related vein, Monique, a white woman who had not finished college, compared herself to another woman, only negatively. Upon meeting her eventual fiancé, Monique assumed that he would be interested in her sister. Monique said:

> I always feel like a little bit of a competition between looks with my sister, 'cause she's always been like naturally skinny and really pretty and I have always struggled with that.

Monique eventually said yes to his marriage proposal, despite some problems in their short relationship, in part because she was surprised that a man as "handsome [...] and fit" as he is would want to be with her.

One might think that the stigma attached to unmarried, adult, heterosexual women would be a powerful incentive for them to propose marriage to men, rather than wait for the reverse. The status that women gain in relation to each other when men choose them, in part, overrides this possibility. Participants in our study also confirm that expressing an interest in marriage makes a woman look desperate, which ultimately may damage her chances of finding a mate. For example, Julia said:

> [...] because I wanted to get married and I wanted to marry the person that I ultimately married, I disciplined myself to not think about it too much because I felt like that's a jinx. Like, the woman who always wants to get married never gets married type thing? So, I intentionally would have in the back of my mind that you know, ultimately I was going to have this like fairy tale wedding, but I never [...] made it real until it was actually happening. And I think that sort of informed the way that I moved around the wedding stuff prior to being engaged.

Participants of this study expressed concerns about the stigma attached to unmarried women and suggested that ease on the marriage market can distinguish women in their relations with each other. Clearly, in the social context of these participants, there is social value in being chosen by a man. Material gifts and romantic experiences add to that value, which we examine in participants' proposal stories in the next section.

Social Status and Romantic Consumption

Siobhan — a white, upwardly mobile, Catholic nurse — was surprised that she would be engaged in her mid-twenties. She assumed that if she married at all, it would be later in life. She also assumed that if she ever married she would not have a diamond engagement ring: her mother did not have one, it would be hard to wear one under her gloves at work, and she disapproved of them as "showy." That perspective changed, however, when her boyfriend suggested they go ring shopping together. From then on, she had her heart set on a particular ring and was eager for him to propose.

> But when I got it on, it was just really pretty [...] I still stare at it. I didn't pull away from a stoplight the other day [when] it turned green and I was looking at how it was catching the color of my shirt. And somebody had to honk at me, and I mean I've had it for like seven months and I still do that. So in that respect — I don't know, it's really pretty and it's symbolic and everything, and it's probably the only thing like this I'll ever own. So I actually had to spend some time kind of almost resigning myself to that. Like it's okay for me to have this. I'm allowed to have this thing.

When Siobhan says that "it's probably the only thing like this I'll ever own," she means a fancy, expensive piece of jewelry, which she was not accustomed to having, but clearly desired. As a special and valuable gift from her partner, it was a powerful incentive to rearrange her life plan and accept his proposal of marriage.

Thirty-six of the 37 women in this study received an engagement ring, all save one with a diamond. Three of the 36, all women of color, did not receive a ring at the proposal, but at a later point in their engagement. All three were among the youngest of the group, with two (and their fiancés) being students at the time. One African American woman's fiancé, also African American, was in law school, while a Filipino American woman's fiancé, who was White, was an undergraduate. The fiancé of the third woman, both of whom were African American, was working in a blue-collar position and she was a paralegal. While the numbers are small here, the delay for these women of color draws attention to the relationship between race and wealth inequality in American society, especially for African Americans. At the same time, both couples challenged dominant trends by getting engaged without a ring instead of waiting until they could afford one. Three of the four members of these two couples graduated from elite liberal arts colleges, which likely provided the cultural capital that made engagement without economic capital possible.

Sentiment and personal meaning can coexist with status considerations. White, Protestant, middle-class Andrea described how the women in her office at work were getting engaged around the same time and she did not like what she saw as the nouveau riche look of their large diamonds. It appalled her that a woman she knew rejected her grandmother's heirloom china because it did not suit her taste. Andrea found it meaningful to incorporate family into her wedding plans. The rings were no different and she and her fiancé planned to use one grandmother's ring for her engagement ring and the other for her wedding band. Yet, after explaining this perspective in the interview, she revealed that they had "upgraded" the diamond in one ring because the original was "really tiny" and added thickness to the other band. Stories such as Andrea's show that one can espouse an opinion where sentiment trumps material value, and yet still want a bigger ring worth more.

In addition to the diamond engagement ring, women in this study received many other valuable items and experiences. One received a second (cocktail) ring at her engagement, a kind of mea culpa for a botched experience while on vacation and a joke to surprise her more during the proposal. The fiancés of more than a fifth of the women who participated in this study proposed while traveling at their expense. Locations include an island in the Caribbean; Savannah, Georgia; Newport, Rhode Island, and resorts on the Maine coast and in Scandinavia. They also proposed on the islands off the coast of Massachusetts: Martha's Vineyard and, for Julia, Nantucket:

> [H]e flew me to Nantucket and we stayed there for the night [...] We went to dinner and not a lot was open on the island then because it was early March. So we just went to the little place

that was open and then we came back to the bed and breakfast and he had like filled the whole place with flowers and like Nantucket baskets and cute things like that. And he asked me to marry him and got down on one knee [...] And he had picked out the ring and everything, which I liked, and it was good [said with a slight laugh]. I said yes.

Here, Julia shares details that express both the affluence of her fiancé and happy relief that he has good taste, as demonstrated by her approval of the type of ring he chose. Proposers treated most of the participants in this study to at least dinner, sometimes at very upscale restaurants, including one featured in *Gourmet Magazine*. Finally, they also often gave gifts that signify romance, such as roses and chocolate-covered strawberries, as well as other special items that appealed to the preferences of the individual woman, such as the Nantucket baskets Julia likes.

There is no doubt that genuine love, convention, and other factors motivated these men. However, Christine's story shows how competition drove some as well. The proposal her middle-class fiancé planned contained virtually all of the elements of romantic consumption identified by Illouz (1997), including a natural setting, romantic commodities, and leisure. He told her he was taking her away for a weekend for her birthday, which she assumed was somewhere they could drive. They ended up going to the airport for a surprise trip abroad. She had to call her employer and family to make last-minute arrangements. They hiked to a beautiful, dramatic vista where he proposed with a two-carat, flawless diamond. When they returned to their luxury accommodations, she found a dress lying on the bed that she had admired in a store six months earlier, along with flowers, chocolate, and other gifts. She wore the dress to dinner, feeling like "Audrey Hepburn."

Marveling at the story, Arend, who was interviewing her, said, somewhat inappropriately, "Wow. That is really amazing [...] I shouldn't be ranking, but I have to say that's by far the best engagement story I've heard yet." She responded:

> You know what? I think that's what he was going for [...] I think especially because it was the last one out of all the sisters. But he said, "I've been thinking about this for a year and a half."

Christine read her fiancé's efforts as making sure her experience did not get lost amid her two siblings, also the recipients of proposals that year. However, she emphasizes that his planning to have the best proposal began before her sisters announced their own engagements. Christine's fiancé is a high school teacher and, according to her, not someone who comes from an affluent background. Yet, competitive consumption can happen at all levels of the income spectrum, relative to those a step lower in class position. Friends and family were amazed at the lengths he went to propose. They were not there to witness it, but through the retelling of the story, her friends now know Christine as the woman so valued that her fiancé gave her the Audrey Hepburn treatment.

Christine's story shows that some women produce the meaning and status associated with the ring and other proposal-related commodities in relation to their reference groups, going well beyond indicating that the engagement is real.

Nicole, a white, middle-class social worker, was not wearing her ring at the interview, so Arend asked her about it. She explained:

> I do [wear it] sometimes. But I'm in social work, and it's really, like most days I [...] I don't know, I spend time with people who maybe don't have as much as I do, and I feel like very uncomfortable about [it] [...] If I remember to wear it or do it, I'll turn it around [so only the band is showing] or whatever. [...] [My fiancé] did an amazing job. It's not the biggest ring or anything, but it's the cut, I think. It's just incredible; it's like fireworks all the time. So it catches the light, and I have to say it's really, really pretty. And it catches people's eye constantly, and I just get attention from it.

Nicole loves the ring her fiancé gave her and had no intention of rejecting it or giving it back; however, the diamond signifies her class privilege, which she feels is inappropriate to emphasize in a setting where she works with those who are disadvantaged economically. Given the class-segregated nature of society, most women interact with members of their own social class. It is to these relationships that we now turn.

Traditional Proposal Stories as Scrip

One way to see the value of a traditional proposal as scrip is to examine what happens when one or more of the conventional elements is missing. Telling the story of how she got her engagement ring *after* her fiancé proposed, Erika, a middle-class African American graduate student, communicated both the tendency of women to note the absence of her ring and the role of her fiancé's mother in making sure she got one:

> I had gotten so accustomed to not wearing it, and that was like the interesting thing about being engaged. Everyone immediately looks at your hand and you have nothing there. So, it was just like, "I'm engaged." "What?" And so I guess he got the pressure from his mom to be like, "you should give her something so that it looks like she's engaged [...]"

Here Erika confirms the research discussed earlier (Schweingruber et al., 2004) that the traditional proposal communicates to secondary audiences that the engagement is real. Her future mother-in-law wants Erika to have a ring so that she appears to others as truly engaged to her son. White, upper-middle-class Olivia, the one woman in this study who did not receive an engagement ring at all (because her partner opposed diamond mining in Africa) further described awkward social interactions. Like Erika, Olivia found that upon learning of her engagement, female friends and colleagues immediately looked at her hand to see her ring. This was stressful for her, since she initially did want one.

> And everybody who I told that [...] I had become engaged [...] said, "oh let's see the ring." And I was like, "what is the deal with the ring?" And I said, "Well I actually don't have a ring, or we haven't decided whether to get a ring." And the look of disappointment on peoples' faces that they didn't get to look at a ring [...] It wasn't like most of my friends are superficial people or anything like that, but it was just like such the association of getting engaged, there's a ring. And I just got grossed out by it, and I thought I don't even want this.

Here, we see Olivia's friends and colleagues also looking for confirmation of the engagement via a ring. However, the interaction implies more, as it seems unlikely that Olivia's friends questioned the reality of her engagement, especially the ones who knew her fiancé. Rather, the lack of the ring challenged their expectations of where the conversation would turn next, which disrupted the interaction and created an awkward social situation.

Participants who received a ring in the normative fashion shed light on the further meaning of the proposal for relationships among women. Some described regular and sometimes omnipresent conversations among colleagues at work about weddings and this includes the topic of proposals. For example, Anna, an upper-middle-class Chinese American physician, described some ambivalence about her ring, but weighed this against her experiences at work:

> Anna: [...] he could have given any ring, to be honest. A ring in itself is just a symbol of commitment to one another basically, and our joy in each other. So, that's basically it. But, you know [...] there's always [...] people. I work on labor and delivery and there's a lot of single women. And as one woman puts it, if you're not getting married or having a baby you're nobody here. Because everybody is in that age group where they're about to get married or they're having babies. And last summer it felt that way, like every other nurse is engaged [...] And all of them are getting married now, actually. So I don't know what the topic of conversation will be once everybody's married. It will be the babies.

> Arend: Their kids, yes.

> Anna: And some people are having babies. And someone's always looking at a bridesmaid dress on the web or looking at rings on the web when there's downtime at night. It's kind of an interesting world of conversation.

Importantly, Anna's colleague conveys that communicating the engagement to others at work is her ticket to social inclusion. It prevents her from becoming a "nobody," meaning someone who does not belong in the daily round of conversation. Repeatedly, even though we did not ask about it, these heterosexual women described how talking about engagement and weddings with their friends and family is a regular part of their everyday life. Deirdre, a 27-year-old, white, former Catholic, communicated this while telling the story of how her fiancé proposed:

> The next week we were going on vacation to Seattle, and we were staying at this spa with a waterfall, and [...] I was like maybe I'm going to get engaged. I mean, my entire office was like, "so which day of the vacation do you think it's going to be?" And I was like, "I've got my money on Tuesday." And so, I mean everybody kind of knew that it was imminent [...]

Interviews with single women from the larger study further suggest that when middle-class, heterosexual women reach that stage in the life course where many of their friends are receiving proposals, if they are not one of them they can feel left out. After her two friends became engaged to each other, Sarah told her boyfriend that if he did not propose by their wedding she would "throw a fit." He made it by four days.

One final observation about the role of the ring as scrip comes from Michelle, a white, middle-class graduate student. Her story shows how a diamond ring communicates more than the reality of the engagement and can actually operate as a source of exclusion from a group of women, depending on the perspective of the women in one's social circle. Michelle described how she would not wear her ring when she attended a graduate-level feminist theory class. Arend asked her what she thought the ring represented that kept her from wearing it to the class:

> Michelle: Well, part of it is that my advisor at [school] is a Marxist feminist; so there's class issues. And she knows [that I have the ring]. I mean she's seen it or whatever. But [...] I feel uncomfortable [...] I don't know. I'm still sort of trying to figure that out. [...] So how exactly it conflicts with feminism [...] is that your question?

> Arend: If you're concerned about what people in feminist theory are going to think about you by wearing it, what is it that you think they think?

> Michelle: That I'm not a real feminist, or that I'm not serious enough about it. Or that I'm a god-awful, liberal feminist [...] you know what I mean? There are certain types of feminists that everyone sort of makes fun of in class, you know? [...] I'm not making a claim that I am or not [...] but just that I'll be categorized [...] I don't want to be labeled.

Rather than connecting her to a peer group, Michelle's ring operates as a potential source of criticism or exclusion. Whether one does or does not have the scrip required for entrance to a social group depends on the group in question. That these groups do not inspire more rejection of the traditional marriage proposal suggests that they are either limited in number or, as in Michelle's case, their effects are local. While Michelle does not wear her diamond ring in front of her feminist classmates, she does in the rest of her life.

That the proposal story and ring operate as scrip can also be seen in the reaction some women have to not having a "good" proposal story to tell, which for some was activated reflexively when Arend asked them to tell her how it came to be that they were getting married. Victoria's fiancé proposed in their living room with the dog sitting on her lap, after he picked up the ring they selected together from the jewelry store. He knelt and professed his love with a "stupid spiel" before asking her to marry him. There were no other romantic commodities or special surprises involved. She reflected:

> I have to say I was disappointed after, because I was really hoping that he would do something—if not spontaneous, if not to make it a surprise, something romantic. But it just was— he made me dinner that night, which was really nice. I don't know, whatever. Like I said, then I told my mom. I was explaining to my mom about the proposal and saying I wish we had a story to tell. I wish we had "and then he took me to the park and he took me to the bench where we sat on our first date and I had no idea what was going on." But I could have that with a guy [...] that I wasn't head over heels for, or I could have [him], who I would love to be my husband. Give me this—whatever, we're in the living room on my couch. What am I going to do about it? He's awesome. You know, there are things that are important in life, and things that aren't, and I'll take a good guy over a great proposal any day.

Victoria clearly communicates her understanding that one needs a traditional proposal for it to be relatable to others in her life as scrip. Rather than stopping there, and without prompting, she proceeded to account for the type of proposal that it was. She created her own story where husbands who are good men who cook dinner are preferable to those who can organize one romantic event. Here, she exhibits exactly the kind of bridging labor that we assumed would happen, if in fact a proposal story operates as scrip. Other strategies employed by participants in this study include the use of humor for covering a botched pro-posal surprise, characterizing a poorly executed proposal as "distinct" or more interesting, and criticizing public proposals or large rings as "showy" or nou-veau riche. This accounting further affirms and reinforces the expectations others will have of a woman's proposal story.

DISCUSSION AND CONCLUSION

For a ritualized social act such as a marriage proposal to become widespread and remain dominant, multiple social forces must line up and be mutually rein-forcing. Previous researchers examined the ritual's dramaturgical qualities for their ability to communicate the seriousness of a relationship (Schweingruber et al., 2004), the commodification of romance and the spectacle of its consump-tion (Vannini, 2004), and essentialized beliefs about men espoused by middle-class women (Lamont, 2014). No doubt, these factors are all in play. Shifting the focus of analysis from heterosexual couples or individual women's beliefs to some women's homosocial relationships with each other throws missing pieces of the explanation into sharp relief.

These proposal stories suggest that incentives exist that encourage middle-class, heterosexual women to wait for men to propose marriage and are not simply defaulting to essentialized culture as "tradition." These incentives include the social status that some middle class, heterosexual women acquire when (1) a man chooses them for marriage and (2) they do well on the marriage market, as indicated by his level of social class privilege and cultural capital as expressed in the gifts and romantic experiences, especially diamond engagement rings. They also include the proposal stories themselves, which are valuable as tickets to social group membership. These gifts and stories can mean inclusion or exclu-sion from peer groups of friends, fellow students, and co-workers that make up the fabric of everyday life. To paraphrase what Madeline told us about her close friends who all got engaged within a year and a half: when middle class, hetero-sexual women reach a certain age they tend to "all line up and fall down at once." No one wants to be the last single woman "standing." On this note, our data confirm Geller's (2001) speculation that some women proclaim their "pop-ularity and desirability" by securing "a formal commitment from a man" though we disagree that "self-congratulation is the controlling idea of the betrothal announcement" (p. 104). Our data suggest that it is more an expres-sion of happy relief and an opportunity to connect with other women in their social network.

For the proposal to operate as scrip, it must take a similar, recognizable form, which accounts in part for the lack of transformation in the ritual. That fact does not preclude variation within and between social classes by cultural capital or taste. Women can receive a tiny chip of a diamond on a gold band or a large, classic emerald cut stone on platinum and still have their ring signify engagement as part of the story of how their fiancés proposed. Though our data are limited here, it suggests that heterosexual women with high cultural capital are in the most significant position to resist at least some aspects of the gendered ritual. They are more likely to have reference groups that use other mechanisms for membership and distinction, including a rejection of the diamond ring. Michelle was reluctant to wear her ring to a graduate-level feminist theory course because she presumed her professor and peers would view her negatively for doing so. Our informal observations corroborate her assumptions. When one of Arend's feminist, academic peers was on the job market, she debated about whether or not she should wear her diamond engagement ring on interviews, concerned about the message it would send about her political affiliations. Another feminist colleague described her own rejection of a diamond in favor of a union-mined sapphire and that it was common among her faculty peers not to wear engagement rings at all. That these women do not wear diamond rings in front of students and that other women, such as Nicole, do not wear rings when working with people of a lower social class suggests that there are opportunities for women with high cultural capital to have broader influence for social change. This is an area ripe for future research. Of course, the fact that Michelle and Nicole both wear their rings in other social contexts suggests that any influence they have is limited in scope.

Why should we care that so many heterosexual, middle-class women will strive for academic and professional achievement and yet will not ask their partners to marry them? From our point of view, the traditional proposal reinforces cultural tropes about gender that undermine the pursuits of full equality and the end of sexist oppression. For women to participate, they must be either passive in waiting for their partner or manipulative in getting him to propose without directly asking. In contrast, men must be or appear to be more assertive and economically well off than their partners. Assertive women are either desperate or dominating; passive men emasculated. These themes apply in other contexts, from double standards in sexual behavior (the slut/stud dichotomy) to seeing women managers as bitches and comparable men as leaders.

Adherence to the cultural norms of the traditional proposal is especially detrimental for people who are working-class or poor. How does an unemployed man approach proposing marriage when he cannot afford a ring or expect to be a "good provider?" All available data suggest that he does not. What might it mean if we could transform this ritual such that anyone could propose and be taken seriously in doing so? What if it were socially acceptable for women to be good providers and men to be stay-at-home fathers? In a service economy that provides more jobs for working-class women, would that not increase the pool of potentially "marriageable men"? If these assumptions are correct, one of the implications of middle-class women's status aspirations as expressed in the traditional proposal and the sharing of the proposal story is that they make it more difficult for working-class and poor men and women to get married, as seen in the most recent recession. Consuming the proposal as scrip comes, as Pugh argues, with a cost, a "savage intolerance of difference" (2009, p. 227). Here, the cost of middle-class social inclusion is the lack of transformation in gender relations. In other words, consciously or not, these middle-class women are choosing class privilege at the expense of full gender equality.

This study is one of very few that examines marriage proposals empirically. Most importantly, we need research on men (in all of their diversity). Under what conditions is a man more likely to accept a proposal from a woman? Do men consider women who propose to be desperate, as some suggest? Do men feel emasculated by a change to the gendered script? Might this be why an expensive ring or other gift is not a status incentive for men? Further research should also address the impact of middle-class social networks for men as they plan to propose. If a traditional engagement does show a man's socioeconomic power and potential as husband, what does that mean when the person proposed to is a man as well? We encourage other researchers to examine our findings and pursue the study of proposals, as well as other cultural norms that remain stalled in the gender revolution.

ACKNOWLEDGMENTS

We would like to thank Harry Dahms, Steven P. Dandaneau, Leah Schmalzbauer, Donica Belisle, Katherine Rye Jewell, Jared Del Rosso, and Ruth Thibodeau for feedback on drafts of this chapter. We appreciate Fitchburg State University for awarding a Special Projects Grant for data analysis.

REFERENCES

Arend, P. (2016). Consumption as common sense: Heteronormative hegemony and white wedding desire. *Journal of Consumer Culture, 16*(1), 144−163. doi:10.1177/1469540514521076

Banks, R. R. (2011). *Is marriage for white people? How the African American marriage decline affects everyone*. New York, NY: Dutton.

Bourdieu, P. (1984). *Distinction: A social critique of the judgment of taste*. Cambridge, MA: Harvard University Press.

Butler, J. P. (1990). *Gender trouble: Feminism and the subversion of identity*. New York, NY: Routledge.

Butler, J. P. (1993). *Bodies that matter: On the discursive limits of sex*. New York, NY: Routledge.

Charmaz, K. (2003). Qualitative interview and grounded theory analysis. In J. Holstein & J. F. Gubrium (Eds.), *Inside interviewing: New lenses, new concerns* (pp. 311−330). Thousand Oaks, CA: Sage.

Cherlin, A. J. (2004). The deinstitutionalization of American marriage. *Journal of Marriage and Family, 66*(4), 848−861.

Dunak, K. M. (2013). *As long as we both shall love: The white wedding in postwar America*. New York, NY: New York University Press.

Edin, K., & Kefalas, M. (2005). *Promises I can keep: Why poor women put motherhood before marriage*. Berkeley, CA: University of California Press.

Engstrom, E. (2012). *The bride factory: Mass media portrayals of women and weddings*. New York, NY: Peter Lang Publishing.

Freeman, E. S. (2002). *The wedding complex: Forms of belonging in modern American culture*. Durham, NC: Duke University Press.

Friedan, F. (1963). *The feminine mystique*. New York, NY: W. W. Norton.

Geller, J. (2001). *Here comes the brides: Women, weddings and the marriage mystique*. New York, NY: Four Walls, Eight Windows.

Gibson-Davis, C. M., Edin, K., & McClanahan, S. (2005). High hopes but even higher expectations: The retreat from marriage among low-income couples. *Journal of Marriage and Family, 67*(5), 1301−1312.

Gouldner, A. (1970). *The coming crisis of western sociology*. New York, NY: Basic Books.

Hobsbawm, E. (1983). Introduction: Inventing traditions. In E. Hobsbawn & T. Ranger (Eds.), *The invention of tradition* (pp. 1−14). Cambridge: Cambridge University Press.

Hollway, W., & Jefferson, T. (2000). *Doing qualitative research differently: Free association, narrative and the interview method.* London: Sage.

Howard, V. (2006). *Brides, Inc.: American weddings and the business of tradition.* Philadelphia, PA: University of Pennsylvania Press.

Illouz, E. (1997). *Consuming the romantic utopia: Love and the cultural contradictions of capitalism.* Berkeley, CA: University of California Press.

Ingraham, C. (1999). *White weddings: Romancing heterosexuality in popular culture.* New York, NY: Routledge.

Ingraham, C. (2008). *White weddings: Romancing heterosexuality in popular culture* (2nd ed.). New York, NY: Routledge.

Jellison, K. (2008). *It's our day: America's love affair with the white wedding, 1945–2005.* Lawrence, KA: University Press of Kansas.

Lamont, E. (2014). Negotiating courtship: Reconciling egalitarian ideals with traditional gender norms. *Gender & Society, 28*(2), 189–211.

Mauss, M. (1990[1925]). In W. D. Halls (Trans.), *The gift: The form and reason for exchange in archaic societies.* London: Routledge.

Mead, R. (2007). *One perfect day: The selling of the American wedding.* New York, NY: Penguin Press.

Montemurro, B. (2002). "You go' cause you have to": The bridal shower as a ritual of obligation. *Symbolic Interaction, 25*(1), 67–92.

Montemurro, B. (2006). *Something old, something bold: Bridal showers and bachelorette parties.* New Brunswick, NJ: Rutgers University Press.

Otnes, C. C., & Pleck, E. H. (2003). *Cinderella dreams: The allure of the lavish wedding.* Berkeley, CA: University of California Press.

Peiss, K. (1999). *Hope in a jar: The making of America's beauty culture.* New York, NY: Henry Holt and Company.

Pugh, A. J. (2009). *Longing and belonging: Parents, children, and consumer culture.* Berkeley, CA: University of California Press.

Sassler, S., & Miller, A. J. (2011). Waiting to be asked: Gender, power, and relationship progression among cohabiting couples. *Journal of Family Issues, 32*(4), 482–506.

Schilt, K. (2006). Just one of the guys? How transmen make gender visible at work. *Gender & Society, 20*(4), 465–490.

Schweingruber, D., Anahita, S., & Berns, N. (2004). 'Popping the question' when the answer is known: The engagement proposal as performance. *Sociological Focus, 37*(2), 143–161.

Schweingruber, D., Cast, A. D., & Anahita, S. (2008). 'A story and a ring': Audience judgments about engagement proposals. *Sex Roles, 58*, 165–178.

Smock, P. J., Manning, W. D., & Porter, M. (2005). 'Everything's there except money': How money shapes decisions to marry among cohabitors. *Journal of Marriage and Family, 67*(3), 680–696.

Storr, M. (2003). *Latex and lingerie: Shopping for pleasure at Ann Summers parties.* Oxford: Berg.

Turner, V. W. (1969). *The ritual process: Structure and anti-structure.* Chicago, IL: Aldine Publishing Company.

Vannini, P. (2004). Will you marry me? Spectacle and consumption in the ritual of marriage proposals. *The Journal of Popular Culture, 38*(1), 169–185.

Veblen, T. (1899/1994). *The theory of the leisure class.* New York, NY: Dover Publications.

Williams, S., & Bemiller, M. (2010). *Women at work: Tupperware, passion parties, and beyond.* Boulder, CO: Lynne Rienner.

Zelizer, V. A. (2005). *The purchase of intimacy.* Princeton, NJ: Princeton University Press.

SOCIOLOGY'S EMANCIPATION FROM PHILOSOPHY: THE INFLUENCE OF FRANCIS BACON ON ÉMILE DURKHEIM

Shawn Van Valkenburgh

ABSTRACT

This chapter examines Francis Bacon's influence on Émile Durkheim and demonstrates that Bacon's theory of mental "idols" has a significant presence in Durkheim's work. Both Bacon and Durkheim sought to demarcate new methods of inquiry against contemporary contenders. Both were wary of unfettered philosophical abstraction, as well as the pseudo-scientist's preoccupation with immediately practical results. Thus, it is fitting that Durkheim would explicitly characterize perceived dangers to sociological knowledge in terms of Bacon's idols – as objective obstacles which habit substitutes for fact in the absence of a sufficiently powerful epistemological mechanism. In preparation against these idols, Durkheim and Bacon offer rhetorically and logically similar remedies of self-imposed discipline and restraint. A close reading of key texts reveals that Durkheim's references to Bacon capture surprisingly deep similarities, suggesting that Bacon influenced Durkheim to a greater degree than is commonly recognized.

Keywords: Durkheim; Bacon; idols; epistemology; enlightenment; sociology

INTRODUCTION

This article stages a systematic exploration of Francis Bacon's influence on Émile Durkheim. Durkheim's indebtedness to the historical giants of science

The Challenge of Progress: Theory Between Critique and Ideology
Current Perspectives in Social Theory, Volume 36, 199–215
Copyright © 2020 Emerald Publishing Limited
All rights of reproduction in any form reserved
ISSN: 0278-1204/doi:10.1108/S0278-120420190000036022

and social philosophy is a well-studied topic. However, while there is no lack of discussion on his relationship to Comte, Hobbes, Descartes, and Spencer (Giddens, 1971; Stedman Jones, 2013; Lukes, 1985; Pearce, 1989), there is heretofore no sustained study of Bacon's presence in Durkheim's work.[1] This oversight is remarkable, as Durkheim (1982[1895], p. 72) himself tells us that "Bacon's theory of the idols has the same significance" for Western thought as Cartesian doubt.

Several factors help explain this lacuna in sociological theory. First, Bacon's reputation as an innovative scientific thinker has fallen considerably over the last several hundred years. Initially, the founders of Britain's Royal Society cited him in order to justify their petition for state funding – and for this reason, Bacon scholars Jardine and Stewart (1999, p. 7) name him the Royal Society's "patron saint." However, despite Voltaire's 1733 claim that Bacon was the "father of experimental philosophy" (Cronk, 1999, p. 51), his genius has long been in doubt from a scientific and historical perspective (Bajaj, 1988; Macaulay, 1837). Thomas Kuhn (1977, p. 45), for example, tells us: "To the conceptual transformations of the classical sciences, the contributions of Baconianism were very small." Alas, Bacon is now commonly remembered as a member of the English elite who was once given too much credit for influencing Western thought. As a result, sociological theorists may be less inclined to carefully tease out Durkheim's reliance on Bacon, an increasingly marginalized intellectual figure.

Relatedly, recent critiques of Bacon have acquired a more pointed political tone, as feminist (Federici, 2004; Keller, 1995; Merchant, 1979), postcolonial (Nandy, 1988), and environmentalist science scholars (Klein, 2015; Leiss, 1994) have demonstrated his work's embeddedness in problematic social projects. Horkheimer and Adorno (2002[1944]) located in his work the seeds of enlightenment thought's self-destruction and regression to barbarism. More recently, Naomi Klein (2015, p. 170) referred to Bacon as the "patron saint" of industrial extractivism. This body of criticism has created a double hindrance to the study of Bacon's impact on Durkheim: modern sociological theorists are less inclined to read Bacon as an important pre-sociological thinker in his own right, and they are also less inclined to study what may be an embarrassing influence on their discipline's founding father.[2]

Finally, Durkheim explicitly cites Bacon only a handful times in his oeuvre, and these references are limited almost entirely to *The Rules of Sociological Method* (1982[1895]) and one closely related essay written in 1908 (1982[1895], pp. 245–247). This would, at first glance, make Bacon appear as a superficial influence on Durkheim's work. However, despite the scarcity of explicit references, Bacon's thought pervades *Rules* and related works at a fundamental though often implicit level. The present article traces the less obvious Baconian thread in Durkheim's scholarship to show that Bacon impacted Durkheim in a deeper and more significant way than is commonly recognized.

Specifically, I will argue that Durkheim's intervention in *Rules* is deeply intertwined with Bacon's well-known discourse on "idols of the mind." In his *New Organon* (2000[1620]), Bacon famously attempted to create an empirically grounded epistemology that would defy a host of alternative contenders: ancient philosophies that were either too abstract or defeatist, as well as the flawed and immoral machinations of alchemists and other greedy pseudo-scientists. Bacon represented these foils — as well as other more "innate" or "inherent" (2000 [1620], p. 18) inhibitions to knowledge — as "idols," defined simply as "*illusions* which block men's minds" (2000[1620], p. 40). For Bacon, these idols present decoy ways of knowing that are so insidious and slippery that they can only be dispelled through empirical induction and sustained study of the idols them-selves. As we will see, Durkheim similarly constructs "prenotions" and abstract philosophies as foils, paralleling Bacon's idols point by point in conceptual essence, rhetoric, and application. Far from being just a formal reference for Durkheim, Bacon's theory of idols infuses the overall scope and argument of *Rules* and other Durkheimian works.

While the present chapter explores the hidden ways in which Bacon influ-enced Durkheim, there were certainly clear *differences* in their agendas. Though Coser (1968, p. 428) notes that Bacon's philosophical treatises "outlined the gen-eral territory" of the sociology of knowledge, Bacon's empirical investigations dealt mostly with the physical properties of nonhuman objects. Durkheim, on the other hand, chose society and human behavior as his primary object of study. Bacon's work set a clear philosophical precedent for Newton, whose mathematical formulae and philosophy of nature proved to be a much more valuable and materially productive version of Bacon's own epistemology. Newton, in turn, inspired Comte's positivist vision for the sciences. However, while Comte is sometimes credited as the founder of sociology, he was primarily interested in the kind of social physics later developed by Adam Smith as a means for quantifying and controlling human behavior at a direct and concrete level. Durkheim, by contrast, was concerned with identifying and explaining more nebulous social phenomena for the edification of policymakers (1982 [1895], p. 104).

Despite these divergences, there are nevertheless fundamental similarities between the oeuvres of Bacon and Durkheim. Before investigating Durkheim's few direct references to Bacon, I will first establish some of the broad similarities between their schemas, establishing a contextual foundation and understanding for any explicit connections.

AGAINST ABSTRACT SPECULATION

While Durkheim's primary point of departure in *Rules* is a critique of psychol-ogy (1982[1895], p. 162) — the science of the individual mind — he also distin-guishes sociology from the *philosophy* of society. This amounts to an attempt to create a *science* of society or a science of the *collective* mind. The significance that Durkheim attributes to this intervention becomes apparent in the conclu-sion to *Rules*, where he summarizes the major methodological premises of his new sociological method: "Firstly, it is independent of all philosophy" (1982 [1895], p. 159). The divorce between philosophy and sociology is clearly of pri-mary importance to Durkheim; it is the subject of this conclusion's very first sen-tence. In this maneuver, Durkheim speaks of the "emancipation of sociology"

(1982[1895], p. 160) from a social philosophy that he describes as "abstract and vague" (1982[1895], p. 109). Unlike the social philosopher who makes "abstract speculations" (1982[1895], p. 68) and "general philosophical statements" (1982 [1895], p. 63), the sociologist's reasoning should be grounded in empirical data, which can therefore feed back into philosophy in a mutually productive relationship (1982[1895], p. 160).

Rules is not the only one of Durkheim's works where we find this attitude toward abstract reasoning. In *Division of Labor*, for example, he writes that "[w]e should judge our researches to have no worth at all if they were to have only a speculative interest" (2014[1893], p. 14). He forcefully repeats this break with philosophy in a polemic against dialectical reasoning in *Suicide* (2002[1897]), and he echoes his disapproving view of speculative knowledge in a book he was working on at the time of his death in 1917: "There is no science worthy of the name which does not end in art; it would otherwise be a mere game, an intellectual distraction, pure and simple erudition" (1994[1920], p. 194). Thus, this skepticism toward esotericism and privileging of practical benefit is not unique to *Rules*; to the contrary, it is present at the beginnings of Durkheim's thought, and extends to his last works.

Here, we can begin to identify broad similarities between Bacon and Durkheim. Like Durkheim in *Rules*, Bacon's primary goal in *New Organon* is to distinguish a new method of inquiry from popular contemporary philosophies and manners of reasoning. Bacon distances his natural philosophy from the "fanciful abstractions" (2000[1620], p. 96) of ancient philosophy, and is wary of the tendency to prematurely abstract and disconnect knowledge from the real world, which he describes as "the destructive and inveterate habit of losing oneself in abstraction" (2000[1620], p. 103). Like Durkheim, Bacon is generally wary of esoteric "speculation." In *New Organon*, the word "speculate" always has a negative connotation: Bacon loathes "speculations and endless discussions [which] are quite insane" (2000[1620], p. 34), philosophies that are "speculative, and not much use" (2000[1620], p. 205), and ways of knowing that are "merely speculative and apparently useless" (2000[1620], p. 92).

Both Bacon and Durkheim counterpose the empty abstractions of philosophy against a kind of genuinely practical knowledge. Durkheim defends himself against possible accusations of idealism as follows:

> this is not to say that sociology should profess no interest in practical questions. On the contrary, it has been seen that our constant preoccupation has been to guide it towards some practical outcome. (1982[1895], p. 160)

Accordingly, Durkheim asserts that the sociologist ought to be a kind of social doctor, diagnosing pathologies in the social organism and recommending ameliorative policy (1982[1895], p. 104). For his part, Bacon (2000[1620], p. 66) deprecates the ancients when he tells us that "[t]he true and legitimate goal of the sciences is to endow human life with new discoveries and resources." He contemptuously reflects on philosophies from which "hardly a single experience can be cited after so many years which tends to ease and improve the human condition" (2000[1620], p. 60). On these grounds, Bacon distinguished himself from those who hurriedly go "leaping or flying to general statements" (2000 [1620], p. 52), and whose inquiring minds therefore ought to be ballasted by the "lead and weights" (2000[1620], p. 83) of systematic and sustained empiricism. Knowledge for Bacon should be based on real-world observations and lead to real-world material benefits.

Bacon scholar Benjamin Farrington (1951, Preface) tells us that Bacon is a true innovator on this front, and explicitly agrees with Karl Marx and Friedrich Engels (2010[1845], p. 166) who crown Bacon as the "founder of English materialism." Farrington goes so far as to suggest that Bacon informed Descartes when the latter wrote that:

> it is possible to arrive at knowledge which is very useful in life, and that instead of the speculative philosophy which is taught in the schools, a practical philosophy may be found. (Descartes, as quoted in Farrington, 1951, p. 16)

Indeed, this practical imperative clearly echoes Bacon's call for materially grounded and technologically productive knowledge. Farrington's claim of direct influence here is more plausible when we see that Descartes concluded this passage by telling us that men ought to be "masters and possessors of nature" (Descartes, as quoted in Farrington, 1951, p. 16). As many have noted, this call for the subjugation of the natural world is a distinctively Baconian narrative (Federici, 2004). If it is true that Bacon is the real originator of British materialism – and therefore indirectly influenced the development of British political economy – then it becomes more plausible that Durkheim was indirectly or directly influenced by Bacon, especially considering Durkheim's direct references to Bacon, which will now be examined.

AGAINST PRACTICAL PRENOTIONS

While Durkheim aimed to "emancipate" sociology from psychology and philosophy, he also defined it against common sense and practical conceptions of society. In *Rules*, Durkheim distances himself from those amateur thinkers who too readily jump to conclusions about society, who "did not wait on the coming of social science to have ideas about law, morality, the family [etc.]" (1982[1895], p. 62). He tells us that in the absence of any formal natural science, people tend to create tentative reflections about the natural world, or "notions about physical and chemical phenomena which went beyond pure perception alone" (1982 [1895], p. 60). In other words, people can have some limited reasoning before the birth of science proper, and these partially formed notions often have some immediate practical value (1982[1895], p. 62). So too in social matters, about which people are inclined to make hasty conclusions. Durkheim reminds us of the insufficiencies of alchemy in order to suggest a need for a social "chemistry." This is where he first explicitly invokes Bacon: the human inclination to rush toward practical results:

> is what characterises alchemy as distinct from chemistry, and astrology from astronomy. It is how Bacon characterises the method followed by the scholars of his day—one which he fought against. (Durkheim, 1982[1895], p. 62)

This reference to Bacon's idols is deceptively apt. While Durkheim demanded more discipline from pseudo-scientists who were concerned exclusively and prematurely with practicality, Bacon also warned about thinkers who "give in to a hasty and premature urge to turn to practical application" (2000[1620], p. 58). Like Durkheim, Bacon refers to alchemy as a negative example, declaring that the "alchemist and magician do meddle with nature (for results); but [...] to little effect and with slender success" (2000[1620], p. 34). Thus, it is not the material goals of alchemy that are suspect, but the means and motivation. Just as Durkheim cautions that people can't help but create imperfect concepts about the natural world without some guiding system (2000[1620], p. 60), Bacon cautions us against the "simple, nonscientific method of discovery which is most familiar to men" (2000[1620], p. 67). If both Durkheim and Bacon are skeptical of pre-scientific methods of inquiry, then, it is partly because these pseudo-sciences were myopically bent on producing *immediate* practical results.

Bacon's skepticism toward the alchemist's preoccupation with immediate practicality may seem to oppose his imperative to discipline the philosophical imagination with "lead and weights." In fact, for Bacon, there is a fundamental error common to both the abstractions of the ancients and the myopic practicality of alchemists: neither addresses humanity's inherent impatience toward the difficult and sustained engagement with materiality that true science demands. Thus, both will fail to bear dependable material fruits. Bacon (2000[1620], p. 57) tells us that:

> almost always men take their experiences lightly, as if it were a game, making small variations on experiments already known; if the thing does not succeed, they get tired of it, and give up.

Similarly, Bacon supposes that the ordinary thinker "rejects what is difficult because he is too impatient to make the investigation" (2000[1620], p. 44). According to Bacon, this childlike restlessness is the source of much failure to produce real-world benefits, failure that is endemic to both philosophy and alchemy. Greek philosophers, for example, "have a characteristic of the child: the readiness to talk, with the inability to produce anything; for their wisdom seems wordy and barren of works" (2000[1620], p. 59). Alchemists, for their part, are distracted from the ultimate pursuit of dependable knowledge by an immature attraction to immediate wealth and practicality – just as Atalanta of Greek mythology is swayed from her footrace by her juvenile attraction to gold: "like Atalanta, they go out of their way to pick up the golden apple, and interrupt their running, and let victory slip from their grasp" (2000[1620], p. 58). By contrast, Bacon's (2000[1620], p. 91) proposed natural philosopher will reap the material rewards of science by delaying gratification:

> We do not grasp at golden apples like a child; but stake the whole race on the victory of art over nature; we are in no hurry to collect moss or cut the green corn; we wait for the harvest to be ready.

Thus, for Bacon, both alchemists and the ancients are guilty of the same episte-mological crime − a childish impatience − and both therefore require discipline from some mental ballast.

Both Bacon and Durkheim bolstered their mistrust of hurried epistemologies with a *moral* rationale. Bacon (2000[1620], p. 13), for one, discourages the pur-suit of knowledge "for profit or for fame or for power or any such inferior ends" and encourages knowledge "for the uses and benefits of life, and to improve and conduct it in charity." He augments this praise of philanthropic knowledge when he condemns "the ambition of those who are greedy to increase their per-sonal power in their own country" (2000[1620], p. 100) as a motivation for learning, and by contrast privileges the discovery of material results whose bene-fits "extend to the whole human race" (2000[1620], p. 99). Embedded here is an implicitly Christian altruism, privileging the common good over egoistic knowl-edge pursuits.

Just as Bacon privileges the production of knowledge for universal benefit and casts aspersion on greedy impatience, Durkheim (1982[1895], p. 163) con-demns amateur social scientists who attempt to prematurely identify social facts, since this can be the product of avarice for immediate financial reward: "We believe, on the contrary, that the time has come for sociology to renounce worldly successes, so to speak, and take on the esoteric character which befits all science." For Durkheim as well as Bacon, then, the pursuit of riches is not only an obstacle to lasting knowledge, but it is also self-centered and thus morally dubious. We can therefore begin to read Durkheim's insistence on philanthropic knowledge as a Baconian enterprise, directed at the disorderly and covetous machinations of alchemists and other pseudo-scientists.

Both Bacon and Durkheim understood the short-sighted pursuit of practical-ity as an *objective obstacle to knowledge*, a distraction that does not merely frus-trate understanding but also falsely replaces truth. Durkheim (1982[1895], p. 62) makes an explicit connection between pseudo-scientific practical ideas and Bacon's idols of the mind:

> Indeed the notions just discussed are those *notiones vulgares*, or *praenotiones*, which [Bacon] points out as being at the basis of all the sciences, in which they take the place of facts.

Far from being a superficial reference, there is a deep affinity between Bacon's idols and Durkheim's prenotions. Durkheim (1982[1895], p. 60) tells us that the short-sighted reasoning of the pragmatist is so common and seductive that it is less appropriate to view as a product of creative human agency, and more as an ingrained part of human nature: "Man cannot live among things without forming ideas about them according to which he regulates his behav-ior." For Durkheim, it is *natural* for human beings to reflect on the world in such an intemperate manner. This is especially true in sociology, and on this matter, Durkheim (1982[1895], p. 62) reaffirms his bond to Bacon: "It is above all in sociology that these preconceptions, to employ again Bacon's expression, are capable of holding sway over the mind, substituting themselves for things." These natural predispositions toward practical knowledge are akin to Bacon's (2000[1620], p. 41) idols of the *tribe* specifically, which are inclinations inherent in "human nature itself and in the very tribe or race of mankind." These particular idols encourage rash judgment, impatience, arrogance, ineptness, weakness, and restlessness in the pursuit of knowledge.

One might presume that for Durkheim such seductive practical notions can nevertheless establish a starting point for real knowledge, even if they are roughshod. To the contrary, Durkheim explains that it is "not by elaborating upon [practical prenotions], however one treats them, that we will ever succeed in discovering the laws of reality" (1982[1895], p. 61). Practical notions are not merely insufficient for producing knowledge; they are counterproductive to those ends. Rather than being a suitable springboard for rigorous science, they become an obstacle. For this reason, Durkheim (1982[1895], p. 61) tells us that prenotions which have only a "roughly appropriate practicality" are not sufficient grounds for "discovering the laws of reality" but are hurdles that must be overcome: "they are as a veil interposed between the things and ourselves, concealing them from us even more effectively because we believe to be more transparent."

Like Durkheim's prenotions, Bacon's idols are not a stepping stone toward true knowledge, but are counterproductive obstructions to it. Bacon's (2000 [1620], p. 35) idols of the theater, for example, are the product of historically specific cultures and philosophies. Thus, Aristotelian logic is "not useful, it is positively harmful": though it may have some pedantic merits for abstract reasoning, in and of itself it does not lead the way to absolute truth, but hinders it. Consequently, Bacon (2000[1620], p. 2) implores us to clear away these shoddy grounds of knowledge — however immediately practical they may be — before building a strong scientific edifice, as the reasoning of his contemporary thinkers is "not well founded and properly constructed; it is like a magnificent palace without a foundation." To Bacon (2000[1620], p. 28), the foundations of contemporary epistemologies were so rotten that he called his own larger epistemological project the Great Instauration: the grand do-over which clears away all extant strategies for producing knowledge. This was a demolition project wherein "the entire work of the mind be started over again." Perhaps most succinctly, Bacon (2000[1620], p. 50) tells us that "if you run the wrong way, the better and faster you are, the more you go astray." For Bacon as well as Durkheim, then, starting from false premises can only lead to more false knowledge.

There are striking similarities between Durkheim's prenotions and Bacon's idols *as objects* which have substantial potential to distract the mind disastrously. Prenotions are not a starting point for knowledge, nor are they the absence of knowledge: they are an objective obstacle which must be cleared away. On this matter, Durkheim explicitly connects his work to Bacon's: Durkheim calls his own prenotions "idola which, resembling ghost-like creatures, distort the true appearance of things, but which we nevertheless mistake for the things themselves" (1982[1895], p. 62). According to Durkheim, we mistake idols "for the things themselves" because idols of the mind *are objects* of a different, obfuscating order. For both Durkheim and Bacon, then, false notions are positively *things*. Whether considered as veils or "phantoms and false images" (Bacon, 2000[1620], p. 151), they have real, objective power to block the mind. It behooves the scientist to think about the false notion as a *something*, rather than as a *nothing*. This affinity between Bacon and Durkheim even extends to their particular rhetorical formations. Previewing Durkheim, Bacon (2000[1620], p. 227) goes so far as to call false notions a "mask and veil" while Durkheim (1982[1895], p. 61) calls them "a veil interposed between the things and ourselves."

For both Durkheim and Bacon, the investigation of these false notions will help dispel them. Bacon's (2000[1620], p. 40) idols, for instance, subtly influence thought from the first instance "unless men are forewarned and arm themselves against them as much as possible." As a result, Bacon (2000[1620], p. 41) tells us that beyond mere inductive reasoning, in the pursuit of knowledge it is "very useful to identify the idols. Instruction about idols has the same relation to the interpretation of nature as teaching the sophistic refutations has to ordinary logic." Because the obstacles to knowledge are so nimble and wily, then, it is not sufficient to merely discern the truth against them: one must study them as forces in their own right in order to fully prepare for their encroachment on human reasoning.

Much like Bacon's idols of the mind, Durkheim's (1982[1895], p. 32) "common sense" is comparably devious and elusive, and therefore necessitates careful observation: "Whilst we believe ourselves to be emancipated from it, it imposes its judgements upon us unawares." Just as Bacon tells us to take up arms against idols, Durkheim (1982[1895], p. 32) remarks that the sociologist "must consequently be on his guard against first impressions." It is precisely because these obstacles are so insidious that the inquiring mind must "always be conscious" of their potential to secretly contaminate knowledge. It is therefore significant that in his 1928 work on socialism, Durkheim (2010[1928], p. 234) explains that if socialism:

> is not a scientific formulation of social facts, it is itself a social fact of the highest importance.
> If it is not a product of science, it is an object of science.

For Durkheim, even ideals and false notions are *true* in the sense that they *exist* and have real consequences for human thought and agency.

The similarities between Bacon and Durkheim continue along these lines. Both Durkheim's crudely formed concepts and Bacon's idols take hold when people lack an extra mechanism for preventing and dispelling them. It is a fundamental premise of Bacon's most famous works that the human mind requires the aid of new mental tools in order to dispel its idols and produce legitimate knowledge. The title *New Organon* can be roughly translated as *New Instrument* − that is, an instrument for clearing away false mental idols. In particular, Bacon's brand of induction − the comparison of diverse concrete particulars resulting in abstraction, often defined against the logical machinations of Cartesian deduction − is "certainly an appropriate way to banish idols and get rid of them" (Bacon, 2000[1620], p. 41). While the human mind has some natural potential for obtaining useful knowledge, it needs the help of epistemological aids in order to make any real progress: "Neither the bare hand nor the unaided intellect has much power," and they therefore require the "tools and assistance" (2000[1620], p. 33) of some special method.

Just as Bacon tells us that the "unaided intellect" requires the "tools and assistance" of induction to comprehend the natural world, so too does Durkheim write that an effective sociology requires a system of methodological rules in order to overcome the pre-scientific tendencies that produce inadequate knowledge about society (appropriately, the title of the work is *Rules of Sociological Method*). In the same way that Bacon defines idols against induction, Durkheim defines his intellectual tools against the mind's dubious tendency to rehash preexisting ideas: under normal circumstances, "[i]nstead of observing, describing and comparing things, we are content to reflect upon our ideas, analysing and combining them" (1982[1895], p. 60). Just as Bacon's idols are counterposed against his method of comparative induction, so Durkheim's abstract philosophies are counterposed against the process of "observing, describing, and comparing things" – the very heart of Baconian empirical induction.

Furthermore, while Bacon tells us that without these methodological tools the mind is too weak to produce useful knowledge, Durkheim warns us of the impotence of the human mind in the face of torrential and bewildering data: "since the details of social life swamp the consciousness from all sides, it has not a sufficiently strong perception of the details to feel the reality behind them" (1982[1895], p. 63). Durkheim writes that perception by itself is not sufficiently "strong" to discern truth from noise, just as Bacon writes that "neither the bare hand nor the unaided intellect has much power" (2000[1620], p. 33). Both thinkers therefore insist that some extra mechanism is required to provide consciousness the foundation needed to move past the obstacles of common mental habit.

AGAINST EPISTEMOLOGICAL DOMINATION

Here, we find a notable congruence in rhetoric: both thinkers feel the need to not only represent idols as objective forces, but also to anthropomorphize them as subjective agents, and as oppressive dominators. Bacon, for example, tells us that Aristotle "utterly enslaved his natural philosophy to his logic" (2000[1620], p. 46) and "parades experience around, distorted to suit his opinions, a captive" (2000[1620], p. 52). Furthermore, as an idol of the theater, Aristotle's philosophy is the cruel master of the unenlightened thinker: "The great majority of those who have accepted the philosophy of Aristotle have enslaved themselves to it" (2000[1620], p. 63). Thus, Bacon conceives of his experimental philosophy as a tool that produces humanity's *freedom* from the domination of abstract logic.

Similarly, Durkheim paints a dramatic portrait of the oppressive power of prenotions when he warns that the sociologist:

> must free himself from those fallacious notions which hold sway over the mind of the ordinary person, shaking off, once and for all, the yoke of those empirical categories that long habit often makes tyrannical. (1982[1895], p. 73)

For Durkheim as well as Bacon, then, habitual reflection is a draconian dictator, against which the sociologist must take up epistemological arms. Remarkably, this language comes just after Durkheim (1982[1895], p. 72) tells us that Bacon's theory of idols is "just as significant" as Cartesian doubt for "systematically discard[ing] all preconceptions."

What both Bacon and Durkheim call for is not the abolition of epistemological authority as such, but the establishment of an *internally imposed mental discipline* that counters the external impositions of philosophy. For example, Bacon (2000[1620], p. 43) wrote that the mind is too "slow and ill adapted" to discover truth "unless it is made to do so by harsh rules and the force of authority." We see a similar tone in Durkheim's (1982[1895], p. 72) antidote for the failures of prenotions, warning us that "inevitably we will relapse into past errors unless we submit ourselves to a rigorous discipline." Just as Bacon sought to weigh down the wandering mind with "lead and weights," so too did Durkheim aim to cure the imperfections of non-scientific reasoning with a strict regimen of epistemological restriction. For both Bacon and Durkheim, then, freedom from false notions comes from a new kind of bondage – one that is internally generated. Thus, we can make sense of Bacon's (2000[1620], p. 24) paradoxical assertion that "[n]ature is conquered only by obedience."

According to Bacon, in order to approach true knowledge, thinking subjects must not only control their internal nature – the mind's natural inclinations – but also external nature. That is to say, real inductive knowledge only emerges out of closely controlled experiments, which Bacon described in remarkably violent terms. He implored the reader to study "nature confined and harassed, when it is forced from its own condition by art and human agency" (2000[1620], p. 20). He wrote in *New Organon* that "the secrets of nature reveal themselves better through harassments applied by the arts than when they go on in their own way" (2000[1620], p. 81). (By arts, Bacon (2000[1620], p. 21) means experiments, or "the experiments of the mechanical arts.") Durkheim (1982[1895], p. 162) mirrors Bacon almost word for word on this topic when he tells us that "only methodical experimentation can force things to yield up their secrets." It is difficult to imagine this as anything other than a direct extension of Baconian thought into the social realm. Like Bacon, Durkheim enacts his critique of false notions and philosophies with rhetoric of domination, and uses the language of discipline and restraint as a remedy against falsity. For both thinkers, then, the pursuit of knowledge is a dynamic drama of domination and resistance: freedom for the subject can only be achieved through domination of mental and external objects.

RULES REPRISED

One might be tempted to believe that Durkheim's reliance on Bacon's theory of "idols" was limited to *Rules*. But, as mentioned above, in an essay written in 1908 Durkheim reaffirmed the fundamental principles of *Rules* and reestablished their connection to Bacon, suggesting that Durkheim held such views while writing *Primitive Classification* and *Suicide* in the interim. In response to a

questionnaire about sociology, Durkheim argued that if sociology is ever to discover causal explanations for social phenomena, it must be *objective*. Durkheim
defined objectivity with explicit recourse to Bacon's works:

> Objective: by this I mean that the sociologist must take on the state of mind of the physicists,
> chemists and biologists when they venture into a territory hitherto unexplored, that of their
> scientific field. He must embark upon the study of social facts by adopting the principle that
> he is *in complete ignorance of what they are, and that the properties characteristic of them are
> totally unknown to him*, as are the causes upon which these latter depend. By the *methodical
> comparison of the historical data*, and by this alone, he will evolve the notions appropriate to
> them. *It is true that such an attitude is difficult to sustain, for it goes against ingrained habits.*
> Since we live our life in society, we possess some representation of these notions, and we are
> inclined to believe that with such usual representations we have seized what is essential in the
> things to which they relate. But these notions, because they have been developed unmethodi-
> cally in order to satisfy needs that are of an *exclusively practical nature*, are devoid of any sci-
> entific value. They no more exactly express social things than the ideas the ordinary person
> has of substances and their properties (light, heat, sound, etc.) exactly represent the nature of
> these substances, which science alone reveals to us. *Thus they are so many idols, as Bacon said,
> from which we must free ourselves.* (1982[1895], p. 246, emphasis added)

Bacon's spirit pervades each sentence of this passage, culminating in an
explicit reference to his theory of idols. Durkheim begins by repeating his claim
in *Rules* that the sociologist ought to approach the study of society with a scientific mindset — in the way that a chemist would study matter, for instance. The
sociologist must accept that he is initially "in complete ignorance of what [social
facts] are, and that the properties characteristic of them are totally unknown to
him." Just as the chemist must abandon the mythic ideas of alchemists, so the
sociologist must abandon popular conceptions about society.

As in *Rules*, Durkheim contrasts a social science against these common sense
representations of society, against notions of an "exclusively practical nature"
that are interconnected with Baconian idols. For Durkheim, the sociologist is in
serious danger of presuming that these social prenotions adequately capture the
truth of society, as it is *natural* for humans to be satisfied with the knowledge
that has limited practicality. The scientific mind is therefore hindered by this
intrinsic inclination to rest in short-term practicality: "such an attitude is difficult to sustain, for it goes against ingrained habits." One hears echoes of
Bacon's tenacious idols of the tribe in these "ingrained habits," as both are
obstacles to knowledge that originate in human nature.

We then see Durkheim reprise his insistence in *Rules* that these prenotions
are so insidious that they can only be dispelled by "methodical comparison of
historical data," just as Bacon's idols can only be dispelled by induction — the
systematic comparison of empirical phenomena which can "banish idols and get
rid of them" (2000[1620], p. 41). Indeed, Durkheim's "methodical comparison"
of empirical data bears peculiar resemblance to Bacon's inductive way of
abstracting essential truths from diverse phenomenological forms, as outlined in
Book II of his *New Organon*. This kind of reasoning may not have been discov-
ered by Bacon, but he was probably the first to devote sustained scholarly attention to its explication and popularization. In any case, it is significant that both

Durkheim and Bacon use a comparable inductive method as a remedy for a perceived human tendency to focus on practical knowledge.

Finally, in the above passage, Durkheim reprises his call for a discipline that relates to society in the way that chemistry relates to chemicals, as physics relates to the physical word — an ascendance from pre-science to science. For Durkheim, there is a need for a new social science because social prenotions:

> no more exactly express social things than the ideas the ordinary person has of substances and their properties (light, heat, sound, etc.) exactly represent the nature of these substances, which science alone reveals to us.

Because of the insufficiencies of practical social prenotions and the natural temptation to create them, the sociologist must hold the study of society to the same standards of rigor as other natural sciences.

At this logically corresponding point in *Rules*, Durkheim invoked Bacon for the first time. Recall that in *Rules*, Durkheim (1982[1895], p. 62) tells us that the tendency of reflective thinkers to create practical prenotions "is what characterises alchemy as distinct from chemistry, and astrology from astronomy. It is how Bacon characterises the method followed by the scholars of his day." True to form, Durkheim refers to Bacon once again at an analogous moment thirteen years later (almost as if he reviewed *Rules* again in preparation for this document), explicitly connecting his own concept of deceptive prenotions to Bacon's denunciation of unmethodically developed ideas: "Thus they are so many idols, as Bacon said, from which we must free ourselves." It is worth noting that in this final direct reference to Bacon, Durkheim chooses to remind us that idols/prenotions *enslave* us in a kind of mental bondage from which we must "free ourselves," reaffirming his tie to Bacon's conception of knowledge as power.

IDOLS OF THE MARKETPLACE

If Bacon was a significant influence on Durkheim, we would expect to see this influence extend past *Rules* (and the short related essay of 1908) into other major works. In fact, we do find certain distinctively Baconian themes in Durkheim's *Suicide*, originally published two years after *Rules*. In particular, we find in both works the implicit but palpable influence of Bacon's (2000[1620], p. 48) "idols of the marketplace," which represent the power of ordinary language to unfairly conflate qualitatively distinct phenomena in the human mind. Jardine summarizes Bacon's thought on this matter:

> At the most basic level, the ascription of names to things, in ordinary language usage, fails to discriminate properly between distinctive phenomena, or names abstract entities "vaguely," so as to give rise to false beliefs about them. (Bacon, 2000[1620], p. xx)

Like other idols, the idol of the marketplace is a habit of nonscientific thinking that becomes an obstacle to knowledge. Its unique character lies in its association with language and is appropriately linked to the "marketplace" as a hub of conversation.

Just as Bacon warns against such false conflation, in *Rules* Durkheim charac-
teristically implores sociologists to define their objects of analysis in a way that
is satisfactorily objective. This means taking care to refrain from fusing separate
phenomena under a false heading. Just as the social fact is a scientific step above
the prenotion, so too is the scientific definition a step above the common definition. In particular, the latter does not conflate qualitatively distinct phenomena
under an unwarranted label:

> when he considers the question of effect, the scientist often distinguishes between what the lay-
> man confuses. In common parlance the word 'fever' designates the same, single pathological
> entity. But for science there is a host of fevers, each specifically different. (1982[1895], p. 153)

This is essentially the same argument that Bacon (2000[1620], p. 49) makes
regarding marketplace idols, which gather under one word "phenomena which
have no constancy or common denominator."

Unsurprisingly, Durkheim's reasoning on this matter extends to *Suicide*,
where it gets a fuller treatment and more clearly parallels Bacon's idols of the
marketplace. With the same attitude promoted in *Rules*, Durkheim (2002[1897],
p. xxxix) is at pains to analyze suicide in a satisfactorily scientific way, cutting
through the ambiguities of common language and identifying suicide's different
manifestations: "Since the word 'suicide' recurs constantly in the course of
conversation, it might be thought that its sense is universally known and that
definition is superfluous." He warns us however that in these "words of
everyday language" and "the confused impressions of the crowd, categories
of very different sorts of fact are indistinctly combined under the same
heading, or similar realities are differently named" (2002[1897], p. xxxix). It
is difficult to understand this as anything other than an extension of Bacon's
idols of the marketplace into the social realm. In applying this lens to suicide
as a social fact, Durkheim mimes Bacon (2000[1620], p. 42) who tells us that
the "crowd" is the source of errors of imprecise language: "Men associate
through talk; and words are chosen to suit the understanding of the common
people. And thus a poor and unskilful code of words incredibly obstructs the
understanding."

In this context, Durkheim's fourth reference to Bacon in *Rules* gains additional meaning. Just as Durkheim takes pains to organize really distinct social
phenomena under different labels, so too does he attempt to parse seemingly
similar societies into different types of social "species" (1982[1895], p. 108) (an
effort clearly steeped heavily in Spencerian and Comtean social evolution). Just
as Bacon seeks to avoid the arrogance of some philosophers and the defeatism
of others, Durkheim seeks to avoid both overgeneralizations produced by a natural human inclination to philosophize, as well as the hyper-particularization of
historical events in studying the social world (1982[1895], p. 108). However, in
the quest to distinguish social species in the face of bewildering particulars, or
the "confused multitude of historical societies" (1982[1895], p. 109), it is easy to
get overwhelmed. Nevertheless, it is possible to locate some social facts that are
more informative than others:

The true experimental method tends rather to substitute for common facts, which only give rise to proofs when they are very numerous and which consequently allow conclusions which are always suspect, *decisive* or *crucial* facts, as Bacon said, which by themselves and regardless of their number, have scientific value and interest. (1982[1895], p. 110)

While this may seem like an offhand or unimportant reference to Bacon, it is instructive on two levels. First, it demonstrates that far from making only a cursory survey of Bacon's work, Durkheim read *New Organon* very carefully. Although Bacon believed that the second book of *New Organon* was his most important, most modern readers dismiss it as one of Bacon's least impactful works. Durkheim, however, read it with close enough scrutiny to find parallels between Bacon's "crucial facts" and his own.

Second, this reference to Bacon's "crucial facts" previews the logical ebb and flow of *Suicide*. Durkheim sets up his sociological explanation of suicide by demonstrating that mental illness, climate, and biological predisposition are insignificant variables in comparison to modern anomie. Bajaj (1988, p. 41) suggests that such a focus on negative explanation is itself Baconian: "[Bacon] strongly emphasizes the importance of the negative instance in carrying out a true induction, a point on which Karl Popper has constructed a whole theory of falsifiability." By "falsifying" individualistic hypotheses in preparation for his sociological theory, Durkheim similarly establishes negative "crucial facts" that do much to eliminate a bewildering array of tempting psychological or biological explanations for suicide.

Indeed, Durkheim's study of suicide may in itself be called a "crucial experiment," insofar as it becomes particularly effective in demonstrating the need for sociology as a discipline that is distinct from psychology. In *Rules*, Durkheim (1982[1895], p. 111) paraphrases Bacon on the subject of crucial facts and experiments: "In many cases even one observation well conducted will be enough, just as often an experiment efficiently carried out is sufficient to establish a law." Fittingly, Durkheim's observation of the social causes of suicide is sufficient to establish the need for sociology as a discipline that will be applicable to a wide variety of social phenomena. If social factors influence even the most intimate of personal acts, who can deny that they influence other more obviously social phenomena? It is clear that Durkheim's relatively minor research investment in *Suicide* resulted in a major explanatory and disciplinary payoff, insofar as the book became one of modern sociology's foundational texts.

CONCLUSION

In this chapter, I have identified heretofore unrecognized connections between the oeuvres of Bacon and Durkheim, suggesting that Bacon's influence on Durkheim was greater than sociologists commonly recognize. While I have sketched their relationship in detail, I have largely left aside the ethical and normative issues at stake in Durkheim's appropriation of Bacon's ideas. These issues are considerable. In the first pages of *Dialectic of Enlightenment*, Horkheimer and Adorno (2002[1944]) connect Bacon to the birth of instrumental reason and locate him at the center of false enlightenment that resulted not in freedom, but the domination of nature and other humans under the guise of progress.

Indeed, while Bacon aimed to produce an epistemology that would be free from royal influence, his philosophical efforts were related to his conspicuous role in promoting England's early colonial efforts – interestingly, the Oxford English Dictionary credits Bacon for coining the word colonize (OED, 2016). Bacon believed that his new natural philosophy could help the English crown subdue the indigenous populations living within its colonies. Specifically, he asserted that the commodities, technologies, and material benefits produced by such a science could convince Irish and Native American "savages" to acquiesce to English rule: "If you plant where savages are, do not only entertain them with trifles and gingles," but also "send oft of them over to the country that plants, that they may see a better condition than their own, and commend it when they return" (Bacon, as cited in Irving, 2006, p. 261). In this capacity, Bacon's proposed natural philosophy could indirectly teach "the peoples to assemble and unite and take upon them the yoke of laws and submit to authority" (Bacon, as cited in Coffey, 2004, p. 267), to the extent that it resulted in "trifles and gingles" and other material benefits that might impress colonial others.

Future work will explore the ways in which these negative aspects of Bacon's thought affected Durkheim's works – which in turn provided the dominant model for sociological research over the past century. In referencing Bacon at a critical moment in sociology's development, Durkheim took advantage of Bacon's fame as a pioneer of enlightenment thought in order to lend legitimacy to his new discipline. The degree to which Durkheim – and by implication, sociology – retained the problematic elements of Bacon's work remains to be seen.

NOTES

1. While La Capra (2001) briefly mentions Bacon's presence in Durkheim's work, and Schmaus (1994) offers some discussion of Bacon's idols, neither of these books elaborates on the connection between Bacon and Durkheim nor explores this connection's full significance. Indeed, Schmaus does not feel the need to revisit Bacon in his 2004 book on Durkheim (Schmaus, 2004).

2. Of course, the same can be said about Comte, Spencer, Hobbes, and Descartes, and this has not prevented sociological theorists from discussing their influence on Durkheim at great length. However, while Durkheim was always at least partly critical of these thinkers, he never wrote anything that was even remotely critical of Bacon, which means a damning portrayal of Bacon may reflect particularly poorly on Durkheim.

REFERENCES

Bacon, F. (2000[1620]). *Francis Bacon: The new organon*. Cambridge: Cambridge University Press.

Bajaj, J. K. (1988). Francis Bacon, the first philosopher of modern science: A non-western view. In A. Nandy (Ed.), *Science, hegemony and violence* (pp. 24–67). Oxford: Oxford University Press.

Coffey, D. (2004). 'As in a theatre': Scientific spectacle in Bacon's New Atlantis. *Science as Culture*, *13*(2), 259–290.

Coser, L. (1968). Sociology of knowledge. In D. Sills (Ed.), *International encyclopedia of the social sciences* (Vol. 8). New York, NY: Macmillan.

Cronk, N. (1999). *Letters concerning the English nation*. Oxford: Oxford University Press.

Durkheim, E. (1982[1895]). *The rules of sociological method*. New York, NY: Free Press.

Durkheim, E. (1994[1920]). Introduction to *morality*. In E. Durkheim & M. Traugott (Eds.), *Émile Durkheim on institutional analysis* (pp. 191–204). Chicago, IL: University of Chicago Press.

Durkheim, E. (2002[1897]). *Suicide*. New York, NY: Routledge.

Durkheim, E. (2010[1928]). *Socialism and Saint-Simon*. New York, NY: Routledge.

Durkheim, E. (2014[1893]). *The division of labor in society*. New York, NY: Free Press.

Farrington, B. (1951). *The philosophy of Francis Bacon*. Oxford: Oxford University Press.

Federici, S. (2004). *Caliban and the witch*. London: Autonomedia.

Giddens, A. (1971). *Capitalism and modern social theory*. Cambridge: Cambridge University Press.

Horkheimer, M., & Adorno, T. W. (2002[1944]). *Dialectic of enlightenment: Philosophical fragments*. Stanford, CA: Stanford University Press.

Irving, S. (2006). 'In a pure soil': Colonial anxieties in the work of Francis Bacon. *History of European Ideas, 32*(3), 249–262.

Jardine, L., & Stewart, A. (1999). *Hostage to fortune*. New York, NY: Hill & Wang.

Keller, E. F. (1995). *Reflections on gender and science*. New Haven, CT: Yale University Press.

Klein, N. (2015). *This changes everything*. New York, NY: Simon & Schuster.

Kuhn, T. S. (1977). *The essential tension*. Chicago, IL: University of Chicago Press.

La Capra, D. (2001). *Émile Durkheim: Sociologist and philosopher*. Aurora, CO: The Davies Group.

Leiss, W. (1994). *The domination of nature*. Kingston: McGill-Queen's University Press.

Lukes, S. (1985). *Émile Durkheim, his life and work*. Stanford, CA: Stanford University Press.

Macaulay, T. B. (1837). *The life and writings of Francis Bacon, Lord Chancellor of England*. From the Edinburgh Review. Edinburgh, Scotland.

Marx, K., & Engels, F. (2010 [1845]). The holy family. In D. McLellan (Ed.), *Karl Marx: Selected writings* (pp. 145–170). Oxford: Oxford University Press.

Merchant, C. (1979). *The death of nature*. San Francisco, CA: Harper & Row.

Nandy, A. (1988). Introduction: Science as a reason of state. In A. Nandy (Ed.), *Science, hegemony and violence* (pp. 1–23). Oxford: Oxford University Press.

OED. (2016). Oxford English dictionary online. Retrieved from http://www.oed.com/view/Entry/36541?redirectedFrom=colonize#eid. Accessed on June 9, 2016.

Pearce, F. (1989). *The radical Durkheim*. Boston, MA: Unwin Hyman.

Schmaus, W. (1994). *Durkheim's philosophy of science and the sociology of knowledge*. Chicago, IL: University of Chicago Press.

Schmaus, W. (2004). *Rethinking Durkheim and his tradition*. Cambridge: Cambridge University Press.

Stedman Jones, S. (2013). *Durkheim reconsidered*. New York, NY: John Wiley & Sons.

ABOUT THE CONTRIBUTORS

Amy Allen is a Liberal Arts Professor of Philosophy and Women's, Gender, and Sexuality Studies and Head of the Department of Philosophy at the Pennsylvania State University. Her areas of interest are twentieth-century continental philosophy, critical social theory (esp. Frankfurt School), feminist theory, and social and political theory. In addition to *The End of Progress: Decolonizing the Normative Foundations of Critical Theory* (Columbia University Press, 2016) discussed in this volume, her books include *The Politics of Our Selves: Power, Autonomy, and Gender in Contemporary Critical Theory* (Columbia University Press, 2007), which was the subject of a special section of volume 29 of *Current Perspectives in Social Theory; From Alienation to Forms of Life: The Critical Theory of Rahel Jaeggi* (Penn State Press, 2018), co-edited with Eduardo Mendieta; *Critical Theory between Klein and Lacan: A Dialogue*, co-authored with Mari Ruti (Bloomsbury Academic, 2019), *The Cambridge Habermas Lexicon*, co-edited with Eduardo Mendieta (Cambridge University Press, 2019), and *Transitional Subjects: Critical Theory and Object Relations*, co-edited with Brian O'Connor (Columbia University Press) are forthcoming. She is currently working on a book on psychoanalysis and critical theory.

Robert J. Antonio is a Professor of Sociology at the University of Kansas and an associate editor of *Current Perspectives in Social Theory*. He specializes in social theory, macroscopic sociology, and economy and society, and his writings have focused on Marx, the Frankfurt School, Weber, Dewey, Habermas, and others in the classical and continental tradition. He has published widely in social theory and sociology, and his essays regularly appear in this outlet, including a prominent essay on climate change that was at the occasion for a special section in volume 26 (see also volumes 16. 23, and 24).

Patricia Arend is an Associate Professor of Sociology at Fitchburg State University. Her work, which focuses primarily on the relationships between gender inequality and consumer culture, has been published in *Race and Society*, *Journal of Consumer Culture*, and elsewhere. She co-edited the book *Culture, Power, and History: Studies in Critical Sociology* (Brill, 2006) and is currently working on a monograph titled *Dream Weddings: Fantasy, Femininity, and Consumer Desire*.

Katherine Comeau is a Post-doctoral Scholar in the Department of Sociology at the University of Notre Dame. She is affiliated with Notre Dame's Center for the Study of Religion and Society and the Kellogg Institute for International Studies. Her work focuses on the relationship between religion, short-term mission groups, and humanitarian aid.

Daniel M. Harrison is Professor of Sociology at Lander University. His teaching and research interests include sociological theory, historical sociology, deviance and social control, and environmental sociology. His book, *Making Sense of Marshall Ledbetter: The Dark Side of Political Protest* was published in 2014. He lives in Greenwood, SC. Harrison's essay, 'Twenty Years in a Culture of Fear,' appears in the fall 2019 issue of *Contexts* magazine.

Lawrence Hazelrigg is a Professor Emeritus of Sociology at Florida State University and an associate editor of *Current Perspective in Social Theory*. His research has included studies of class, status attainment, perceptual fields, comparison behaviors and expectations, and time discount, among other topics. Theoretical threads uniting those studies have come from a long range of theorists, from Adam Ferguson, Adam Smith, and David Hume, to Kant, Hegel, Marx, and Nietzsche, thence Georg Simmel, Emile Durkheim, Max Weber, and George H. Mead, to present-day theorists such as Judith Butler, Jacques Derrida, John Dunn, Erving Goffman, Michael Hannan, Charles Manski, Thomas Sargent, Thomas Schelling, Aage Sorensen, Arthur Stinchcombe, Nancy Tuma, Harrison White, and Peyton Young, among others. His main works include the trilogy, *Social Science and the Challenge of Relativism* (University of Florida Press): *A Wilderness of Mirrors − On Practices of Theory in a Grey Age* (vol. 1, 1989), *Claims of Knowledge − On the Labor of Making Found Worlds* (vol. 2, 1989), and *Cultures of Nature: An Essay on the Production of Nature* (vol. 3, 1995). Presently, he is completing a long monograph on processes of sociality.

Reha Kadakal is an Assistant Professor of Sociology at California State University Channel Islands, and was previously a Harper Fellow and Lecturer at the University of Chicago. His research interests include normativity in social theory, conceptions of truth, and forms of modern subjectivity. Building on the original project of critical social theory, his work investigates the normative foundations of social theory not only in order to evaluate those different paradigms, but also as a means to address the unresolved dilemma of modernity, namely the relationship between knowledge, truth, and the good society. In his secondary, empirically oriented research, he brings to bear his interest in normativity on the rise of Islamism in Turkey within the larger, global context of religious politics. Among his publications are "Toward a Critical Ontology of the Social: Hegel, Lukács, and the Challenge of Mediation," which appeared in the 2015 volume of *Current Perspectives in Social Theory*, and currently he is completing a book manuscript on truth in social theory.

Timothy W. Luke is a University Distinguished Professor of Political Science in the College of Liberal Arts and Human Sciences as well as Program Chair of the Government and International Affairs Program, School of Public and International Affairs at Virginia Polytechnic Institute and State University. He is an associate editor of *Current Perspectives in Social Theory* and on the editorial boards of many journals, including *Capitalism Nature Socialism, Critical Social Policy, Culture and Politics: An International Journal of Theory,* *e-Learning and Digital Media, Fast Capitalism, International Political Sociology.* and *Telos.* His areas of research and teaching specialization include the comparative and international politics, environmental politics, cultural studies, international political economy, and modern critical social and political theory. He has published widely, including several books – e.g., *Gun Violence and Public Life* (Paradigm, 2014), *A Journal of No Illusions: Telos, Paul Piccone, and the Americanization of Critical Theory* (Telos Press, 2011); *There Is a Gunman on Campus: Tragedy and Terror at Virginia Tech* (Rowman & Littlefield, 2008) – all co-edited with Ben Agger; and *Capitalism, Democracy, and Ecology: Departing from Marx* (University of Illinois Press, 1999) – and many articles.

Karen Ng is an Assistant Professor of Philosophy at Vanderbilt University and a Member of the editorial board of *Current Perspectives in Social Theory*. She specializes in nineteenth-century European philosophy (with a focus on Hegel and German idealism) and Frankfurt School Critical Theory. Her book, *Hegel's Concept of Life: Self-consciousness, Freedom, Logic*, is forthcoming with Oxford University Press in 2020. Her recent publications include "Life and the Space of Reasons: On Hegel's Subjective Logic" (in *Hegel-Bulletin*, 2018), "From Actuality to Concept in Hegel's Logic" (in *The Oxford Handbook of Hegel*, 2017), "Hegel and Adorno on Negative Universal History: The Dialectics of Species-life" (in *Creolizing Hegel*, 2017), and "Ideology Critique from Hegel and Marx to Critical Theory" (in *Constellations*, 2015). In 2018, she was a Research Fellow at the Center for Humanities and Social Change at the Humboldt University, Berlin.

Kevin Olson is a Professor of Political Science at the University of California, Irvine. His research areas include contemporary political theory, insurgent and popular politics, postcoloniality, cultural politics, poststructuralism, and critical theory. His publications include *Imagined Sovereignties: The Power of the People and Other Myths of the Modern Age* (Cambridge, 2016), *Reflexive Democracy: Political Equality and the Welfare State* (MIT, 2006), *Adding Insult to Injury: Nancy Fraser Debates Her Critics* (editor; Verso, 2008), and numerous articles in various journals, such as *Political Theory, American Journal of Political Science, Journal of Politics, Constellations*, and *Current Perspectives in Social Theory*. He has served as an Albert and Elaine Borchard Foundation Scholar in Residence at the Château de la Bretesche, France, and an Erasmus Mundus Scholar at Utrecht University, The Netherlands.

George Steinmetz is a Charles Tilly Collegiate Professor of Sociology at the University of Michigan and a Corresponding Member of the Centre de Sociologie européenne, Paris. His research areas include Comparative and Historical Approaches; International Sociology; Politics and Social Change; Qualitative Approaches; Sociology of Culture; Theory, Knowledge, and Science, and he is a social theorist and a historical sociologist of states, empires, and social science. His books include *The Devil's Handwriting: Precoloniality and the German Colonial State in Qingdao, Samoa, and Southwest Africa* (University of Chicago Press, 2007) and *Regulating the Social: The Welfare*

State and Local Politics in Imperial Germany (Princeton University Press, 1993), and as editor, *Sociology and Empire. The Imperial Entanglements of a Discipline* (Duke University Press, 2013), *The Politics of Method in the Human Sciences: Positivism and Its Epistemological Others* (Duke University Press, 2005) and *State/Culture. State Formation after the Cultural Turn* (Cornell University Press, 1999). He is currently completing a book on the emergence of sociology in the former British and French overseas colonies between the 1930s and the 1960s, as well as on a reconstruction of sociology as historical socioanalysis. In 2017−2018, he was Visiting Professor at the Institute for Advanced Study, School of Social Sciences, Princeton, NJ; in 2020 he will be a Fellow at the American Academy in Berlin.

Shawn Van Valkenburgh is a PhD candidate in the Department of Sociology at the University of California, Santa Barbara. His research interests include science and technology, gender, critical theory, and criminology. His current research project examines anti-feminist ideologies in online forums.

INDEX